The Authors

This book is an outgrowth of a series of study and discussion meetings in which the authors, together with others, participated over a period of years.

The authors—college and university professors and educational administrators—include: William H. K. Narum, Warren A. Quanbeck, Howard V. Hong, Sidney A. Rand, Harold H. Ditmanson, Stanley Olsen, Arthur C. Paulson, Loring D. Knecht, Richard Solberg, Bartlett R. Butler, Arnold Flaten, Carl L. Bailey, Albert F. Wessen, Olaf Millert and Kenneth W. Thompson.

Christian Faith and the Liberal Arts

Edited by • HAROLD H. DITMANSON • HOWARD V. HONG • WARREN A. QUANBECK

VERITAS OMNIA VINCIT

Augsburg Publishing House
Minneapolis 15, Minnesota

CHRISTIAN FAITH AND THE LIBERAL ARTS

ACKNOWLEDGMENTS

The editors and the publishers are grateful to the following for permission to use material contained in this book:

Abingdon-Cokesbury Press, Nashville, Tenn.; George Allen & Unwin Ltd., London, England; The American Historical Review, Washington, D. C.; Edward Arnold Publishers, London, England; Association Press, New York, N. Y.; Cambridge University Press, New York, N. Y.; Century House, Watkins Glen, N. Y.; T. & T. Clark, Edinburgh, Scotland; Columbia University Press, New York, N. Y.; J. M. Dent & Sons, Ltd., Don Mills, Ontario, Canada; Faber & Faber Ltd., London, England; Harper & Brothers, New York, N. Y.; Harvard University Press, Cambridge, Mass.; Hazen Foundation, New Haven, Conn.; Henry Holt and Company, Inc., New York, N. Y.; MacMillan Co., New York, N. Y.; McGraw Hill Book Co., Inc., New York, N. Y.; Muhlenberg Press, Philadelphia, Pa.; New American Library of World Literature, Inc., New York, N. Y.; James Nisbet & Co. Ltd., London, England; Oxford University Press, Fair Lawn, N. J.; Random House, Inc., New York, N. Y.; The Ronald Press Company, New York, N. Y.; Routledge & Kegan Paul, London, England; Scott, Forseman & Co., Chicago, Ill.; Charles Scribner's Sons, New York, N. Y.; C. Alphonso Smith, Groton, Conn.; Stanford University Press, Stanford, California; The University of Chicago Press, Chicago, Ill.; University of Oklahoma Press, Norman, Oklahoma; The Westminster Press, Philadelphia, Pa.; Yale University Press New Haven, Conn.

Manufactured in the United States of America

Preface

Ten years ago the Association of Lutheran College Faculties, meeting at Augustana College (Rock Island, Illinois), was faced with a disturbing question. One of the principal speakers argued that Lutheran colleges in America operated according to no distinctive Lutheran or even Christian philosophy of education, but had simply imitated secular patterns to which they had added chapel services, religion classes, and a religious "atmosphere." This was not, of course, the first time this charge had been heard by Lutheran educators. But on this occasion it was decided to try to do something about finding an answer.

The chairman of the Association, Edward Nervig of Augustana College, Sioux Falls, commissioned Norman Nordstrand, then Dean of St. Olaf College, to assemble a representative committee of Lutheran educators to consider the question: "Is there a Lutheran philosophy of higher education?" A planning committee met to discuss ways and means of attacking the problem. It appeared that the question could best be explored, not by a large number of scholars meeting annually, but rather by a small working committee which could achieve genuine rapport through prolonged association and the fullest sort of opportunity for frank and informal discussion. It was felt that such a committee could come to agreement on basic presuppositions and move on to a productive handling of further issues without having to go back to the beginning on every occasion.

The feasibility of including within the committee representatives of all the various synods and geographical areas of the Lutheran community was ruled out by lack of financial resources. Thus the committee took shape as a group of teachers and administrators from six schools: Augustana College, Sioux Falls, South Dakota; Concordia College, Moorhead, Minnesota; Luther College, Decorah, Iowa; Luther Theological Seminary, St. Paul, Minnesota;

St. Olaf College, Northfield, Minnesota; and Waldorf College, Forest City, Iowa. In proceeding to explore the question as fully as possible this committee regarded itself as a voluntary working group, rather than as a committee of the Association of Lutheran College Faculties.

Over a period of ten years the group met three or four times a year. Although certain important areas are not treated in this volume, papers on nearly every phase of collegiate education were read and subjected to thorough and critical discussion. Each paper was re-written in the light of criticisms and suggestions offered by the group. As the editors reflected upon the essays, the pattern of organization outlined in the Table of Contents suggested itself. For the group had in fact addressed itself not only to the teaching of specific courses, but also to the very purpose and structure of the curriculum and administrative organization and to certain wider problems relating to the Church's historic stake in liberal arts education, to the theological basis of Christian education, and to the nature of man and of truth.

Although these essays represent the study and discussion of a group which hammered out a common platform, it is clear that the writers do not agree with one another on all points. Individual differences in thought remain and have not been ironed out for the sake of uniformity. Beyond agreement on certain fundamental religious and intellectual points, the committee experienced the same tensions that prevail throughout the educational community in general. The committee would not be disposed to claim that what it here sets forth is a distinctively "Lutheran" position. There are frequent references to the Lutheran tradition and to Lutheran schools. But it would be fair to say that the point of view is broadly representative of the classical intellectual tradition of the Western church, qualified in important ways by Reformation concerns.

The following persons have participated either consistently or from time to time in the work of the committee and were at the time of its formation associated with the designated colleges:

AUGUSTANA COLLEGE: Stanley Olsen, J. Jorgen Thompson, Jr., Richard Solberg, Edward Nervig, Ed. Gunberg.

CONCORDIA COLLEGE: Carl Bailey, Allan Hanson, Reidar Thomte, Sigurd Mundhjeld, Olin Storvick.

LUTHER COLLEGE: Gerhard Belgum, Gerhard Frost, Sherman Hoslett, Bartlett Butler, O. W. Qualley.

LUTHER THEOLOGICAL SEMINARY: Warren Quanbeck, George Aus.
ST. OLAF COLLEGE: Howard Hong, William Narum, Harold Ditman-
son, Arthur Paulson, Arnold Flaten, Norman Nordstrand.
WALDORF COLLEGE: Sidney Rand, Tom Kilian.

Inasmuch as the rather informally assembled group did not
include representatives of all the disciplines which it would be
desirable to discuss in a book of this sort, contributions were solicited on sociology from Albert Wessen (Yale), on political science
from Kenneth W. Thompson (Rockefeller Foundation), on foreign
language from Loring D. Knecht (St. Olaf), and on psychology
from Olaf Millert (St. Olaf). It should be noted that the article
by Arnold Flaten, "The Church's Stake in the Visual Arts," has
appeared in *Frontiers* magazine. Parts of William H. K. Narum's
chapters were incorporated in *Integration in the Christian Liberal
Arts College*. Versions of Howard Hong's chapters were published
in *This World and the Church* and in *The Christian Scholar*
magazine.

The editors wish to express their gratitude to all the men who
have contributed to this volume or participated in the extended
discussion for the faithfulness and seriousness with which they
have fulfilled their tasks. The ten-year dialogue has been for all of
us a delightful and stimulating experience. We also wish to record
our appreciation to the faculty wives and to the administrative
officers at the host colleges for the generous hospitality given to
the committee during its meetings.

Special thanks are due Dr. William Narum and Audrey Johnson,
a student at St. Olaf College, for preparing the index.

This volume is sent forth as a modest contribution to the current
discussion of educational philosophy and procedures. As teachers,
administrators, churchmen, and citizens we must all take our part
in this lively conversation which is of such crucial importance for
the future of higher education and the relationship of the Christian church to our culture.

THE EDITORS

Contents

vi

Contents

Part One

Presuppositions

CHAPTER 1

The Role of the Liberal Arts in Christian Higher Education

by William H. K. Narum

The liberal arts tradition in the history of education is an old one. Even church history reveals it to be the kind of education that the church has believed to be the most significant. A case could be made out, in fact, for considering the terms "education" and "liberal education" to be identical terms, although the term "education" has come to be applied indiscriminately to all kinds of instruction. The thesis of this chapter is that the church has a definite stake and a special interest in liberal education. Since the liberal studies deal with the central powers and the core studies of human knowing, they constitute the unique and decisive area of education where the Christian viewpoint can and must make its impact. Furthermore, since the liberal studies are the prerequisites of all human learnings, they should also be the first concern of the church in its program of higher education. Only when the liberal education program has been "secured," and that not in a half-hearted way, should the church feel able to turn its attention to the subsidiary and, incidentally, far more costly specialized vocational, graduate, and technological studies.

Let us turn our attention, therefore, to an investigation of the meaning of liberal education, after which we shall evaluate its role in Christian higher education.

LIBERAL EDUCATION ITSELF

History

The Greeks and Romans. The liberal arts originated with the Greeks, and chiefly with the sophists. Werner Jaeger has written of the sophists:

Before them we never hear of grammar, rhetoric, and dialectic . . . clearly the systematic expression of the principle of shaping the intellect, because it begins by instruction in the form of language, the form of

3

oratory, and the form of thoughts. This educational technique is one of the greatest discoveries which the mind of man has ever made: it was not until it explored these three of its activities that the mind apprehended the hidden law of its own structure.[1]

Men had followed the laws of grammar or reason by custom, but with the sophists these laws were consciously studied. The sophists blunted their own influence, however, by a relativizing theory of knowledge which regarded logic as merely rhetorical tricks whereby one might win an argument and "make the worse appear the better cause." In this respect their views were a threat to a serious philosophy of education, and it was Socrates and Plato who especially combatted their relativism by an affirmation of the absolute value of truth and logical principles. Plato's Academy and Aristotle's Lyceum were major forces in the history of Western education. One might speculate what would have happened if the ancients had turned toward Plato's mathematical emphasis, "measuring," rather than towards the "classifying" emphasis of Aristotle (a more biological approach), or to rhetoric as such. C. N. Cochrane has pointed out that the historical importance of the victory of rhetoric cannot be exaggerated:

> For, by imparting to Classicism precisely that "literary and aesthetic bias" which Plato had so earnestly deprecated, it modified the whole complexion of Western culture, giving to it a rhetorical cast from which it was hardly to free itself under the most powerful stimulus of modern mathematical and physical science.[2]

Thus grammar, rhetoric, and logic became the chief educational instruments of formal education in Europe (not until the Seventeenth century did mathematics come into its own again). In late antiquity these studies were called the *trivium,* and with the *quadrivium* (arithmetic, geometry, music, and astronomy) made up the seven liberal arts.

Cicero and Quintillian made the chief Roman contributions in the history of the liberal arts. Cicero's emphasis was the relation of law, philosophy, and history to the liberal arts, whereas Quintillian made a special treatment of rhetoric. In general the Romans propagated the Greek ideal of liberal education, but with major emphasis upon rhetoric.

---

[1]*Paideia,* trans. Gilbert Highet (New York: Oxford University Press, 1945), I, p. 314.
[2]*Christianity and Classical Culture* (New York: Oxford University Press, 1944), p. 146.

The early church and Augustine. The early church was so occupied with its missionary task that its educational task was exhausted in its instruction of the catechumens. By the time of Augustine, however, as the church became more and more a part of the historical scene, it began to interest itself in the total task of education. In *De Ordine* (Concerning Order), Augustine remarked:

And those who are content with authority alone, and expend their efforts on good morals and holy desires, condemning the liberal arts or not being up to them, I do not see how they can be really happy among mortal men, though I believe with unshakable faith that they will be free and happy to the greatest extent in the next life, who have lived best here.[3]

Augustine saw in liberal education a way whereby the church might combat heathen philosophies by requiring such an education of its own leaders. "This is the order of learning, or there is none," he remarked of liberal education.[4] Augustine planned to write treatises on the various liberal disciplines, but succeeded in writing only one, *De Musica*. According to his intentions philosophy was to be substituted for astronomy in the quadrivium. Augustine recognized that the earliest disciples were not educated men, that God had chosen the weak things of the world to confound the wise. But he saw also that the utmost effort of intellect was necessary to understand the ways of God to man, and along with Jerome and Ambrose he desired to consecrate human learning to the uses of the Christian life. The liberal arts would be indispensable aids to the study of the Bible. In Greece the liberal arts had paved the way for philosophy; in Rome, for oratory; in the Church, for the good life and the study of scripture and theology. *Credo ut intelligam*—I believe that I may know—faith aids reason, and understanding is the reward of faith—so Augustine believed.

The Middle Ages. In this period the church carried on the wider educational task, and the seven liberal arts (trivium plus quadrivium) were the basic studies. In the Carolingian age logic began to assume more importance, and the study of the trivium easily eclipsed that of the quadrivium. Theology was the central study,

---

[3] *De Ordine*, II, 9, 26.
[4] *Ibid.*, II, 17, 46.

of course, with the seven free arts and a rudimentary sort of medical study as the handmaids of the queen of the sciences.[5] Philosophical and theological problems dominated the intellectual scene from the Eleventh to the Thirteenth centuries. The medium of expression was Latin, its rhetoric being the chief emphasis of South Europe, whereas its dialectical (i.e., logical) use was stressed in Northern Europe. The realm of knowledge moved up a ladder from grammar, rhetoric, and logic to metaphysics, with theology at the top ruling and encompassing all.

The founding of universities in the late Middle Ages bore witness to the central importance of the liberal arts for the church. The universities of Naples, Paris, Oxford, Prague, and the like, were all centers of liberal learning as well as famed for certain professional schools, such as Paris for theology, or Bologna for law. In them all the classical heritage was enriched with the treasures of the Fathers of the Church, not least the writings of Augustine, all of which had been until then preserved in monasteries. The tremendous intellectual achievement of a Thomas Aquinas in his *Summas* was only possible by means of this tradition. Aquinas did not give an explicit treatment of the liberal arts, but he saw that they freed man's highest powers, his intellect and his will, for their proper activity. The liberal arts studied man, and the study of man trained man's highest powers.

The Reformation. Luther once remarked, "When schools flourish, then things go well, and the church is secure. Let us have more learned men and teachers." Like Aquinas, Luther did not treat the liberal arts in any specific way, but it is clear from his writings that he valued liberal education highly. He himself was a university professor, after all, and often spoke disparagingly of "the same old blockheads, unable to converse on any subject or to be of assistance to anyone."[6] He thought that children should receive instruction from learned schoolmasters on languages, history, and the other arts especially, in order for them to be able to see as in a mirror the character, life, success, and failure of the whole world.

As a result of this knowledge, they could form their own opinions and

[5]H. O. Taylor, *The Medieval Mind* (London: Macmillan & Co., Ltd., 1938), I, p. 302, argues that the indifference of Augustine and Ambrose to natural knowledge was the most palpable intellectual defect of these men, leading to the result that there was no incentive in the Middle Ages to study the natural world.

[6]*Works of Martin Luther,* (Philadelphia: A. J. Holman Company, 1915), IV, p. 122.

adapt themselves to the course of this outward life in the fear of God, draw from history the knowledge and understanding of what should be sought and what avoided in this outward life, and become able also by this standard to assist and direct others.[7]

Luther disparaged philosophy because he identified philosophy with scholastic philosophy, and that with Roman Catholicism, and condemned both in the same breath. This had unfortunate consequences for the relations of faith to reason in the centuries that followed, for Protestant thinkers felt they had to be nominalists rather than realists in philosophy, although Protestant theology was always realistic. The result was an ever-widening breach between natural science and theology in the modern period.[8] Melanchthon hoped to save the day for philosophy, but his Aristotelian predilections were not calculated to provide a permanent basis. Melanchthon and Luther were quite agreed in their estimate of education: "the school must be the next thing to the Church."[9] Since their time the Lutheran church has been characterized by its strong interest in education.[10]

On the Reformed side of the Reformation the same emphasis on liberal education obtained. John Calvin was himself a great humanist who became a great reformer, never regretting or denying his education. The great Swiss educator, Pestalozzi, comes from this tradition. In the United States the public school is very largely an outcome of the establishment of schools by the early Calvinist Puritans in New England. Harvard, Yale, and Princeton, great bulwarks of liberal education to this day, were established by Calvinists.

The Counter-Reformation movement in the Roman Catholic Church was no denial of the importance of liberal education either, as can be seen with the Jesuits. Under Ignatius Loyola the Jesuits established a system of studies that was a particularly effective method of developing man's intellect. In the Nineteenth Century a significant reaffirmation of the liberal arts viewpoint came from Cardinal Newman's *The Idea of a University*, which argued that a Christian university must be centered around the liberal arts.

As to the present day, and in the American scene, the presence of

---

[7]*Ibid.*
[8]Cf. Otto Piper, *God in History* (New York: The Macmillan Company, 1939), p. 54.
[9]*Works* (Holman Edition), Vol. V, p. 298.
[10]Cf. the folk-school of Grundtvig, the Danish Lutheran, notable for the fact that liberal studies are the chief studies of the curriculum, especially theology, philosophy, literature, and history.

hundreds of Christian liberal arts colleges is a testimony to the attitude of the Church toward liberal arts education. To cite only one theologian, Dean Jerald Brauer of the University of Chicago's Federated Theological Faculty writes:

There is one thing that the Christian college has done and can continue to do in distinctive fashion for higher education in America—education in the liberal arts as the background for professional or graduate study. It is precisely at this point that the major debates in higher education now rage; it is here that the implications of Christian faith can be most fully articulated; it is in the liberal arts program that the Christian college should concentrate.[11]

Thus, down through its long history the Christian Church, whether Protestant or Catholic, recognizing the liberal arts as the core learnings, has seen their peculiar closeness to the concern of the Church in education.

The Renaissance and Secular Education. The Renaissance also reaffirmed the tradition of liberal education, although its stress lay on the humanistic and Greek intellectualistic aspects. The Greek language was emphasized, and a "humanistic" education as distinguished from a church-dominated education, had to embody a knowledge of both Greek and Latin, plus a study of the classical works, especially the newly-discovered Greek classics. Theology was ignored or neglected. Plato's works were brought to light, and perhaps it is not accidental that mathematics came to dominate the Seventeenth and Eighteenth Centuries, and the quadrivium the modern age. The Nineteenth Century may be said to have been dominated by biology, whereas mathematics and physics seem to be more dominant in our times.

Nature and Content

Having now surveyed the history of the liberal arts (in brief) with special attention to their place in the educational thinking of the Church, we now turn to a systematic approach to these studies. What are the liberal arts? What are the relationships among them?

---

[11]"The Christian College and American Higher Education," *The Christian Scholar* (Autumn, 1958, Special Issue), pp. 240 f. (Dean Brauer's article is a transcript of his address to the Second Quadrennial Convocation of Christian Colleges meeting at Drake University, Des Moines, Iowa, in June, 1958.)

Answers to questions like these will help us to see their significance for Christian higher education. In general we may say that while human learnings are almost infinite in number, there is a core to them—namely, the liberal arts, for these learnings are the specifically intellectual ones. All other human learnings depend on them and presuppose them. The liberal arts are prerequisite arts to all other studies, and are thus the basic human learnings. Let us examine these core studies, then, from two viewpoints: (1) as disciplines of the human mind, whereby the mind is sharpened and taught how to think and make judgments, and (2) as sciences of the human mind, whereby the mind is brought into relationship with knowledge.

As disciplines. Theodore M. Greene has suggested that we could define the curriculum as the arranging of tasks or disciplines which guide the learner. He lists the following aims of these disciplines:

to communicate clearly — language, mathematics, artistic idiom
to inquire accurately — natural and social sciences, historical and literary methodologies
to evaluate wisely — the humanities
to understand synoptically — history, philosophy, theology.

We could also say that logic, which is the basic liberal art, ought to be included as well, and its aim as a discipline might be said to be—

to reason validly — logic (and mathematics)

Let us next look at these in turn, starting with the latter as the most basic.

To reason validly. No matter what one studies in the liberal curriculum, one must use his intellect, and the art that governs this "use" is logic. "If the purpose of liberal education is to form our judgment, then the theory of judgment, which is logic, makes it aware of its own principle."[12] Logic is the common structure of all knowledge, whether theoretical or practical. It is the structural coherence of all knowledge, and the formal unity of all scientific learning.

[12]Gustav E. Mueller, *Education Limited* (Norman, Oklahoma: University of Oklahoma Press, 1949), p. 63.

To communicate clearly. This is chiefly the function of language study, to be found in both English and foreign study. Grammar investigates how a language is put together, how one should read; rhetoric, how human beings express themselves, whether by writing or speaking. Besides word symbols, there are other symbols of communication in more specialized media—such as mathematical, musical, and technical notation, and artistic idiom, which might be called the "grammars" of these fields.

To inquire accurately. The mind is disciplined to make accurate inquiry into experience by means of the natural sciences, the social sciences, and also the various methodologies. The natural and social sciences are not viewed here in terms of content, but in terms of ways of knowing. The natural sciences, for example, train the mind in the exacting methods of experimental inquiry. The social sciences train the mind in the various methods whereby social phenomena are investigated and described, such as by the case method, sampling, and the like. The various methodologies—such as in literature, or history, or philosophy—reveal that method is not of a piece, but depends on what is being examined. Literary method, for example, is like nothing else as a method of analysis, but necessary to inquire accurately into literature.

To evaluate wisely. Literature and the other fine arts, ethics (philosophical and theological), and esthetics help the mind to make more adequate judgments of beauty and ugliness, right and wrong. To study and to become acquainted with the fine arts is both to cultivate one's ability to make esthetic judgments and to increase one's capacity for esthetic delight—both of which enhance a man's perception of everyday human experience. The arts illumine human experience through drama, novel, painting, sculpture, etc., and by so doing strengthen and discipline the imagination which conditions moral insight. All works of art pass judgment on the world as it is, and endeavor to move beyond what is. As to the moral realm, ethics is a direct cultivation of the mind to make distinctions between right and wrong, good and evil, by studying the criteria whereby such judgments may be made. Axiology (philosophy of value) is the critical study of the nature, criteria, and status of all values. Finally, the systematic study of religion also enables one to appreciate values, chiefly that "value" which we call "holiness." The beautiful, the good, and the holy—in all the student should be taught to evaluate more sensitively and objectively.

To understand synoptically. The study of history, philosophy, and theology enables the student to get an outlook on the whole, to integrate his study. The integrative synoptic aspect proper is given by history and philosophy, whereas the integrative center is provided by Christian theology, for the Christian college has been defined as the kind of college which finds its integrating faith and philosophy in the Christian religion.[13] History trains the mind to make synoptic judgment in terms of *time*, whereas philosophy does this in terms of *system*. All things are related in both a temporal and a systematic way. The historian weaves artificially separated strands of life together in the relationship of time. Through history (rightly taught) the student can integrate his knowledge temporally, bringing all fields into historical perspective. Within the Christian college, it should go without saying that history is to be regarded as itself integrated in and through the Incarnation and God's redemptive purpose in history.

The philosopher seeks to understand human existence and experience in terms of value (axiology and ethics), in terms of beauty and creativity (esthetics), in terms of knowledge (logic and epistemology), and to understand reality as a whole by means of metaphysics (the study of being as being, or the meaning of reality *as a whole* and not its aspects, which is the province of the special sciences). Through philosophy (rightly taught) the student learns to integrate his knowledge by ordering it. Greene comments that philosophy is even more synoptic, therefore, than history, because "it surveys all spatio-temporal phenomena in their essential diversities and similarities, their basic causal interconnections, and, in addition, their relation to actualized and ideal values."[14]

The historical and philosophical axes complement each other— the philosopher cannot ignore historical event, and the historian cannot ignore basic interpretative principles.

The study of the Christian religion is the very center of integration for the Christian college, of course, for theology is man's ultimate attempt to relate time and eternity, the profane and holy, fact

---

[13]By the 1951 workshops on "What Is a Christian College?"

[14]"A Liberal Christian Idealist Philosophy of Education," Chap. IV of *Modern Philosophies and Education*, ed. Nelson B. Henry (Chicago: University of Chicago Press, 1955), p. 126.

and value, etc. to each other in terms of the Christian Revelation. Theology deals with the philosophical questions of the origin and destiny of man and the universe, and answers them in terms of divine revelation. In this manner it trains the mind to see all things and all knowledge from a theological perspective, and prepares the way for that personal integration (the self and God in fellowship) which is superior to intellectual integration alone.

These, then, are the five great families of disciplines—although sometimes they are reduced to four when the first two are combined as a "logical-linguistic" skill. Every student should have the opportunity for as adequate a training in each as his time and ability permit.

As sciences. Secondly, we may discuss the liberal arts from the aspect of content. Any curriculum attempts to present a "course of courses," and thus strives to be a system of knowledge. In his study of *The System of Knowledge,* Paul Tillich has pointed out that the principle of such a system must be grounded in the nature of knowledge itself. Knowledge regarded merely as a *fact* of human history has appeared in a number of subject matters, and one could write a history of each one as so many historical facts. Or one could write a sociology of knowledge, as Karl Mannheim did. In this way the various sciences would be objects of knowledge, and there would be an integration of sorts. However, as Tillich has pointed out, the various sciences of the human intellect are essentially creations of the human "Geist" (mind, intellect), and thus "they stand under the norms and under the criticism of the *Geist*."[15] The normative order is thus logically prior to the empirical. As to the centrality of theology Nels Ferré has commented:

Theology ought to be avowedly the center of the curriculum. The curriculum should be anchored unashamedly on the absolute will of God. . . . Theology would . . . center the curriculum in truth, provide cohesion at its directive center, make necessary the creative distinctiveness and relative autonomy all the academic disciplines, and offer guidance and incentive to the creative and cooperative Christian community.[16]

In the same context Ferré pointed out that the academic life should, of course, center in the total life of the Christian commu-

---

[15]*Das System der Wissenschaften nach Gegenständen und Methoden* (Goettingen: Vandenhoeck & Ruprecht, 1923), p. 1.
[16]*Christian Faith and Higher Education* (New York: Harpers, 1954), pp. 121 f.

nity where worship would be primary.[17] Thus as sciences the same family of studies discussed as disciplines comprise a system of knowledge with logic at its perimeter and theology at its center. Only through such an ordering can the Christian college be a university, not a pluriversity of unrelated subjects. First, the formal sciences, then the factual, then the normative, and finally, the synoptic. This is the way that Greene suggests, and we shall use his classification along with modifications from Tillich's previously cited study of the system of knowledge. Looking at the sciences in order, we shall again begin with logic and language.

The formal studies. Because in the United States the term "science" has come to be restricted to the natural (and perhaps the social) sciences, we shall use the term "study" as a neutral usage, even though the term "science" merely means systematic knowledge. Thus logic and mathematics (Tillich called these the *Denkwissenschaften*—the sciences of thought, or "Sciences of the Ideal"), the study of language is general, and the several languages in particular comprise the formal studies. There are disciplines explicitly connected with language—linguistics and semantics—but the study of grammar and rhetoric within a given language would no doubt be the normal way most students would learn language.

The empirical studies. In Greene's terms these are the "factual" sciences (natural and social), whereas Tillich called them the "*Realwissenschaften*"—sciences of the real. Here we would find the natural sciences (primarily physics, chemistry, biology, but also aspects of psychology), and the social sciences (sociology, psychology, economics, political science, anthropology, social psychology, political and economic history and geography, insofar as these are scientific in orientation rather than concerned with social policy). By saying as Tillich does that they are sciences of the real no metaphysical judgment is being made about the object of these sciences. Rather it expresses the fact that unlike logic these studies are laying hold of what is other than thought—the object.

The normative studies. In Tillich's and German usage generally, we are here in the realm of the *Geisteswissenschaften,* which also includes the synoptic disciplines. As Tillich has said, these norma-

---

[17]*Ibid.,* p. 123.

tive disciplines have created the objects which they study. This might sound like logic, but in the formal studies the object is "found," whereas here the object is "created." Thus it is *"Geist"* and of the *"Geist."* The normative studies would include:

1) The arts. First and foremost, the arts quicken our esthetic sensibilities, strengthen and discipline our imagination. Only first-hand acquaintance with great art can develop our artistic taste. Besides this task, another objective of the arts would be to develop technical proficiency in each art, which would be more limited in scope than the former, but an important aspect nevertheless. And finally, a study of the arts gives us knowledge and appreciation of the works of art themselves.

2) Criticism. Criticism is a province of each art, and is each art's self-reflection as to what should be the norms for critical appraisal within the art in question. It presupposes art experience.

3) Explicitly normative studies: ethics, esthetics, and the philosophy of religion. Some call these the three "value studies."

The synoptic studies. History, philosophy, and theology are the synoptic studies because among the matrices of significant relationship are time, causality, and value. History operates along the axis of time (and corollary to it would be geography as the study of space), whereas philosophy seeks to find systematic interrelationships. Finally comes theology, the study of the Christian religion, as the very center of integration for the Christian college. The whole curriculum may be seen as demonstrating the claims of theism, for this is a *universe* because there is *One* God, and it is an *intelligible* universe because the One God created *through His Word* and thus the entire universe is logos-natured.

We now have seen the same four families of studies first examined as disciplines here examined in terms of their content—as sciences, in other words. In this connection it might be instructive to remember Aristotle's division of the sciences into the theoretical and practical. A cursory examination of Aristotle's division would soon make it clear that the formal, the factual, and the synoptic studies we have discussed would be theoretical sciences, whereas the normative studies would be practical sciences. Logic and language might be treated as practical sciences, but in and of themselves they are theoretical. Let us briefly examine the Aristotelian division, for it may help us understand how the Christian college should approach the teaching of these areas.

Theoretical sciences. Aristotle stated that the aim of the theoretical sciences was simply "to know." Knowledge is *the* end of such studies. That the knowledge gained may be utilized for other purposes goes without saying, but the object of studying them is to gain knowledge. On the other hand, the practical sciences aim not merely at knowing, but at knowing for the sake of something else—the practical. Whereas theoretical sciences aim at *truth* as the goal, practical sciences aim at either *the good* (ethics) or *goods* (the arts), which are not "the" good but nevertheless good.

The aim of the Christian college in teaching the theoretical sciences must be truth—but this means the whole truth. And the whole truth is certainly the opposite of a pathetic bifurcation of faith and knowledge. Teachers whose knowledge in their field is expert and mature often combine this with a theology that is inept and naive. And it is just this kind of teacher who, not knowing theology, fears it as a threat to the autonomy of his field. Theology is no threat to the relative autonomy of any field—to its methods of study, and the like. It is a threat only to a false philosophy about any field—that it has no presuppositions, for example, or that the particular field can be extrapolated to cover everything, as when an anthropologist might assume that relativity of customs means that all ethics is relative, or if a physicist would assume that all reality is physical. These are extreme cases, perhaps not found within a church college, but they are examples of possible expertness within the particular field combined with naivete in philosophy and theology. Value judgments and synoptic interpretations, which are made by everyone wittingly or unwittingly, require study and attention—and what is more—they must not be the province of the philosophy and theology specialists in the college alone. To avoid the charge of "education plus," Christian educators should strive to become more aware and more perceptive of the philosophical and theological presuppositions of their task in the Christian college. It is not that they alone of all educators in their field will have philosophical-theological presuppositions to worry about, but it may be that they will be among the few in their field who know that everyone has them, and who prefer to be alert to them rather than asleep about them. And being cognizant of these presuppositions may illumine aspects of their subject matter that are dark to others.

Practical sciences. What has been said about the theoretical sciences would apply here too, but there are some problems that are unique to this area. The practical order was divided by Aristotle into two spheres, the sphere of action and the sphere of making. Action is the use to which we put our freedom, which depends on our will. According to Christian teaching, however, the unregenerate will is bound in slavery to sin. This does not mean that man has no good left in him,[18] nor that he can make no choices, but it means that all his choices are made within the sphere of law, or morality. Thus he can never satisfy God, for no man can keep the law perfectly. St. Paul described this situation in Romans 7. To Christian thought human action is good only when it is freed from the law and becomes free for the "spontaneity of the good." We attain to an approximation of this in the "first fruits" of the indwelling of the Holy Spirit, although we are at the same time the natural man. Therefore, goodness must be evaluated religiously, not merely from a moral standpoint. The Christian must still observe the law, but he is no longer "under" it, no longer under its curse. He is accepted of God, justified before God, for quite another reason than keeping the law—he is justified by grace through faith. Christian ethics cannot by its very nature be something merely "learned" in the classroom—it must be learned in the everyday discipleship of the believer before God. One cannot conclude that this means the denial of criteria or standards, on the one hand, or a self-regarding ethic on the other. The freedom of the Christian man, as Luther put it, means that the believer is freed from concern over his own salvation, and free to turn toward his neighbor in love. For the believer, then, religion and ethics are inseparable, although for the purposes of study and reflection one may study doctrine and ethics separately.

In measuring action from a purely human standpoint, however, we do judge humanly—that is, on the basis of law, for everything human is under the reign of law. The Church calls its own people as well as the pagan to obedience to the laws of creation. The believer's ethical behavior ought to exceed the requirements of the law, however, although he can do no less than the law. Christianity did not introduce the ethical consciousness into human life. Natural ethics or philosophical ethics exists in men's spontaneous or reflective value judgments, and can profitably be studied by itself or in

---

[18]This is the lame charge made so often by Roman Catholic thinkers against Luther and Calvin in John Wise, *The Nature of the Liberal Arts* (Milwaukee: The Bruce Publishing Company, 1947), p. 193. If man had no good left in him, he would be the devil, or even worse, non-existent.

preparation for study of Christian ethics with its unique answer. Natural ethics may be taught indirectly by reference to its embodiment in literature, social studies, and philosophy, as well as directly in philosophical ethics.

As to fine arts, in Aristotle's terms we find ourselves in the province of human making or productive action, not in the sense in which we use our freedom (ethics), but in relation to the *thing produced*. This kind of action may be regarded as good if the work produced conforms to the end peculiar to it, so said Aristotle. Criticism would be normative within each field, whereas esthetics would be the normative science of the entire province of making. Art is intellectual because in its method of working there can be discerned the pondering, the brooding, and the maturing of the creative imagination. The artist desires to impress his idea upon a given matter, whether this matter be metal, sounds, building materials, pigments, people, or even concepts. Thus the arts are wider than the fine arts, although the latter are included among the liberal arts because of their intrinsic value and more intellectual character. That is to say, the products of the fine arts are ends in themselves and have intellectual substance. Plato would have used the word "artisan" about the workers in the applied arts. Today we usually call such arts "crafts."

The fine arts, then, are "finished" arts (which is what the word "fine" means here), for the products of these arts are works of beauty which are finished creations, objects of contemplation, designed for no other purpose than contemplation.

Education as a subject matter is really a practical science too, and thus an art. It aims at the "making" of men and women, or as one sometimes hears the word, "molding" them. Such an art must respect the nature of its materials, as any art must, and since the "matter" is the personalities of men and women, education becomes one of the most difficult of arts.

Knowing, then, concerns what is; action and making are governed by what ought to be. The formal science of logic is sometimes regarded as a "normative" science, in that it sets down norms for proper thinking. The fact that there are such sciences as logic, ethics, and esthetics reveals that man does not, as a matter of fact, reason correctly, act rightly, or create beautifully. Furthermore both scientist and artist must realize that they are first *men* before they are scientist or artist. That is why ethics is the most important of the normative studies, and for the Christian, this means Christian ethics. Why is there no Christian logic or Christian esthetics then? The answer, we believe, lies in the fact that our thinking and making are structured by the laws of creation, and the end of these studies (aside from theology) lies in either understanding creation or in creating within the bounds laid down by creation. Our moral action, on the other hand, is under the imperative of the Gospel. The believer as a person is a new creation, and as a member of the new aeon should express the motivations and qualities of the new creation.

The Structure of Liberal Education

We turn now to an examination of the structure and interrelationship existing between the various liberal arts. This might be described as the relation between the inner, central studies of man and God to the outer, less central studies. The "inner to outer" relationship is what Brunner calls "the law of closeness of relation."[19] Man's relationship to God is central, then man in relation to man, next man in relation to nature, and finally man in relation to the symbols whereby he expresses himself (logic, language, mathematics). The latter are *basic* studies, but not *central* studies.

The study of religion is central in the Christian liberal arts college, for man's ultimate concern is God and His relationship to man, and central to religious study itself would be systematic theology (or church doctrine) and Christian ethics. Next would come philosophy, for "the co-ordination of the various spheres of life is the task, not of the theologian, but of the philosopher.[20]

[19]Emil Brunner, *Revelation and Reason* (Philadelphia: The Westminster Press, 1946), p. 383. The nearer anything lies to the center of existence—man's relation to God and the being of the person—the greater is the disturbance of rational knowledge by sin. The disturbance is the greatest in theology, the least in the exact sciences, and zero in the formal (logic and mathematics). Thus we can distinguish Christian conceptions of the good, freedom, community, and God especially. In this way rational knowledge is corrected by faith. In theology it is no more correction, of course, but a substitution. In mathematics or logic this correction disappears altogether, except when we are concerned with their foundations. In the sphere of law, the State, history, and the like, purely rational knowledge and faith are necessarily intermingled. When we are concerned with human beings as persons, therefore, rational knowledge needs correction by faith. "In other words, the more we are concerned with the world, *as* the world, the more autonomous is the reason; but the more we are concerned with the world as God's creation, the less autonomy is left to the reason." p. 384. (Preceding *passim*, pp. 383 f.)

[20]Brunner, p. 395. In the same connection Brunner writes of the relation of theology to philosophy in this wise: "They both stand under Christ, the one in an inner, and the other in an outer, circle; the one with the task of understanding the message of Jesus Christ in its inmost depths of meaning, and thus of purifying the proclamation of the Gospel and ever anew basing it upon the Word of revelation; the other with the task of making clear the truth of faith in order to throw light on the problems of Christians living in the world, and to help them to deal with these problems in a creative way." p. 396.

Then would come literature, history, the other arts, the social sciences, the natural sciences, and finally, the basic studies of mathematics, language, and logic.

No judgment is made by virtue of this arrangement as to the dignity of one's specialization. The Christian concept of vocation contains the notion that all vocations are on an equal level of dignity before God. Yet, this does not remove the fact that some areas of knowledge deal with questions of more central concern *to all men* than do other areas. For example, no matter what one's future occupation, he will be reading literature, listening to music, conversing, and constantly judging, acting, and thinking within the context of a philosophy of life and a theological understanding of the world. He will require understanding of these areas more than the descriptive understanding of human behavior or of nature, notwithstanding the importance of the latter, simply because the major problems of man are moral and spiritual. If one asks about the nature of the good state, how can one answer the question unless he first inquires into the nature of man and the ends of life in theology and philosophy, and then moves to the mastery of the political wisdom of the race in history, ending up with the more technical aspects of the question in political science and sociology?

If one is to secure a "formed" education, then, with some structure to it, the curriculum cannot be a mere encyclopedia of sciences, where the student in what Nicholas Murray Butler referred to as "the rabbit theory of education" roams about nibbling here and there at whatever attracts or tempts.

Purpose

Having now discussed the nature and content of the liberal arts, we turn to their purpose. The liberal arts are called arts because they aim to "make" or "produce" a certain kind of mind. What is the purpose of liberal education as historically conceived? It is to form the human mind—and by so doing, to set it free, to liberate it —thus, "liberal" or "liberating" arts. Christian liberal education no doubt aims to educate "the whole man"—body, mind, and will—but it remains true that education is of necessity intellectual, of the mind, and that it aims to form the intellect, to enable the student to gain an intellectual grasp on human experience.

The liberal artist, then, is a person who is making his mind, and the liberal educator is the educator who is interested in providing the opportunity for persons to become liberal artists. To reiterate, the aim of liberal education is the formation of the mind so that the student may gain an intellectual grasp on human experience. This should have a decisive effect on his being and action both. The Christian cannot say that the liberal arts are absolute ends in themselves, but they are worth pursuing for their own sake nevertheless. Liberal education is both an education in the practical (or artistic) rules of good thinking (discipline, means) and an education by the acquisition of knowledge, in a real grasping of truth and beauty and goodness (the ends of intellectual effort). Christian liberal education aims not only to produce a free mind by forming the intellect, but a person who is devoted with his free mind to the service of the Lord Jesus Christ. Nevertheless, its primary aim is intellectual also, or else it could not be called "education." By inculcating precision of thinking and the understanding of truth, beauty, and goodness, the liberal arts, Christian or secular, aim at the liberated mind, freed *from* shoddy thinking and undiscerning judgment and in Christian education freed *for* service to God and mankind.

The Limited Character of Liberal Education

By restricting their attention to the core learnings the liberal arts are in a position to accomplish their end. There is no attempt to study everything, for such an attempt is doomed to failure so far as education is concerned. The result would be a formless, not a formed, mind. Thus there is a narrowness about liberal education, a narrowness that is so wide in its implications, however, that it is a liberating narrowness. In order to form the mind, liberal education rules out certain areas, not as being inferior to the liberal arts, but as being exterior to them. Training of any kind is not the same as education. Training deals with a function of man with regard to some special subject. Education concerns the essential man by dealing with all forms of activity that are ends in themselves. Various fields are really training: engineering, industrial arts, business education, physical education, music education, nursing education, parish education, home economics, or "education" (skills and techniques of teaching). The same is true of professional training—medicine, law, journalism, theology, and the graduate study of any field. To say this implies nothing against training, but it does suggest that we clarify the meaning of education so that we do not confuse it with training. Liberal education is sometimes impugned as "useless," an epithet which identifies the useful with the utilitarian. There are activities that are not utilitarian but are far from useless. That a formed mind is useful to society and to the individual himself should hardly be questionable. The liberal arts study those activities of man for the sake of which everything else is done—activities concerning man as man, namely, his intellectual, moral, and spiritual interests. We need to learn how to do well what we are called upon to do as moral agents, or to do well what we must for the cultivation of our minds. This is not only preparation for an educated citizenry, but for enlightened church-manship as well. Both education and training are needed, but education is both prior to and indispensable to any training.

There is also a limitation in liberal education due to its intellectual nature. It does not propose to encompass the whole of a man's life. Man is not merely intellectual. He is a physical, moral, and spiritual being also. Physical education, intramural sports, and intercollegiate athletics are essential to maintain a more wholesome atmosphere on the campus, and to remind students they are not disembodied intellects. Moreover, sports are not merely physical—they provide an opportunity to play, a needed activity in a place where study is the main concern. As to morals and religion, there are many people both of virtue and sainthood who have not gone to college. Liberal education is concerned with man as a moral and spiritual being, but as "education" it must perforce deal with these aspects of man from an *intellectual* approach. Otherwise it would hardly be education. But by an intellectual approach not everything about man's moral and spiritual nature is grasped. An educated person ought to be aware of the more extensive implications and profounder aspects of ethics and theology through classroom instruction, but even so, he too needs moral experience and religious living to discipline the will and bring knowledge and action into effective harmony. Christian ethics would point out that the power and aid of the Holy Spirit are indispensable to the Christian life—which means hearing the Word of God, partaking of the Sacrament of the Altar, prayer, meditation, and the like. Thus there is a distinction between instruction and preaching. The instruction of youth in ethics and religion should not pretend to be preaching, or it violates its purpose. Rather such instruction is instruction about the Church up to date and what the Church has recognized and confessed to be the right faith. "As such, instruction of youth has to teach, not to convert, not to 'bring to a decision,' and to that extent not to proclaim."[21] The crossing of the boundary line into proclamation will be unavoidable, but is not normative, since the teaching of religion is science, instruction, and investigation. For this reason the liberal arts disclaim any grand purpose to shape the entire human being. The Church, the chapel, the dormitory, the playing field, the commons—all of these help to form a human being, too. Let the classroom do what it is capable of doing—forming the intelligence. As Robert M. Hutchins has asked: must the liberal arts college do what the church, the family, the state, and society in general are doing?

Even the campus educates, and college administrations must be concerned with what kind of education the campus is giving. It is not the function of the campus to educate the intelligence—this is the function of the classroom. But any college is a campus as well as a classroom. Therefore, in its community life a Christian college in particular has a duty to promote a favorable physical, moral and spiritual atmosphere for the growth of its members. Its campus should be conducive to study and should foster the Christian spirit in college life, defined by someone as: humility, unselfishness, helpfulness, generosity, objectivity, freedom from envy, personal relations among students and faculty both.[22]

As a *community* of scholars, both junior (students) and senior (faculty), the college campus must be a place where there is concern for the social competence and moral character of its members. As a community of *scholars* the primary basis for unity in the college community should be the college's belief in and propagation of the "intellectual virtues." Baron von Hügel listed these virtues as: candor, courage, intellectual honesty, scrupulous accuracy, chivalrous fairness, endless docility to facts, disinterested collaboration, unconquerable hopefulness, perseverance, manly renunciation of popularity and easy honors, love of bracing labor and strengthening solitude.[23]

The college as a whole must accept responsibility for the moral and spiritual formation of its students, since the classroom with its intellectual investigation of morals and religion is only a part, albeit central, of the whole. The dormitory life, social functions,

[21]Karl Barth, *Church Dogmatics*, trans. G. T. Thomson (Edinburgh: T. & T. Clark, 1936), I, 1, p. 55.
[22]A. John Coleman, *The Task of the Christian in the University* (New York: Association Press, 1947), p. 19.
[23]Quoted in *ibid.*, p. 58.

eating places, and the like, should strive to promote a true collegiate community life—an integration of intellectual, ethical, and religious interests. In this connection the all-too-prevalent cafeteria system in our church colleges might be called in question for not providing that community aspect which ought to characterize the mealtime in a college community. But all of these aspects are secondary to the central aim of the college—the formation of the human mind. This is the college's *raison d'etre*, without which it would not be a college at all. Unless the central aim is being met, especially by means of a top-grade faculty and a solid curriculum, then the other features are meaningless.

The restrictiveness of liberal education suggests also that education does not end in college. Liberal studies prepare a man for a life-long devotion to them. A liberal college recognizes that life cannot be composed merely of liberal arts—it only insists that for four years the student devote himself to them as if they were everything. Only in this way can mastery of these arts be assured. Furthermore, these arts are so demanding that extraneous studies should not be allowed to crowd them out. Not all parts of man are of equal importance—his dress, his food, his health, his business, important as they are, are not as important as his intellectual, moral and spiritual nature. The studies that occupy themselves with these aspects of man are the liberal studies—therefore, let the liberal arts college be what it is supposed to be. Let it have the opportunity to concentrate all its energies on the infinitely important task of teaching the student how to think, how to communicate thought, how to make accurate inquiry, how to discriminate values, how to see relationships—how, in fact, to become an integral human being, with an intellect that is formed rather than formless.

SUGGESTIONS TOWARD A CHRISTIAN PHILOSOPHY OF LIBERAL EDUCATION

We have now said that the liberal arts are the arts and sciences of the human mind. These arts and sciences also constitute what we call "culture," or the realm of culture (not in the sociological sense, however). The Lutheran Church throughout its history has always emphasized that culture is a God-given realm of creation.[24] Man did not create this realm, but God gave it to man as both a

---

[24]See, e.g., Dietrich Bonhoeffer's *Ethics*, tr. Neville H. Smith (New York: Macmillan, 1955), pp. 140-141, 252-253.

gift and a task. God gave to man his reason whereby he might create the arts and investigate the sciences within this realm of culture. The Christian, therefore, enters the realm of culture, not because he ought to, but because he wants to. It is the God-given gift of reason that impels him to cultural activity. The believer's commitment to Christ not only gives him a faith but also an outlook, a new outlook within which he sees all the spheres of life.

Fundamentally this is an ethico-religious outlook, wherein the personal meaning of life is affirmed as central. Using Pascal's terminology, the order of charity (i.e., *agape*, love) is higher than mind, and mind is higher than body. While this order was always present in the creation from the beginning, it was not unambiguously revealed until the coming of Christ. The fact of creation indicates the reality of the object (it is created, and one can love only what is other than oneself), and the reality of the subject (it is not a by-product of nature, but a unique person) both, as well as the relation of God to nature. The doctrine of creation, moreover, rules out all secular attempts to explain the world (mechanism, materialism, pantheism, deism, etc.) or to assert that the world is wholly inscrutable. The world is intelligible—this is the grand assumption of all knowledge—but such a belief is justified only if one realizes that things are intelligible because the divine light shines on them. The world is uniform—this is the grand assumption of natural science—but such a belief is justified because the world is the creation of the one true God. The grand assumptions of knowledge, therefore, are justified only by faith in the God and Father of our Lord Jesus Christ, in whom it is revealed that higher than intelligent understanding is love.

Next to the ethico-religious center of man, then, there is nothing more human than the arts and sciences, the products of the human mind as ends, not as the application of the mind to other purposes. The order of mind, as Pascal said, is next to that of love, and the inner core of the uses of mind (arts and sciences) is presupposed in all applications of intelligence (such as the useful arts, applied sciences, technologies, etc.). There is no implication here that mind is excluded from the order of love, for each order takes up into itself the order below it, and consequently we can understand why everything in the order of the mind must serve human life as a whole. Nevertheless, each sphere has a relative autonomy, such that no scientist "who does not carry on his researches simply and solely for the sake of truth is no true scientist, and the artist who does not work simply in order to create a work of art is no true artist."[25] Through the order of love we shall not learn how to think, but love should impel us to learn how to think better in order that we might thereby better serve God and fellow men in love. Moreover, we do not come to faith without our minds. The old Lutheran dogmaticians used to speak of faith as consisting of knowledge, assent, and trust (*notitia, assensus,* and *ficucia*). In the last analysis faith is primarily trust, but the other aspects are involved too.

While we grant, then, that life is more important than knowledge, nevertheless knowledge is of great importance. In culture the mind is exercised upon elements that are ends in themselves, relatively speaking, but in the state, in marriage, or in one's job, one must also exercise his mental abilities. The unexamined life is not worth living, said Socrates. Experience teaches man nothing unless he reflects on his experience. Man must learn by a sort of trial and error method, however, for he is not God. Therefore, a man must pause and reflect before he acts, and his life is a constant "withdrawal and return," to use Toynbee's phrase. What the believer's action ought to be in the local community, or the church, or the state—all call for his reflection on the ends of man in these communities. He must also be able to assess the contemporary situation in these communities. But then he must act, even though he does not have full knowledge or understanding. He must act from confidence in Christ, that is, by faith and hope. All of the orders in which man lives—political, economic, cultural, etc.—are provisional, awaiting the final redemption in the coming of our Lord. Then these orders will be fulfilled, for Christ is the fulfillment of the law, not its destroyer. The earth will not be destroyed, but renewed. No work of culture will endure, but culture itself will be fulfilled in that new heaven and new earth.

For the student, then, who finds himself at a liberal arts college, his duty is to become acquainted with all the areas of culture, as well as eventually to concentrate upon one. For the time being the life of learning is his calling. At the same time he lives also in the other spheres of life—as a child of parents, as a citizen of his country, as a member of the church, and the like. His major task in college is preparation for adult life through learning. The college can equip him in his intelligence primarily; all the other orders

---

[25]Emil Brunner, *The Divine Imperative* (Philadelphia: The Westminster Press, 1947), p. 485.

help him, along with college, to grow in moral and spiritual stature as he lives in fellowship with God. The aims of a college, to help him to know how to think, and so on, are invaluable for the student no matter what his future "job" will be, inasmuch as intelligence is required in any job he may have. But this is not all, for no occupation is an end in itself, and with the interests he gains in college, he may put his leisure time to more rewarding use. This should not be thought of selfishly, but in terms of service to others. The more educated a man is, the more service he can render. Not only love of man and God will characterize his life, but love of truth, beauty, and goodness as well, and actually this is to love the values that God has placed in His creation. Culture is a symbol of the future truth, beauty, and goodness we shall enjoy in God's new creation.

Therefore, while we would indeed insist that the ethico-religious is essential to man, culture (or the intellectual) is next to it. This relation is the *fides quaerens intellectum* ("faith seeking understanding") of Anselm. The personal meaning of life is first, and culture does not enable us to be more personal than the most uncultured of men who know Christ. Even so, the order of mind, the gift of reason, obscured as it is by sin, is certainly to be regarded as one of man's most treasured endowments, to be used for the glory of God. Its cultivation is the task of man, not merely in school and college, but also in his leisure hours no matter what the nature of his "job" may be.

THE SERVICE OF THE CHRISTIAN LIBERAL ARTS COLLEGE TO THE CHURCH

It Provides Educated Churchmen

While many of our colleges were founded to give a cultural education for men going into the ministry, this should not be our view today. That is to say, we believe in liberal education as the indispensable background for community leaders in any vocation whatsoever, including the ministry. If the sphere of culture is a God-created order, then the church stands for the best kind of culture, just as it stands for the best kind of economic, political, and material life. It stands for the best, although it cannot determine the inner technics of any sphere. The church, however, does know the ends for which these orders exist and to which the means must be subordinated. Perhaps the best analogy one can use here is that of "conscience." The church in Norway during the last war spoke of the church as the "conscience of the state." The church as the communion of true believers cannot be identified with this creation, for it is a new creation. But as organized, which organization exists only to serve the true believers, the church is of this creation, subject to its laws. Although the purpose of the organized church is to serve the true church, the organized church nevertheless stands in an indirect relation to the other created orders, namely, as their "conscience," just as the spiritual church is its conscience. In relation to politics or economics, for example, the organized church should speak out to champion and encourage justice, and protest against injustice wherever it occurs. This means it must have some notion of justice, and call into play all the capacities of its enlightened laymen in these fields. In the realm of culture, the church was not called into being to create culture, but since the Incarnation did not abolish the Creation, the church can be the spiritual and moral conscience of this realm too, defending the ideals of truth and beauty in the name of Christ the Word through whom the entire Creation was made, and protesting against untruth and ugliness wherever they appear. And vice versa, the church college can be the intellectual conscience of the organized church—for it is the church in higher education.

Many would insist that the church should be the conscience of these spheres in an official manner; others would say it should be indirect, that is, ethically through the individuals who make up the church. Either way it is the individual who in particular must work out the implications of the pronouncements of the church. The Christian liberal arts college exists to provide the men and women who as members of the church are also these responsible individuals in the community to which they belong. Churchmanship and citizenship may be said to be the all-embracing terms for this aim.

In this respect, as Nels Ferré has pointed out, the college (or university) can help these prospective shapers of the destiny of our society "by enabling them to develop creative solitude." Without solitude there can be no depth of society, and church colleges must refuse to become nursemaids to their students' intellects. Students must be put squarely on their own! Somehow the college must then "breed the spirit of personal insight and creative adventure," as Ferré has put it—perhaps by the contagion of creative

thinking in the faculty (which also can be won only through solitude).[26]

Not only is this a question of the relation of the college to the
church, but the church itself ought to be an example to others as
well as to her own people. That is, the church must set a high
standard in its own worship, witness, and work. The church does
not witness to God's implanting of beauty in His creation when it
constructs ugly church buildings or provides furnishings for them
that are repugnant to an educated esthetic judgment. The church
does not witness to this order either when a sermon reveals illogical
thinking. A sermon cannot be mere logic either. But the church
should stand for the best in any sphere of human activity—be this
in building a church or in thinking a thought. Anything less would
be an insult to God's created order—to the God of measure, order,
and number.

This does not mean that God cannot work his will without a
beautiful church or logical thinking, but it does mean that the
church can raise unnecessary obstacles to others if it offends taste
and understanding. Here an educated laity can be of invaluable
service to a local congregation, and can take the lead, for example,
in seeing to it that only the best goes into a church building. We can
also expect that a pastor's education in the liberal arts will be of
aid, not hindrance, to his work. If we believe otherwise, we have
no right to continue in the highest possible education of our ministry. The Lutheran Church has never considered ignorance or
lack of culture a virtue in its ministry. The minister should be one
of the most highly cultured men of his locality, but not that he may
glory in his "cultivated" intellect or lord it over others, for this
would be a sad misunderstanding of the aim of a liberal education.
The really cultured man is not a high-brow snob at all; properly
understood he is the kindliest, most considerate of men. He can
adapt himself to all people. He knows that intelligence is not an
end in itself; only the snobbish intelligentsia believe this. The
church has no place for the latter. Thus culture is not *the* end for
the minister, but it is a good means. The vices of culture, intellectualism, and estheticism, occur when culture is regarded as an end
in itself. But the minister, for example, should read widely, not
merely in theology, lest he become out of touch with his people
and with the significant issues of the times.

[26]Ferré, p. 241.

Likewise the church must have concern for its members' mental culture as well as their moral culture. If the church does not feel it ought to speak officially, let the members of the church, and here we think of the Christian college graduate particularly, urge upon the community that it is robbing man of his due if it does not provide certain instruments of culture for them. Libraries, museums, picture galleries, parks—all are as much a need of any community as better sewers and street lamps. The church must be the conscience of the community not only in respect to politics, then, but also in respect to culture. In both, the education of the Christian liberal arts college ought to be giving its graduates a sense of responsibility in the community. All men live by nature in the created orders, but not all men understand the true meaning of these orders. Here is the mission of the Christian college graduate: to let this understanding become known by his thoughtful actions.

In this way the Christian liberal arts college can help the church itself to overcome a tragic obstruction which sometimes appears in opposing faith to knowledge or faith to art—as if somehow knowledge and art were outside the orbit of God's will. The church dare not make any particular culture its end, or the sphere of culture as such an end, but as long as this creation lasts, the church does have a responsibility to uphold the order as a God-created order. Even its first task of evangelism and teaching is hindered if people cannot read or understand. Are we in danger of realizing William Temple's warning that our modern mechanical education is producing a generation adept in dealing with things, indifferently qualified to deal with people, and incapable of dealing with ideas? Hence the contention of the British Bishop of Carlisle that "for a revival of religion there is needed a great rebirth of poetry and of the highest literature."[27] Our church colleges can produce men and women who will never let such things atrophy, and, no more than we make the state an end in itself when we defend good citizenship, no more do we make culture an end in itself when we encourage the cultivation of intelligence and cultural responsibility on the part of believers.

We must not fall into a notion of religious life as separate from secular life. All life is sacred, under God's rule—in Luther's terms, the Kingdom of God on the left hand (Law, the old creation) and the Kingdom of God on the right hand (Gospel, the new creation).

---

[27]*Towards the Conversion of England* (Toronto: J. M. Dent & Sons (Canada) Ltd., 1946), p. 13.

We must not commit the "angelic fallacy" of thinking that faith takes us away from the world. On the contrary we are not to be of the world, but we are to remain in it. We are to use the world, not abuse it. Therefore, Paul tells people to get back to their jobs. As a Christian a man is not going to read nothing. C. S. Lewis puts it this way: "If you don't read good books you will read bad ones. If you don't go on thinking rationally you will think irrationally. If you reject aesthetic satisfactions you will fall into sensual satisfactions."[28] Under the church's influence, learning and the arts have flourished. The spiritual life is not a renunciation of God's creation, but using the world in the service of God.

It Stands for a Christian Philosophy of Life

The theological seminary of the church is a professional institution, preparing men for the ministry and the teaching of theology. The college has a special place. It is the educational arm of the church which is engaged in the study of all areas of culture. The universe of knowledge, then (not on the level of the graduate school, however), is the concern of the liberal arts college. But why should the church be interested in having such institutions?

As C. S. Lewis has said: "If all the world were Christian, it might not matter if all the world were uneducated. But, as it is, a cultural life will exist outside the Church whether it exists inside or not."[29] Therefore, as he argues, for Christians to be uneducated and simple would be to throw down our weapons.

and to betray our uneducated brethren who have, under God, no defence but us against the intellectual attacks of the heathen. Good philosophy must exist, if for no other reason, because bad philosophy needs to be answered. The cool intellect must work not only against cool intellect on the other side, but against the muddy heathen mysticisms which deny intellect altogether.[30]

Bad philosophy needs to be answered, and this means not only in the philosophy department, but in the philosophy that molds the Christian attitude to any particular area of study—in the natural and social sciences, and in the humanities. Do our colleges teach sociology and psychology in the same way as a secular university?

[28]*The Weight of Glory* (New York: Macmillan, 1949), p. 46.
[29]*Ibid.*, p. 50.
[30]*Ibid.*

Or does the essentially Christian philosophy of society, thus the Christian notion of man and God as applied to society, affect the teaching? This is only one example, and it could be multiplied throughout the curriculum. Are we giving all students a consciousness of the unity of learning and the organization of truth within a Christian outlook? This is a problem of curriculum and teaching. We know that in secular universities either a naturalistic or an idealistic theory of education, or at least an indifference to religion in education, is apparent. What does it mean for us to make religion central? Unless the Christian college is providing a leadership that can see life steadily and see it whole within a philosophy of education that makes Christ and His truth central, we are yielding by default to pagan philosophies and secularization.

It should be apparent now why the church has such a stake in liberal education. It is here where the battle of ideas is joined—not in the engineering school, or the business college, or in the vocational training programs. It is in the humanities, the social sciences, and the natural sciences that a Christian philosophy can and does make a tremendous difference, and where the Christian Church must combat pagan philosophies of culture. In these areas ideas are the important things, and anyone who doubts that ideas make a difference has only to look at the world in our day, split in two by an idea broached by a Karl Marx. In the battle against secularization the Christian liberal arts college can be a mighty arm of the church. Ours is no time for weakening the liberal arts program— now is the time for its strengthening up to the limit of our resources and men.

It Promotes Creative Culture and Research

Lastly, the Christian college also aims to make a contribution to the world at large through the creative and research work of its faculty in particular. It will be unable to command the manifold research facilities of the large university, but it can succeed on a smaller scale. In some areas it can easily compete with and even excel larger universities. In the realm of the creative arts, for example, especially music, the Lutheran church college has already made a real contribution to American culture. In some of our colleges truly creative work in the visual arts is being done. Literary efforts of various kinds have come from our colleges that are noteworthy contributions to literature. But there can also be fundamental research into the basic and general aspects of knowledge. In developing and unfolding the implications of Christianity for knowledge the church college can make a significant contribution to education. The church college ought to be making some exciting experiments in curriculum interrelationships that might affect all education. Creation, research, educational achievement—all within the context of Christian wisdom—should characterize the church college. Then the church college can become "more than an incubator of character and community; it must become the final training ground for scientific, social, and political leadership."[31] But the church college will not succeed in this unless it works in the light of the Wisdom of God—the Lord Jesus Christ. That is why the teaching of the Christian religion is by nature central to the church college. "In such teaching inheres the coherence of the curriculum."[32]

When all is said and done, the Christian college's aim at heart is to be the best college it knows how to be, and its real task is to give its students the finest possible education. It will not put research above teaching, but keep them both as equally high aims. The church college will have the courage of its convictions—to be a college of liberal education with a Christian philosophy radiating from its center and permeating all its parts.

CONCLUSION

Today the Christian liberal arts college is a very necessary arm of the church in the church's never-ending battle against the secularization of life. The Christian liberal arts colleges of our church are a standing testimony to the church's concern for the best culture of its members, a learning that is to be gained within a true community of scholars with a common mission, and a learning that is integrated within the context of a Christian outlook on life and knowledge. Because cultural expressions are the weapons in the battle of ideas, the church's stake in liberal education is most crucial. The church must see in its liberal arts colleges the essential sphere of its mission in higher education, the place where it can make a contribution impossible in any other kind of higher education.

[31]*Ferré*, p. 243.
[32]*Ibid.*

CHAPTER 2

The Theological Basis
of Christian Higher Education

by Warren A. Quanbeck

"What are the basic theological convictions of the Lutheran teacher, and how do these convictions give a unified and comprehensive view of the entire task of education and illuminate and clarify studies in special fields?" Putting our question in these terms makes it unnecessary to argue here for the existence of theology or for its relevance to our discussions. What follows is no attempt at a comprehensive discussion of the relation of theology and education, but rather a brief indication of the nature of theology, its source and norm, and what illumination is afforded the teacher by its answers to certain key questions, the nature of man, of truth, and the world and man's place in it.

THE NATURE OF THEOLOGY

Much has been written in recent years on the status of theology as an empirical science. Some of its friends would repudiate such status for it from distaste for exposing the holy things of God to the atmosphere of a laboratory. Its foes would deny it that dignity because they consider its subject matter as incapable of intelligent examination. An increasing number of theologians, however, lay claim to just such status for theology. They point to its use of its own categories, e.g., revelation; its irreducibility to the terms of another science such as psychology or sociology; and its use of scientific method. Theology, according to this view, is a human endeavor, and while it concerns itself with the revelation of God it ought not therefore to be confused with revelation. That theologians themselves are prone to do so is demonstrated by the existence of the "fury of the theologians" of which Melanchthon complained, and which is by no means limited to the sixteenth century. Theology is the church's examination of its preaching against the background of historic events which constitute God's entry

33

into human history and specifically in terms of the prophetic and apostolic testimony to the divine inrush as it culminates in Jesus Christ. This backward look is, however, accompanied by a concern for the problems of the day, lest the theologian should preach in Greek to a congregation ignorant of it. Theology is then a concern with the problem of communication, of which so much is being written in our day. It needs to understand its message, but also to convey this message intelligently to people involved in the perplexities and complexities of life in the world.

THE SOURCE AND NORM OF THEOLOGY

The knowledge of God was sought in ancient times along three main roads: (1) Speculation, whether by the examination of human consciousness or by a study of man's environment. (2) Moral endeavor, seeking knowledge of God by performance of his will or obedience to his law. (3) Mystical experience, seeking an intuitive, emotional, or ecstatic encounter with God. All three pathways assume that God is in some way accessible to man and that the properly instructed man can find him. The Biblical tradition rejects this assumption; convinced that God so transcends man and the world that knowledge of him is possible only where he chooses to reveal himself. Man's relation to God is not a natural one, which can be effected by man's activity, but is based on the grace of God. Knowledge of God is first granted to Israel under the Old Covenant. Israel knows God not because its leaders have been clever enough to discover his secrets, but because God has revealed himself by his acts in history on behalf of his chosen people. He delivered a helpless nation from captivity in Egypt, he sustained them during the vicissitudes of the wilderness experience, he drove out the nations of Canaan in order to provide them the promised land, he raised up leaders to deliver them from their enemies. The Exodus is the ground of Israel's knowledge of its God and its call to serve him, and thus the constant focus of its religious life.

The experience of the Exodus is deepened and purified by the Exile and the return. Israel's constant tendency to take its relation to God for granted and to develop a national self satisfaction is here exposed to humiliation and disgrace. The prophets of the exile give powerful expression to Israel's vocation as servant of God. God has chosen them not to be privileged pensioners but to make them the messengers of his glory to all nations.

The historical character of God's revelation is reaffirmed and deepened in the Incarnation of the Word of God. The God who dwelt among His people in tabernacle, temple, and Shekinah now becomes flesh, and reveals Himself, shockingly enough to the pious Jew, in the limited historical existence of a Jew from Galilee, Jesus of Nazareth. In him God makes known his purpose for mankind. He is the fulfilment of Israel's history and hopes; he accomplishes the redemption of his people; he ushers in the new age, the kingly rule of God. Because he comes as Messiah of Israel, he makes it clear that the history of Israel is not just two millennia of marking time for the propitious moment of unveiling. Only in Israel's history, institutions, and hopes can we understand him who comes as Israel's Messiah. He cannot be assimilated to any casual religious tradition but must be seen in the context of the Old Testament as the fulfilment of God's redeeming purpose prepared in the life of his people.

Another indication of the historical character of revelation is the Bible. Jesus Christ was historically contemporaneous only with his own generation, but succeeding generations have not been dependent upon rumor or legend for their knowledge of him. The witness of the New Testament prophets and apostles has been preserved in written form to testify to Jesus as Messiah of Israel. Just as Israel's history is used in the providence of God to prepare for the Messiah, so the circumstances of the early Christian community provide the matrix for the revelation of the word. Quite possibly none of the New Testament authors wrote with the intention of forming a canon of authoritative books. But the letters and Gospels written for specific situations in the life of the early church are available when the eyewitnesses have passed from the scene and a reliable testimony is necessary. For later generations of Christians the writings of the Old and New Testaments are the instruments by which the revelation of God in Christ becomes contemporary and capable of apprehension.

It is important to understand the precise sense in which Scripture is authoritative in the Church. For the Church of the middle ages, the revelation of God in Christ took place in the experience of the Eucharist. The Scriptures were significant not for the revelation of Christ but as the law of the Christian life. And since the use of Scripture in a legalistic way raised many serious problems of interpretation, the four-fold method of exegesis was used to bring difficult points of Scripture into harmony with the practice of the

Church. The Bible thus had considerable theoretical authority; for practical purposes authority was vested in the hierarchy. The reformation, reasserted the authority of Scripture, not just as a *legal* authority, but as an *instrumental* authority, that which reveals Jesus Christ the Son of God. This had also significant consequences for Biblical interpretation, some of which are coming to be appreciated anew in our day.

The significance of the Bible is not so much that it declares the law of God as that it reveals the Gospel. The perception of the Gospel in Scripture is the Reformation's contribution to the interpretation of Scripture. For example, some schools of interpretation stress the literary, historical, devotional, or dogmatic values of Scripture. The Reformers recognize the existence and value of these elements, but point out that they are all secondary to the evangelical content of the Bible. The Bible is not just a haphazard collection of Jewish law, poetry, history, and wisdom, like a mound of earth covering an ancient village. It is rather architectural, and its structure is given by the redemptive purpose of God active in history. It is Jesus Christ who is the meaning of Scripture, and this not by allegorical imposition but by historical exposition.

The authority of the Bible is therefore not the authority of a new law, as though Christ were only a second Moses, but it is the authority of the Lord Jesus Christ who is revealed in it. This, of course, raises the same problems for unbelief as did the Incarnation of the Word in the flesh. Jesus could be recognized as the Christ only by those to whom the Father granted the eyes of faith. To others he was the carpenter's son, the thaumaturge or the blasphemer. In the same way Scripture has the divine authority of the Gospel only to those who have faith; to unbelievers it may indeed be an impressive book of wisdom and devotion or an authoritative guide to conduct, but they do not hear the voice of God addressing them in it.

Still another aspect of the historical character of God's revelation is the Christian church. The kingly rule of God has not ceased with the ascension of Christ, nor has it been delegated to earthly authorities, but it continues to be exercised through the Christian church, the Body of Christ. Those who have been baptized into the name of God, who have perceived by faith that Jesus is Lord, who participate in the anamnesis of his atoning work in the Lord's Supper, they are the presence of God in Christ in the world. The church shares the servant form of her Lord; just as his identity was perceived only by faith, so only the believer can recognize in this ordinary band of men and women the presence of the Living God. And as Christ's glory is revealed in the shame of a crucifixion, his power in the weakness of submission, his Lordship in his humility and service, the Church sets forth the claims of God not in proportion to its statistical impressiveness but to the extent that it shares the mind of Christ who came "not to be served but to serve, and to give His life."

The Christian community is the context within which theological thinking must be carried out. Because faith is of the essence of Christianity, theology necessarily has an existential character. Just as music criticism is not the proper domain of the tone-deaf, nor visual arts of the blind, so theology requires participation in the life of the Christian Church for its effective prosecution. The recent history of theology is sufficient commentary on the fallacy of aspiring to an impossible objectivity in this realm. This, of course, does not suggest that the theologian may defy the canons of logic, indulge in superficial thought, or disdain to concern himself with data or a rigorous methodical discipline.

As an assertion and reminder of the existential character of theology, the Lutheran church puts forward the three ecumenical creeds and the confessions from the sixteenth century as testimonies to the way the Gospel has been understood in certain critical periods in the life of the church. Recognizing that the Bible is a large and difficult book and that it is easy to miss its point, historic Lutheranism points to the creeds and confessions to help us find the kernel of the Gospel. These confessional writings are not to be understood as a new form of church law but, as they themselves assert, as guides in the understanding of the Scriptures, which alone are authoritative for faith and life.

SOME SIGNIFICANT PROBLEMS

The revelation of God in Christ provides a religious standpoint for the understanding of the whole of life. The all too common fragmentation and compartmentalization of life have no excuse in view of the religious perspective offered by revelation. Three areas so illuminated are especially significant for education.

The problem of man. Perhaps the most important question of our time is the question: What is man? In the confusion of competing viewpoints it is well to remember that the Bible has its own contribution to make. This contribution, as seen from the centrality of the revelation in Christ, has a number of elements.

Man is *created* by the living God. As distinct from all anthropologies which view man from naturalistic, mechanistic, or materialistic premises, the Bible asserts that he is the creation of an intelligent and beneficent God. This does not deny or minimize his kinship with the world of animals in terms of bodily structure or function, but it singles out man's uniqueness in being created to reflect the face of God. No treatment of man which ignores his bodily reality can be adequate, but neither can one which assumes that the satisfaction of bodily needs exhausts the meaning of human life. Man's dignity as one created in the image of God and for fellowship with God must be the starting point of any anthropology which aspires to adequacy.

But lest this provoke a rapture of idealism, the Bible adds the sobering thought that man is also a *fallen creature*. His dignity as a creature of God is indeed lofty, his destiny as one made to share the life of God glorious, but unfortunately the fall into sin has intervened and spoiled what might have been an idyllic picture. Man as we know him does not reflect his Creator. The harmonious life in the world has been destroyed by the entry of pride, malice and greed.

Thus the Bible avoids both the extremes of optimism and pessimism concerning the nature and destiny of man by the sober realism with which it discusses man's dignity as creature of God and his tragedy as sinner.

Man, the fallen creature, is also the *object of God's redeeming love*. The Incarnation of the Son of God brings the good news of redemption, reconciliation and atonement. God has not left man to the consequences of his sin, but has himself intervened to rescue him. Christ is the second Adam, the new humanity, the bringer of the new age, the pioneer of life. He who is joined to Christ through baptism and faith is "in Christ" and shares in the life of the new humanity. The redemptive work of Christ offers new possibilities to fallen men. They still continue to live in the body subject to the same limitations, diseases, and accidents that are the lot of fallen humanity, but by faith they share in the risen life of Christ. The Bible's treatment of this aspect of work of Christ is both realistic and eschatological. There is both present reality and future fulfillment. The life in Christ is not the old life under sin, but ameliorated by possession of a certificate of forgiveness. It is a new life which the Christian has in Christ and which he strives to manifest in daily life in accordance with the ancient exhortation, "Become what you are in Christ." The Biblical emphasis upon the person of the Holy Spirit and his work of sanctification are a part of this Biblical realism, as is also the prominence of the sacraments in the life of the Church.

But the eschatological aspect must also be noted. The old aeon is passing away, the power of sin and Satan is broken, but the Parousia is not yet. The Christian does not experience the fullness of the promise. He continues to be plagued by temptation, by sin, by disease and all the other accompaniments of life in a fallen world, but he has the confidence that He who has begun the good work in him will complete it in the day of Jesus Christ. It is precisely the tension between the old age and the new which makes him long for the deliverance from present imperfections even while he rejoices in present forgiveness and present assurance of the grace of God.

The Biblical answer to the question about man has received a great deal of attention in the history of theology. The same thing cannot be said concerning the second question. *What is truth?* Here theologians have most frequently been content to take for granted the epistemological presuppositions of their own philosophical tradition. The consequences have been not only confusion on this issue but serious disturbances of the life of the church.

In the history of Christian thought, the Greek epistemological tradition handed down from Plato and Aristotle has been only rarely challenged. The traditional understanding of this position assumes that truth is an intellectual concern, a quality of propositions. Truth is accessible to man, can be perceived by the intellect, and can be used by man to gain mastery over his environment. It is important to recognize that the Biblical tradition does not placidly accept these assumptions but challenges them strenuously. The comparative dearth of philosophical speculation among the Biblical writers is not due to a lack of capacity for reflection but to the presence of entirely different presuppositions. One of the most important characteristics of the Biblical tradition is its theocentric point of view. In opposition to the Greek tradition which assumes the accessibility of truth, the Biblical writers begin with the conviction that truth is in God and therefore accessible only to the extent that He reveals it. Truth is not available to any one clever or perceptive enough to find it but is for those to whom God wills to make it known. It is not contained in propositions but transcends them; it is not logical but ontological; it is not a matter of statements only but of realities to which statements can refer. Therefore it cannot be perceived by the intellect alone, but requires the focusing of man's total personality in faith, the recognition, acknowledgement and complete trust in the God who makes Himself known.

Two points must be made here incidentally. First, the Biblical conception of truth does not exclude propositions, logic, or intellect. It recognizes that all are necessary but are not sufficient for the knowledge of the truth. Propositions or symbols are necessary, but they do not contain the truth. They point beyond themselves to the truth which transcends them. Truth is not illogical, but its frame of reference is wider than an anthropocentrically conceived universe.

Intellect is not absent from the act of faith, but faith involves the whole man, not just his reasoning abilities.

It is important that faith be defined in Biblical terms as the confrontation of the *totus homo* with God in Christ and not in its rationalistically truncated version as acceptance of the truth of propositions.

A second contrast should be observed. The Greek seeks truth in order to dominate his environment. The Biblical view is characteristically theocentric: knowledge of the truth is for the sake of obedience to God's will or correspondence to the right order of reality. God grants man knowledge of the truth in order that he may do the truth, a typical Biblical expression which has a strange ring to those nurtured in the Greek tradition.

To grasp the Biblical understanding of truth is to perceive a new dimension in its understanding of man. Modern thinking attempts to comprehend man as a self-explanatory, self-sufficient being. This is foreign to the thought of the Bible, which always approaches man in his relation to God. Man is not truly man, except as he stands in the proper relationship to God. It is precisely his desire to be autonomous, to escape his obligation to God, that constitutes his sin. Just as man's physical organism suffocates when deprived of the atmosphere, so personality can develop properly only in relationship to God. Refusal to trust the God who speaks in Jesus Christ is rejection of the truth, however many substitutes may be offered in its place.

A *third* question of importance to the understanding of education

is that concerning *the world and man's relation to it.* The Bible asserts that the world is created by the same God of love who made
man and that the entire creation reflects the goodness and wisdom
of God. This is to reject first of all the idea that the world is an
accident or that it is devoid of meaning and purpose. It rejects
also the idea, sometimes offered under religious auspices, that the
physical universe is the product of another, less skilful deity, and
is therefore hostile to man. This idea frequently operates in popular
religion, as the notion that man's body is the seat of sin (reminiscent
of the *soma-sema* theory of the Greeks) or that the material
world is evil in itself. The Bible asserts that God made the whole
world and everything in it and that the result of His creative work
is "very good."

But the Bible also recognizes the realities of the present situation.
Since the fall of man the world does not exhibit the harmonious
proportions of the original creation but rather reveals the judgment
of God against human sin and pride. The world as we know it is
not a place of perfect freedom, rationality, and justice. The innocent suffer, scoundrels are given high honors, the fool is counted
noble, and many endure hunger or cold through no fault of their
own. All of this comes under the heading used by modern theologians, "the cosmic consequences of man's sin." But along with
this emphasis there is also the indication that the entire creation
awaits with longing the fulfilment of redemption. The realism of
the New Testament extends to the transformation of the creation in
the fulfilment of the saving purpose of God.

Even within this world, however, God continues to exercise His
sovereignty. He does not withhold the consequences of sin, but He
limits and curbs them through the "orders" or institutions built
into the fabric of the world. Political authority with its power to
punish the transgressor is one such "order"; the family, the institutions of culture, such as education, are others. These are "masks"
of God, as Luther called them. We see the face of God and have
knowledge of His love only in Jesus Christ. But God operates as
the "hidden God" behind these masks which exercise His sovereignty in the "kingdom on the left hand." Only one who knows
God in Christ can perceive Him at work behind these masks;
those who are not convinced of His love may regard them as arbi-
trary, despotic, perhaps even demonic. But the Biblical tradition
regards even these authorities as having a qualified religious value
as manifestations of the activity of God.

Man's relation to the world is therefore a complex one. His attitude toward it cannot be one of unconditional approval, both because of his own sinfulness which perverts even good things and because of the ambiguous character of the world itself. Nor can his attitude be one of rejection, both because of the practical difficulties of the hermit's existence and because of the fact that God's Lordship is exercised even in the kingdom on the left hand. He is called to live in the world with the freedom of God's children who are not of the world. His vocation is to serve his God by serving his fellowmen, to accept what comes to him as from the hand of God, and to live in the glad confidence that the God who has called him is faithful and will accomplish what He has promised.

CHAPTER 3

What Man Thinks of Man

by Howard V. Hong

Francis Bacon is sometimes called the one who blew the bugle rallying the shaping forces early in the modern age. Scornful of the past and confident in man, he emphasized the need for an inductive approach to the external world with the aim to "lay more firmly the foundations, and extend more widely the limits, of the power and greatness of man."[1] Freed from restraints and strengthened by a growing knowledge of nature, men would build a satisfying life through the use of technical reason and instrumental knowledge. Two hundred and fifty years later André Malraux, himself in the tradition of Bacon's Kingdom of Men, spoke to the opening session of UNESCO and stated:

At the close of the nineteenth century Nietzsche's voice re-echoed that ancient oracle whose voice was once heard crying over the Archipelago: "God is dead!"—and he restored to that cry its tragic import. And everyone knew well what it meant: it meant that the world was awaiting, ready for, the Kingdom of Man.

The problem facing us today is that of knowing whether or not, on this old continent of Europe, Man is dead.

The main reasons why this problem has arisen and confronts us now are obvious.

To begin with, the nineteenth century nursed vast hopes, founded on science, on peace, on the quest of human dignity.

A hundred years ago it was assumed that the great hopes the men of those days bore in their hearts would lead inevitably to a series of discoveries that would serve man's welfare a series of ideas to serve the cause of peace, and a new range of feelings that would promote man's dignity.

As for the furtherance of peace—well, it would be idle to press that point.

As for science, we have our answer in Bikini.

As for human dignity. . . .

The problem of Evil was by no means ruled out in the nineteenth cen-

[1] Francis Bacon, *Novum Organum*, CXVI.

tury. But when it makes its reappearance amongst us today, it is no longer merely through the antics of those dark and tragic puppets manipulated by the psychoanalysts. It is the huge and sombre figure of the Dostoevskian archangel that once again appears in our midst, and again we hear him say: "I refuse my mission if the torture of an innocent child, by a brute, is to be the ransom of the world."

Above all we see, above the phantom towns . . . hovers a yet more terrible presence; for Europe, bloodstained and ravaged though she be, is not more ravaged, not more bloodstained than the face of the Man she had hoped to bring into this world.[2]

Malraux is joined in his sombre evaluations by others sharing the modern confidence in man with his "knowledge of power" whereby he can manipulate the physical and social worlds. Bertrand Russell interpreted "*A Free Man's Worship*" in terms of man's recognition of his ephemeral existence and evanescent fictional ideals essentially unsupported by man's knowledge of reality. Max Otto, also of the Baconian tradition, in 1949 considered E. B. White's "*Hymn to the Dark*" to be a truer appreciation of our state than is shown in the usual declarations of great scientists and great religionists.[3]

> This is the prelude to darkness, this great time
> Of light and war and youths who follow Hate
> Shaped like a swastika, sadist economies,
> The dominance of steel and the sword stainless,
> The dissenting tongues cleft at the root and bleeding,
> Singers with their throats cut, trying
> (While there's yet time) to point out where the venom is,
> Ink never drying
> On the insatiable presses.
> Science triumphant, soy beans more than edible,
> And the stud chemist, with his lusty pestle,
> Serving the brood mares of hysteria,
> Getting the gases and the incredible
> Sharp substances of our enlightened dying.
> This is the light that failed, O Christ,
> Make us an end of light if this be light,
> Make us an end of sound if this ethereal
> Babble, caught in the glowing tubes, translated into waves,
> Be sound. If darkness comes, let the dark be
> Velvet and cool . . . kind to the eyes, to the hands
> Opened to the dust, and the heart pressed
> To the rediscovered earth, the heart reclaimed
> For the millionth time by the slow sanity
> Of the recurring tides.

[2]In *Reflections on Our Age* (New York: Columbia U. Press, 1949), pp. 84-85.
[3]*Science and the Moral Life* (New York: New Am. Lib., 1949), p. 88.

The most significant change in outlook in the past decade has been the realization that knowledge of the external world is not the whole of tenable, significant knowledge. Man's critical problem is not the conquest of nature. We have been like the odd mother who was very proud and happy that her little boy had found father's razor—because it was so sharp. Just as the mother soon discovered that the boy and not the razor was the main problem, so are men in our time coming to the realization that man's central problem is man. Man's greatest task is not the amassing of what Conant calls "accumulative knowledge."[4] Man's predicament as man far outweighs his remaining ignorance of the physical world. Man's central imperative labor is understanding and mastering himself.

Contemporary disillusionment over the Kingdom of Man has reached the point of disillusionment over what James Harvey Robinson called "Civilization, Man's Own Show." A version of Bacon's scientific humanism is still a current secular hope, but this, too, is a reflection of the new concern about man as the main problem, as attested by the awakening ethical consciousness of many atomic physicists. Other more persuasive climates of opinion are less hopeful because the ground of hope in the rational, ethical character of man has been destroyed by wholesale evidences of the scientific, bestial inhumanity of men. Nihilism and despair constitute a large part of the new outlook on man and the future and mark the dwindling of Baconian optimism.

The most hopeful aspect of man's present predicament is that he is beginning again to ask questions about himself. Man is unique, it seems, in that he can transcend not only his world of things but can look back upon himself. He can ask who he is, what is his origin and destiny, and what is his relationship to what is not-himself. What men think man is represents a cluster of questions and answers about reality, knowledge, values, and time. What we men think man is epitomizes our basic outlook and guides the direction of our activities. Men may try to avoid asking this intimate question, but even in our age when the important questions have been about external nature, social organization, and commerce, these very preoccupations have been an expression of what men think man is—a consuming animal immersed in nature and society. The tragedy is that by regarding man as a thing we have

---

[4]*On Understanding Science* (New Haven: Yale U. Press, 1951), p. 21.

lost man and are terrified by the monstrous deeds of these things called men. But the human glory of this tragedy is that men can try to understand it, and in the process we are now coming back in agonized seriousness to the question of the psalmist—what is man?

How men have consciously or unconsciously answered this key question in modern times is a pocket survey of secularism. What men think of man is essentially a metaphysical answer about the nature of reality. If secularization of human life has been the progressive trading of eternity for time, the theoretical and practical abandonment of God, and the loss of spiritual reality, the active point of the transaction has been man and his thinking about himself. A change in the concept of man embodies a change in consciousness of reality and man's relationship to it. When men ceased asking about the nature and destiny of man, concern for the ultimately real also ceased.

The aim of this chapter is, therefore, that by examining what men have thought about man we can discern the inner movement underneath the multiphasic development termed secularization. Ideas have legs; they have a way of running themselves out into practical consequences. Now at the desperate bottom of the trough of secularization, we are, it is here contended, harvesting the consequences of a shift in men's dominant answers to the psalmist's question.

SOME VIEWS OF MAN

Modern views of man have not been of whole new cloth. To understand them we must go back to earlier Greek and medieval concepts of man from which modern doctrines were derived or against which modern views were directed. Our aim in this section is secondarily systematic and primarily developmental because of the dialectical relationship of these views and their consequences.

To begin we cannot help going back to the so-called Greek view of man, inasmuch as the basic view of Greek thinkers has been of permanent influence. There was no single unvaried Greek view of man any more than a single, homogenized Greek view of knowledge and the good. Yet even the nature philosophers from Thales on down, thinkers who were little concerned with man, nevertheless presupposed something about man—primarily that he was a rational being and that by the exercise of human reason he could hopefully raise the question "What is the ultimate stuff of the

universe?" Pythagoras and the Eleatics, and even the Sophists in
their scepticism, were captivated by the orderliness of things and
the power of reason to grasp and express that order. The too cus-
tomary presentation of the "Greek man" as disembodied intellect
is, however, short of being accurate. In Plato and Aristotle man
is regarded as being a tripartite unity of the appetitive, the spirited,
and the intellectual, with the corresponding virtues of temperance,
courage, and wisdom. In his *Republic* Plato's discussion of justice
applies to the individual and to organized society. Justice is "mind-
ing one's own business"; justice is achieved when each fulfills his
proper role. This means that for the individual life is to be rationally ordered, with each aspect of man in its proper functional
relationship, all subordinated to the end of life, which is the good.
In Aristotle, the highest good is the contemplative life. The physical and emotive aspects of man are not therefore denied, but they
are denied pre-eminence. The highest in man is reason, and the
end of man, the highest good for man, is the exercise and dominance of ontological, not technical, reason. Modern versions of
this view, in spite of their attacks on Greek intellectualism and
although without the metaphysical background of a Plato or of
an Aristotle, are the various movements to "rationalize" human
activity, such as the programs of the scientific humanists.

By Socrates and Plato a very significant second emphasis was
made in their elaboration of the Delphic oracle's motto: Know
Thyself. The indirection and inconclusiveness of the Socratic dialogue are in keeping with Socrates' assertion in his trial (Plato,
Apology) that "the unexamined life is not worth living." This was
his way of saying that man is man's central problem. Diogenes
Laertius recounts the story (if apocryphal, yet illuminating) that
Socrates, credited with having sculptured figures of the three graces
on the Parthenon, abandoned the art because it was ludicrous to
spend one's life making blocks of stone look like human beings
and to be careless about one's own life to the point of letting it
become as shapeless as a block of stone. Likewise when charged
with having taught novelties about the universe, he answered that
he long ago gave up looking up into the stars and peering into
things of natural philosophy, because men have the ethical task of
understanding what man essentially is and of transforming one's life
in accordance with that understanding. In Plato this primary emphasis on self-knowledge as the intellectual and ethical task is
anchored in the doctrine of recollection. Man possesses the truth,

not simply the truth about himself, but knowledge of reality. The knowing subject, then, is the key to himself and to reality. The anthropocentrism of Socrates thereby becomes cosmocentric in Plato.

The most important phase of later Greek thought, one of the most enduring and pervasive of philosophies, Stoicism, continues in the line of Socrates, with a difference. Stoicism is an ethical-religious view embracing concepts of reality, man, and history. Marcus Aurelius enjoins his followers:[5]

> If thou findest in human life any thing better than justice, truth, temperance, fortitude, and in a word, any thing better than thy own mind's self-satisfaction in the things which it enables thee to do according to right reason, and in the condition that is assigned to thee without thy own choice; if, I say, thou seest any thing better than this, turn to it with all thy soul, and enjoy that which thou hast found to be the best. But if nothing appears to be better than the deity which is planted in thee, which has subjected to itself all thy appetites and carefully examines all the impressions, and, as Socrates has said, has detached itself from the persuasions of sense, and has submitted itself to the god, and cares for mankind; if thou findest every thing else smaller and of less value than this, give place to nothing else, for if thou dost once diverge and incline to it thou wilt no longer without distraction be able to give the preference to that good thing which is thy proper possession and thy own; for it is not right that anything of any other kind, such as praise from the many, or power, or enjoyment of pleasure, should come into competition with that which is rationally and politically good. All these things, even though they may seem to adapt themselves in a small degree, obtain the superiority all at once, and carry us away. But do thou, I say, simply and freely choose the better, and hold to it. But that which is useful is the better. Well then, if it is useful to thee as a rational being, keep it; but if it is only useful to thee as an animal, say so, and maintain thy judgment without arrogance; only take care that thou makest the inquiry by a sure method.

Stoicism expresses the conviction that what happens to a man from outside is relevant only insofar as one permits it to become important. Man is divine by virtue of his oneness with the soul of the universe, by virtue of his reason. Man's concern, therefore, should be primarily with that which makes him unique, his reason, "the deity which is planted in thee." Rational judgment is the sphere of man's essential activity, the one ground of both truth and morality. This explains the Stoic maxim: "Follow nature."[6] By reason and rational judgment man is united with reality (nature) and is

---

[5]Emperor M. Aurelius Antonius, *Thoughts* (New York: G. P. Putnam's Sons, n.d.), Bk. III, para. 6.
[6]*Ibid.*, II, para. 17.

at the same time morally superior to it. By concentrating his being on the eternal truths apprehended by reason one preserves filial reverence for the goodness of all that is (pantheism) and simultaneously maintains this moral superiority possible to man; thereby he achieves release or salvation (apathy).

Stoicism sums up the two dominant themes in the Greeks' views of man. In self-knowledge man discovers that which places him above the flux of time and above meaningless immersion in nature: the Logos, reason. By reason he can systematize experience and discern rationality (order) also in the external world, thereby reducing the chaos of multiplicity to rational discourse (knowledge or science). On the other hand reason is more than human reason. It is the divine spark which man derives from the inmost character of reality. In man the divine principle which orders the Cosmos becomes human knowledge. In reason man has his essential humanity; in reason he simultaneously is united with the divine, the rational, orderly cosmos which is man's true ground and center.

In the greatest of the church fathers, Augustine, there are two emphases of particular importance in a consideration of views of man. Augustine came to Christianity with a wide and detailed knowledge of Greek philosophy. More like Paul rather than like Tertullian, Augustine both challenged and used what Greek thought had to give. In his criticism of Greek rationalism Augustine held that reason by itself is not able to attain the limits of truth possible to man. Reason, he held, is that which man uses to understand his experience. Christian thought is not the way whereby a man becomes a Christian but is the way whereby he understands and formulates Christianity. *Credo ut intelligam;* I believe in order to understand. Faith, then, is not opposed to reason, but faith, Christianly conceived, is indispensable to true understanding. Preoccupation with pure reason, which the Stoics considered to be the ground of man's independence of external nature, Augustine believed to be incapable of bringing man to wisdom, the intellectual apprehension of the eternal. In fact, man's very thought and desire of independence he held to be illusory and sinful.

One of the best expositions of Augustine's view of man (exemplified in his *Confessions*) is his *De Trinitate*. His starting point is the unquestionable fact of self-consciousness. He challenges the sceptics on their own ground and goes to the bottom of the barrel, asserting that even though one were to doubt everything, he could not doubt that he doubted. The essential point here is that self-knowledge is unique, because it is knowledge from within and is thereby basically different from knowledge of the external world.

But, more important, the unique knowledge of one's own self-awareness is not self-contained. In this knowledge of self, there is also the apprehension of being finite, derived. This self-knowledge is knowledge of being a creature and not a self-creator, a being dependent as are all other finite beings upon the unlimited and the infinite. "In order to know God do not go outside yourself, return into yourself. The dwelling place of truth is in the inner man. And if you discover your own nature subject to change, then go beyond that nature. . . . Press on, therefore, towards the source from which the light of reason itself is kindled."[7] It is this kind of metaphysics of self-consciousness which Ralph Harper no doubt had in mind in concluding that when men ceased to be concerned about man they also lost the deeper reality upon which men are dependent.[8] Of decisive significance for Augustine was the fact that the Christian gospel drove him to an examination of himself. Although there is a genuine Socratic element in Augustine, had there not been the personal Christian confrontation it is doubtful that there would have been the profound depth in his view of self-knowledge and knowledge of God.

If this concentration of self-knowledge and inwardness in Augustine, this high value placed on the unique subjectivity of the person, can be traced to the Christian view of God as a person, as infinite subjectivity, the Augustinian stress on the individual is an outcome of Patristic Christology and the uniqueness of a historical human being. This is no place to explore the question; yet this, together with the uniqueness of self-consciousness, the Christian view of individual responsibility before God and immortality, posited the significance of the individual human being in a way considered in Greek thought only by Socrates.

Although Aquinas shifted the center of Christian thought from this Augustinian metaphysics of consciousness to a metaphysics of nature (Aristotelianism modified by the Christian view of reality and the created order), he sought vigorously to combat Averroes and Aristotle on this point of individual immortality. His *On the Unity of the Intellect* is concerned primarily with the worth of the individual person and maintains that his worth is rooted in his

---

[7]*De Vera Religione*, xxxix, 72, quoted by Langmead Casserley, *The Christian in Philosophy* (London: Faber and Faber, 1949), p. 45.
[8]*Existentialism, A Theory of Man* (Cambridge, Mass.: Harvard U. Press, 1949), p. 12.

relationship to God. From the philosophical view his argument against a Universal Intellect and general immortality was based on the implication that there would be no human will and that human mortality and individual responsibility would be destroyed. In opposition to the growing influence of the Averroists the Lateran Council of 1512 considered it necessary to enunciate for the first time the immortality of the soul as a dogma of the Church.

The essential difference between the medieval Christian view of man and the main Greek view of man is that the Christian estimate regarded man as more limited in his finitude and separated (fallen and sinful) from truth and reality. Although neither Augustine nor Aquinas categorically condemned the Greek glory of man, his reason, this unique power requires an act of faith and divine illumination (Augustine) or the supplementation of revelation and infused theological virtues (Aquinas) to be effective and not to be the occasion for the sin of pride. On the other hand, because of an anthropological personalism rooted in a theocentric personalism the Christian view of man elevated man above the lofty level on which the Socratic concept culminating in Stoicism had placed him.

It was the Christian elevation of man which the Renaissance humanists exploited. The Christian view had freed man from immersion in nature. In spite of monastic asceticism the Christian view of man did not consider the battle of man to be primarily against his body (man's point of participation in the natural world common to all temporal beings). Men themselves in all their powers, the individual totality made of dust and divinely destined, were the primary problems of men and the object of divine judgment and love. Therefore it is understandable the vitality of Renaissance humanism in its emphasis on man was within Christianity and not outside it. This point is reiterated by contemporary scholars like Brunner and Berdyaev.

Freed by the Christian view of man from immersion in nature and from cosmic determination or Fate, the man of Renaissance humanism was regarded as God's highest creation, a creature of freedom, indeterminacy and limitless power. Pico della Mirandola conceived of God speaking to man:

Neither a fixed abode nor a form that is thine alone nor any function peculiar to thyself have We given thee, Adam, to the end that according to thy longing and according to thy judgment thou mayest have and possess what abode, what form, and what functions thou thyself shalt desire. The nature of all other beings is limited and constrained within the bounds of laws prescribed Us. Thou, constrained by no limits, in accordance with thine own free will, in whose hand We have placed thee, shalt ordain for thyself the limits of thy nature. We have set thee at the world's center that thou mayest from thence more easily observe whatever is in the world. We have made thee neither of heaven nor of earth, neither mortal nor immortal, so that with freedom of choice and with honor, as though the maker and molder of thyself, thou mayest fashion thyself in whatever shape thou shalt prefer. Thou shalt have the power to degenerate into the lower forms of life, which are brutish. Thou shalt have the power, out of thy soul's judgment, to be reborn into the higher forms, which are divine.

O supreme generosity of God the Father, O highest and most marvelous felicity of man! To him it is granted to have whatever he chooses, to be whatever he wills.[9]

Even though this humanism had its ground in the Christian elevation of man, it was at the same time a truncation of the Christian view of man and a corresponding exaggeration of that which it retained from Christianity. Therefore the Renaissance ignoring of the limited, sinful character of man, his dependence on God, and involvement in nature, in order to exalt the freedom and dignity of man, of the individual man, was repeatedly challenged by the Reformation and also by the growing natural sciences, by both, but in quite different ways.

Luther, for example, does not deny the Greek glory of reason and the natural dignity and freedom of man. But he does insist repeatedly that the essential point of departure for man in his consideration of himself is that he is a sinner before God. Luther's emphasis is on a God of love and judgment and man as the object of God's love and judgment. Freedom of choice and moral responsibility man has and reason is an exceptional weapon in meeting the heretics, but man is apart from God in pride and rebellion. In sin he is bound; not only because of the limitations of his finite mind but because of his polemically egocentric will he cannot find God and come to Him. There are those who charge Luther with debasing man in order to exalt God just as the humanists progressively relinquished God in order to exalt man. If this is true of some Lutheran apologists, it nevertheless misses Luther's concern with

[9]Quoted in Paul Kristeller and John Randall, Jr., *The Renaissance Philosophy of Man* (Chicago: University of Chicago Press, 1948), pp. 224-5.

man in his predicament. Luther's central problem is not God but man, the salvation of man, the problem of a foundering ethics when man realized that he is caught in the lime of his guilt and rebellion.

The story of modern views of man is complex in all its divergencies, but we can discern two basic developments. One of the main streams has been a continuation of Renaissance humanism expressing itself primarily in humanitarianism and in the political philosophy of democracy (Locke, Rousseau, the American Revolution, and the French Revolution), with the Christian elevation of man in the background in the forms of Rationalism and Deism (the Enlightenment, American and French Revolutions, the Encyclopedists, Paine, and Jefferson), an optimistic primitivism (Rousseau), and the cult of humanity (French Revolution and Comte). Humanitarianism and political humanism have often been intrinsically incompatible with the second main stream, but the issue has not been joined.

The second main stream has been the naturalism of empirical philosophy and the natural sciences. This is an enormous subject in itself and can only be sketched here. And happily for our needs the literature and views in this area are well known and need not be cited at length in this brief study.

An important clue to modern anthropology in this second aspect of the modern tradition is given by Descartes:

> Give me matter and the laws of motion and I will build a universe exactly like the one that we behold, with skies, stars, sun and earth, and on the earth minerals, plants and animals; in short, everything that experience introduces to us, except the rational soul of man.[10]

This is an expression of Descartes' well-known radical dualism in the interpretation of man: mind or thinking stuff and matter or extended stuff. Thus when he looks out and sees men and women he asks, ". . . yet what do I see from the window beyond hats and cloaks that might cover artificial machines, whose motions might be determined by springs? But I judge that there are human beings from these appearances, and thus I comprehend, by the faculty of judgment alone which is in the mind, what I believed I saw with my eyes."[11]

---

[10]Quoted by L. Levy-Bruhl, "Essay on Descartes," Rene Descartes, *The Meditations* (Chicago: Open Court, 1931), p. xxiii.

[11]*Ibid.*, p. 39.

Carrying this empirical analysis of man further, David Hume ventures to affirm "of the rest of mankind"

that they are nothing but a bundle or collection of different perceptions, which succeed each other with an inconceivable rapidity, and are in perpetual flux and movement. . . . There is properly no *simplicity* in it (the human mind) at one time, nor identity in different; whatever natural propension we may have to imagine that simplicity and identity. . . . In order to justify to ourselves this absurdity, we often feign some new and unintelligible principle, that connects the objects together, and prevents their interruption or variation. Thus we feign the continued existence of the perceptions of our sense, to remove the interruption; and run into the notion of a soul, and self, and substance, to disguise the variation. . . . The identity, which we ascribe to the mind of man, is only a fictitious one, and of a like kind with that which we ascribe to vegetables and animal bodies.[12]

From Descartes' split-man, through Hume's loss of the self in a succession of perceptions, through La Mettrie's one-legged Cartesianism in *L'Homme Machine,* through successive spectacular developments which gave rise serially to modern astronomy, physics, chemistry, and biology, man's concept of man as developed in the tradition of the natural sciences culminated in nineteenth century Darwinism. One of the two most important effects (for this inquiry) of Darwinism was that it seemed to give ground for a materialism and a mechanism, rendering unnecessary or untenable supernaturalism or an idealistic metaphysics. Nature is the totality and self-explanatory. The second result was the total immersion of man in nature as part of the unified physical world. Darwinism and its interpretation are characterized by William Dampier as

the complement on the biological side of the contemporary tendencies in physics, tendencies which pointed to a complete account of the inorganic world in terms of eternal, unchanging matter, and a limited and strictly constant amount of energy.

The application to living beings of the principles of the conversion of matter and energy led to the exaggerated belief that all the various activities, physical, biological and psychological, of the existing organism would soon be explained as mere modes of motion of molecules, and manifestations of mechanical or chemical energy. The acceptance of the theory of evolution produced the illusion that an insight into the method by which the result had been obtained had given a complete solution of

[12]*A Treatise of Human Nature,* together with *An Enquiry Concerning Human Understanding* (Chicago: Open Court, 1907), pp. 247-54.

the problem, and that a knowledge of man's origin and history had laid bare the nature of his inward spirit as well as the structure of the human organism regarded from without.[13]

It was at this time that slogans appeared like "Thought is a secretion of the brain just as bile is a secretion of the liver" and a man "ist was er iszt." Ernst Haeckel in his widely-known *The Riddle of the Universe* gave a complete and rigorous expression to this point of view. In it God is the Great Gaseous Vertebrate and life and psychic activity depend solely on the material changes in the protoplasm which has arisen somehow from non-living nitrogenous carbon compounds.

Although Haeckel's attempt to draw out the implicit assumptions and consequences of Darwinism and the nineteenth century natural sciences did not constitute a unanimous voice, the direction that it clearly expressed was consistent with the view of man which had been developing within the naturalist tradition: Man is an animal, although a very complicated animal. This view is essentially a rationalized interpretation of man with the data of the physical and biological sciences as the only relevant knowledge. Of great significance has been the fact that the most humane of the sciences, psychology and sociology, have sought to transfer methods and basic principles from the physical and biological sciences, with additions and variations, with a resultant effect on the concept of man. Psychology, the most social of the natural sciences and the most natural of the social sciences, reveals this borrowing of methods and basic assumptions.

From a prior concern with man as a thinking, feeling, purposive being, the development in American psychology has been toward a quantitative consideration of man as a complex of receptors and effectors. Behaviorism (Matson and Pavlov) regards man as an aggregate of atomized responses to stimuli. A later eclectic behaviorism, as expressed in one of the most widely used American psychology texts, regards man as an adaptive animal motivated by physiological drives molded by social forces.[14] Gestalt psychology,

---

[13]*A History of Science* (New York: Macmillan, 1944), pp. 340-1.

[14]Floyd Ruch, *Psychology and Life* (Chicago: Scott, Foresman and Company, third edition, fifth printing, 1948): "Man is an organism, but one far more complex and far more adaptable than the lower animals . . . both in body structure . . . and in brain, which is man's greatest resource and the basis of his unique material and spiritual achievements." pp. 8-9.

"Drives, appetites, aversions—all these are inborn; they have a biological origin, they are basic. But obviously there are many forms of human motivation besides these direct biological reactions. . . . Complex motives and simple bodily needs seem far apart. Yet

less atomistic and physicalistic, emphasizes a more organismic view, man as a whole, characterized by whole-responses to whole-situations. Vitalist psychologists such as Freud and Jung go far beyond the observation of behavior and assert the primacy of the irrational and the unconscious, an aspect of man the rationalistic humanists had not denied but had tended to minimize.

The most effective promoted views of man in our time have been more in the naturalistic tradition rather than in the stream of humanistic anthropology and revolutionary political philosophy. The main spokesmen for these persuasive views have been Nietzsche, Marx, and Freud. Freud has often been called the Darwin of psychology, and Marx considered himself the Darwin of economics and sociology. Nietzsche, though critical, welcomed Darwinian naturalism as background for his irrationalism. (One who thinks with his body.) Yet none of them merely appended his view to Darwinism. The great common link binding these three in the main naturalistic stream is their view of man as immersed in nature and as being totally the product of natural forces. A second link is that they were all engaged in an overwhelming protest against the humanist-revolutionary "ideal abstraction" of man as a rational being. Nietzsche accepted the moral implications of Darwinism (morals as chance instinctive variations preserved and deepened by natural selection) and taught that Christian morality was a slave morality subverting the key to man, Will to Power. The "struggle-for-life" becomes elevated in Nietzsche to the gospel of the Super-man. One is tempted to oversimplify Nietzsche and term his view a Darwinian vitalism. Freud finds another clue to the nature of man: the sex impulse and sexual desire, which lie at the root of all man's activities and thought. Marx, in a materialistic inversion of Hegelian dialectics, sees man as an economic animal and all the activities and thought of man as functions of production, distribu-

---

these motives grow from bodily needs just as the adult grows from the child, with old, simple forms taking on complexity and variety. This process of development is a complicated one, with social influences and inherited bodily structures in combination to make the individual feel intellectually curious or content to read dime novels, make him seek or withdraw from outstanding success, make him a solicitous or indifferent parent.

Just how do the biological tissue needs develop into complex motives? It is instructive in this connection to study the rise of the exploratory motive." P. 143.

"Thus we have passed from the simple physiological drives to the more complex derived motives we see around us every day. P. 149.

"Of course these social motives are based on biological drives shared by all humans, but the way they are organized into derived motives depends on the particular environment. A person will be selfish or generous, will believe in Jesus or in tree spirits, will be interested in making money or in working for a better government, according to the attitudes and behavior that he has all his life heard called 'good' or 'bad.'" P. 151.

tion, and consumption. A third link binding together these three contemporary leading interpreters of man and placing them in main stream of naturalism is their abandonment of metaphysics and their emptying religion of its significance. (Freud's psychologizing of religion, Nietzsche's passionate anti-theism, and Marx's materialism and economic interpretation of religion.)

THE CHRISTIAN VIEW OF MAN

As we look back over the shifts in man's thinking about man we recognize that a nihilism has been implicit in the whole development of emancipated humanism on the one side and scientific naturalism on the other. The essential clue to the dialectics of the humanistic view of man is that having declared himself the independent, self-determining lord of all things, man in the course of four centuries has lost his humanity. Many contemporary scholars have penetratingly analyzed the ironical dialectics of humanism. Brunner summarizes it this way:

. . . Greek humanism had not been a *creatio ex nihilo*. It had been the rational transformation of ancient pagan religion and drew much of its power of conviction from the religious-metaphysical presupposition. Now this presupposition could not be reproduced, pre-Christian religion having been completely destroyed by Christianity. The humanism of the Renaissance and even of the beginning of the Enlightenment could remain unconscious of this fact as long as it still drew its life from the metaphysical substance of the *Christian* tradition. But in so far as this connection was lost, or consciously cut out, the idealistic humanism was hanging in the air. The systems of philosophical metaphysics could not be an equivalent substitute for the lost religious basis, if only for the reason that they were accessible only to a small elite of philosophical thinkers. This metaphysical background was definitely and purposely pushed aside by the positivist movement and from that moment humanism had lost its basis. More and more it was replaced by a naturalistic inhumanism, by a materialistic collectivism, by a pseudo-Darwinian principle of ruthless extinction of the weaker by the stronger, or by a pseudo-romantic principle of the powerful individual dominating the mass of the hero people.[15]

Benjamin Constant epitomizes the development of that humanism: "De la divinité par l'humanité à la bestialité." Having lost God,

---

[15]*Christianity and Civilization* (New York: Scribner's, 1949), I, pp. 97-98. See also a contemporary novelist on this general theme: Werner Bergengruen, *A Matter of Conscience*.

man has lost man. Proudly presuming an eminence and independence he does not have, man has come to see himself as a victim of the forces of nature, a victim of the irrationality of his own consciousness, and a victim of the instrumentalities of economic production.

The clue to the dialectics of man's view of himself in the naturalistic stream seems to be two-fold. The implicit mechanistic materialism, however sophisticated, has presented a world of blind, brute force inimical or indifferent to man's values and his esteem of himself in terms of those values. Second, man viewed as an object of analysis within the quantitative categories of scientific methodology, emerges as a creature produced by the interaction of the given of heredity and the given of environment, or, viewed by narrow descriptive introspection he emerges as a creature rooted in physiological drives.

The net results of the two streams seem to merge. From the high vision of Baconian scientific humanism and exalted Renaissance humanism, through a loss of contact with reality, through methods which necessarily regard man solely or primarily as a thing, man has in his own eyes become a loose, enigmatic bundle of fragments, a creature produced by indifferent or irrational forces which he cannot control, and he himself has ironically become his own greatest enemy. The nihilism of this entire development of man's view of man has cynically been expressed by Mencken: " 'Man is a sick fly taking a dizzy ride on a gigantic flywheel. . . . He is lazy, improvident, unclean. . . . Life is a combat between jackals and jackasses.' " That this is not simply a bit of Menckenian witticism (except in form) is attested to by contemporary European nihilism and man's growing inability to ground his actions otherwise than upon a self-destructive appeal to physical power and mass domination. The debased secular Kingdom of Man characterized by man's inhumanity to man is the corollary of man's loss of God and man's rootless exaltation of himself, resulting in the final loss of awareness of what it is to be a man. It is not surprising that concentration camps, mass annihilation, and a cynical preoccupation with force and violence have come out of a culture subscribing to views that man is essentially an economic animal or a creature of race and blood. This is the paradoxical outcome of man's self-deification and his vision of a secular paradise of men.

Yet there is more to be said. On a wall of the crematory in the Dachau Concentration Camp, where hundreds of men and women, dead or alive, had been reduced to ashes, a G. I. Pascal scrawled these words:

They were mixed together when the world was made—the murderer and the lover. This is the eternal journey of a man. He gets tricked and bamboozled and he louses up his life. But if it is a sadness to be a man, it is a proud thing, too, and no demon ever foaled can know that great journey.

This much must be said, and more, too. The Christian view of man, his nature and his destiny, although attacked from two sides by the humanists and the naturalists, is not dead. It is precisely now when man is crushed by the destructive outworking of these two monopolistic streams of partial truths about man, that men are becoming excruciatingly aware that he is neither a totally free lord nor merely a thing, and that there is a larger, more profound truth about man. The Christian philosophy of man, not simply as a conceptual formula, but as an appropriated living grasp of man and reality, is that truth.

A philosophical anthropology consonant with the Christian faith is characterized by an adequacy in the treatment of its object (man) which cannot be claimed for other views. A sketch of a Christian philosophy of man would include the following constructive and critical elements:

A. Considerations in the approach to man.

  1. Starting point: man's awareness of himself; unique self-transcendence; critical awareness of self-awareness.

  2. Wholeness of man: an individual not to be reduced to the fragmentary analytical abstractions of the natural and social sciences.

  3. Concreteness of individual existing men: a reality not to be lost in the generalized abstractions of statistical data of the natural and social sciences and the eclectic syntheses of some philosophies.

  4. Method: primary data of immediate consciousness (whole range from self-awareness to religious encounter of God and men); value of analytical, descriptive data of empirical sciences; value of critical eclectic formulations of philosophy; value of normative disciplines (ethics, political philosophy, aesthetics, and theology).

B. Christian view of man.

1. A person, a subject, not essentially a thing. (Critique of scientific approach and of naturalism.)

2. A finite, derivative being: naturalism and supernaturalism. (Critique of humanism.)

3. A conceptualizing being: comprehensive understanding. (Relevance of Greek rationalism.)

4. A symbolizing being. (Re-creative, transforming power: art, science, and philosophy.)

5. A valuing being. (Purposive; instrumental knowledge.)

6. A normative being. (Criteria of thought; moral obligations, regret, guilt, and sin.)

7. Individuality. (Particular and universal and individual.)

8. A historical being with a destiny. (Continuity—individual, social, and metaphysical.)

9. A being of freedom and dependence. (Natural, moral, and metaphysical.)

10. Tragic optimism in Christian view of man. (Partiality of rationalistic and naturalistic views of man; inclusive polar Christian view of man and history.)

11. Christian Theanthropocentrism:

It is through this God-given dominion over nature that he is given the power and the right not merely to use natural forces, but also to investigate nature by his own God-given reason. But the man who knows himself as bound by the word of the Creator, and responsible to Him, will not misuse his scientific knowledge of the world by using his reason to raise himself up against the Creator and to emancipate himself from Him by a false pretense of autonomy. He will not become one who, detached from God, is the prisoner of his own technical achievements. . . .

This doctrine of the *imago dei* does not, however, stand on its own right, but is comprehensible in its deepest meaning only from the center of divine self-revelation. Behind Christian humanism stands, as its basic foundation, the faith in that Man in whom both the mystery of God and the secret of man have been revealed in one; the belief that the Creator of the Universe attaches Himself to man; that He, in whose creative word the whole structure of the Universe has its foundation, has made known as His world purpose the restoration and perfection of His image in man; that therefore not only the history of humanity, but the history of the whole Cosmos shall be consummated in God-humanity. It is this aspect of the Christian conception of man that gives him his incomparable and unique place in the Universe.

Nothing that astro-physical science has brought or will bring to light about the structure of this Universe, and nothing that biological science has discovered or will discover about the connection between sub-human organisms, can shake or even touch this truly Christian theanthropocentrism. If it is true that God created man in His image, and that this image is realized in Christ's God-manhood—and faith knows this to be true—then nothing, either in the sphere of nature or in that of history, can uproot this humanism, unless it be the loss of this faith.[16]

This study has been based on the conviction that the secularization of human life, leading to profound disillusionment and universal terror in our time, has been the dialectical consequence of fundamental concepts of man, his nature and purpose, and of man's shifting concept of reality to which he is in some way related. The conflict within philosophical anthropology has been three-cornered, between (1) classical cosmocentric rationalistic humanism, (2) neo-Epicurean–Democritean materialism of modern scientific naturalism, Marxism, and Nazism, and (3) polar theanthropocentrism of Christianity. Renaissance humanism, losing its Christian background of Greek cosmocentricity, elevated man, the creative intellect, the lord of creation, the free individual. Naturalism, whether biological evolutionism, economic materialism, sociological determinism, psychological behaviorism, or expanded scientific humanism, immersed man in nature: man became a creature of earth somehow nursing ephemeral illusions about a dignity and a destiny unfounded in the nature of things.

The Christian view of man is at home with both views and in conflict with both. With Pascal the Christian view of man vocalized would say to the humanist: "When you exalt man, I debase him and show him to be not only a child of the natural-social order and of physical nature, but a creature in whose highest activities of nature-transcending reason and creativity there is irrationality or destructiveness, evil, and heaven-scaling pride. He is a creature who comes from dust and returns to dust, a creature who sinfully rebelling against his ties to nature and against his dependence upon God lays waste nature and himself."

To the reductionist naturalist the Christian view says: "When you debase man I exalt him and show him to be a creature endowed with freedom and intelligence, to be the crown of creation, a discerner of values beyond descriptive data, knowing good and evil,

---

[16]Brunner, pp. 88-9.

a being born of earth and time but with a destiny beyond both, a being called to be a son or daughter of God."

The exalted Renaissance view of man was combatted by Reformation emphasis on the nothingness of man without God. The victor in this battle, however, was not the Christian view of man but a rootless humanism which became inverted and merged with an antihuman naturalism. In our time as never before in the modern age men know in a vague or directly terrifying way the truth of the negative pole of the Christian view of man. The potentially tragic character of man's freedom and transcendence has been played out in the five-century drama of secularization. The Christian church can well say, "We told you so." But the witness of the church to a bleeding, despairing humanity must be to help men to see themselves not only as they are, stewing in their own juice. The work of the Christian church, not forgetting the reality of God's judgment on man's cosmic impiety, must be to witness with hands and word the true humanity of man in the called-life of fellowship with God in Christ and with other men. In its tragic optimism about man the Christian church does not have an immaculate judicial platform apart from man's crucifixion of himself. Without dismay, surprise, or bitterness over man's perversion of his high calling in theory and in act, the Christian church must be more than ever a redemptive demonstration of the reality of God in human life, of the true nature and destiny of man, to a generation that has lost faith in both God and man.

SIGNIFICANCE OF THE CHRISTIAN PHILOSOPHY OF MAN FOR HIGHER EDUCATION

The center of concern in Christian higher education in all education, should be the learner, the developing person. This is the test to distinguish between education and training. The aim of education is the realization in the individual of that which is uniquely and universally human. The aim of training is the development of a particular function. The problem, then, in education is the growth of a person as a thinking, valuing human being with a history and a destiny. Occupational and professional training have their place for particular individuals with special interests, but this is not education. The clue to such training and its defect as education (and therefore can only in its accidental characteristics be considered essential education) is that it is aimed at men as sociological or economic functions, not as persons. Education as conceived in the Christian Liberal Arts college ought on the other hand to aim at the individual's fullest possible realization of himself in the context of his essential humanness rooted in the divinely created natural order and called to a divine destiny which is relevant for every man now and for eternity.

Whatever studies reveal man in his capacities and limitations and consider his origin and destiny and the norms of his judgments —whatever studies make men more transparent to themselves and in their context and thereby make them realize more clearly that man is our central problem—these are the subjects which ought to constitute the core of the curriculum. Chemist and University President James B. Conant gives a clue in his discussion of "Accumulative Knowledge, Philosophy, and Poetry." In pointing out the progress or advancements in accumulative knowledge, he says:

I put no halo over the words advance and progress; quite the contrary. In terms of their importance to each of us as human beings, I think the very subjects which fall outside of my definition of accumulative knowledge far outrank the others. To amplify this point would be to digress too far. I need only ask two questions: How often in our daily lives are we influenced in important decisions by the results of the scientific inquiries of modern times? How often do we act without reflecting the influence of philosophy and poetry which we have consciously and unconsciously imbibed over many years? A dictator wishing to mold the thoughts and actions of a literate people could afford to leave the scientists and scholars alone, but he must win over to his side or destroy the philosophers, the writers, and the artists.[17]

The core, then, it would seem to me, should be the humanities, defined broadly to include the study of language and literature, the fine arts (aside from technique), history, philosophy, and religion, these areas of human knowledge and activity which are concerned with man in his uniquely human characteristics, his creativity and his questioning of himself. Sociology and psychology conceived as humane studies would likewise be valuable as part of this broad core of the humanities. This core should also include, I believe, the natural sciences taught as an attempt of men to understand the physical world and their relationship to that world. If they are taught as a corpus of information and pattern of tech-

[17]*Op. cit.*, pp. 22-23.

nique they lose their educative value and become training. The President of the California Institute of Technology spoke recently of the educational loss resulting from the confusion of the natural sciences as a human enterprise with technology. The loss, however, is not quite as shocking as that which results from the pseudo-scientific, routine teaching of the humanities, in which the aim of education is lost and the central issues and concerns of the humanities as subjects is obscured by fact-gathering chronology and formal analysis for their own sakes.

Such an aim in education and such a central emphasis in the subject matter of education would be the most practical, the most valuable, kind of education, for it touches on man's chief problem, himself, and in a Christian context not only is this understanding deepened, but there is a solution for man in his predicament.

Part Two

Structures

Objectivity and the
Christian Teacher . . . . *Howard V. Hong*

The Administration of the Christian
Liberal Arts College . . . . *Sidney A. Rand*

The Problem of
Curriculum . . . . *William H. K. Narum*

CHAPTER 4

Objectivity and the Christian Teacher

by Howard V. Hong

Diogenes is supposed to have replied to Alexander, in answer to a magnanimous offer to grant his wish, "Please move aside. You are standing in my light." In like manner a charge is sometimes brought against some teachers, not least against teachers with Christian convictions, that they interpose themselves between the students and the subject of study, that some teachers take advantage of their position to seduce their students into accepting their point of view, and that some repress variant points of view or aspects of the subject matter. Objectivity as an ideal in learning and teaching is advocated as a positive aim in teaching and as a remedy for such malfeasance, nonfeasance, or misfeasance in the pedagogical office.

The ideal of objectivity, most simply stated, is that the object of knowledge or the subject to be learned should dominate the learner or knower. The idiosyncrasies and predilections of the learning subject are to be reduced to a minimum in order that the object may more clearly be known as it is. Above all, the teacher as match-maker should not seek to dominate or mislead. He should never be subject to Stravinsky's contempt for conductors who speak of "my Beethoven's Fifth." Practicing rigorously the same openness towards the object (subject matter) which he covets for the learner, he will as teacher seek to facilitate the discovering of the object in its depth and varied fullness and simultaneously the discovery of the object by the learner. Objectivity, then, in a teacher is an expression of respect both for the object to be known and for the learning subject.

If the ideal of objectivity in learning and teaching is essentially as sketched, a number of obvious themes require consideration: (1) the possibility of objectivity, (2) a possible re-interpretation of objectivity, and (3) the Christian faith and objectivity in teaching.

THE POSSIBILITY OF OBJECTIVITY

The assumption of the possibility of thoroughgoing objectivity in learning and teaching involves one in fundamental problems of knowledge and ways of knowing. Exhaustive treatment of the problem is out of place here, but some points must be touched upon. Foremost is the subject/object structure in all knowing. One need not accede to the claims of the sophist or of the sceptic or even of a Kant to conclude that no knowledge is entirely objective for the incontrovertible reason that knowing involves the knowing subject with his enabling and/or distorting subjective conditions or capacities which are necessary for knowledge of any kind or degree. The devising of effective methods to minimize individual predilections and to reduce the role of the knowing subject can never be radical, unless it be the elimination of the knower and thereby the possibility of knowing itself. Russell's treatment of the perpetual elusiveness of common error makes clear that even the achievement of public-ness or universality only accentuates the fact that the knowing subject, however, de-individualized, is nevertheless a pole in a realistic (apart from any idealistic view) concept of knowing. Effective delousing by methodological controls cannot, therefore, yield entire objectivity in knowing unless the host is gassed along with the epistemological vermin. The object may then reign in unrivalled splendor—and unknown.

One of the most disconcerting factors in maintaining a radical objectivist view is the paradox of the objectivist natural sciences. Viscount Samuel claims that contemporary physics has abandoned the "object"[1]; the natural sciences as "free conventions" (Einstein)[2] or as "intellectual constructs" (Margenau),[3] which are not claimed to be descriptions of a world of objects but rather to be conceptual vehicles for integrating experience, are significantly removed from a confident objective empiricism. "While the concepts are developed in close connection with the data of observation, they are not derived from these data by a process of abstraction but clearly reveal our intellectual domination over the data; and, basically, we understand only what we have put into our concepts."[4] It

---

[1]Viscount Samuel, *Essay in Physics* (Oxford: Blackwell, 1951).
[2]Albert Einstein, letter in appendix to Samuel's *Essay*. See also Einstein, "Reply to Criticisms" in *Albert Einstein, Philosopher-Scientist*, ed., Paul Schilpp (New York: Tudor, 1951).
[3]Henry Margenau, *The Nature of Physical Reality* (New York: McGraw-Hill, 1950).
[4]W. H. Werkmeister, *A Philosophy of Science* (New York: Harpers, 1940), p. 316.

seems, therefore, that objectivity and the correspondence test of truth are significantly qualified in the subject matter areas and in the way of knowing in which they are traditionally considered best exemplified. The role of the knowing subject is vastly more important in its selecting, organizing, hypothesizing, and experimenting activity than earlier objectivist empiricism allowed.

Selectivity in the natural sciences is also found in the limiting of categories of description of objects to quantitative coincidences and analysis of the object in terms of cause and effect. Does not this, however, permit knowledge of only certain aspects of the object? Münsterberg maintains that in this limited approach of quantification and analysis the object is fragmentized and finally dissolved. He goes further and presents the case for the artist as a knower more concerned with the whole object as it is, reposing in the object and plumbing its depths.[5] The artist, in spite of the freely acknowledged selective-creative activity in shaping the art work itself, may well claim objective truth value for his presentation. In the same vein Whitehead characterizes the natural sciences as high abstraction from the object and insists that the romantic poets exhibited a concreteness and objectivity which more adequately render the object as it is. "In thus citing Wordsworth, the point which I wish to make is that we forget how strained and paradoxical is the view of nature which modern science imposes on our thoughts. Wordsworth, to the height of genius, expresses the concrete facts of our apprehension, facts which are distorted in the scientific analysis. Is it not possible that the standardized concepts of science are only valid within narrow limitations, perhaps too narrow for science itself?"[6]

The preceding discussion does not presume to be an adequate treatment of theory of knowledge and certainly does not aim at impugning the objective truth claims of the natural sciences and their methods. It is important, however, to note that these disciplines, assumed to be the quintessence of objectivity in knowing, are characterized by abstraction from the object, by restricted selection from among various possible categories of description, and by significant intellectual organizing activity. If selection of data and organization (Planck says "any scientific treatment of a given material demands the introduction of a certain order into the

---

[5]Hugo Münsterberg, *The Principles of Art Education* (New York: 1905).
[6]A. N. Whitehead, *Science and the Modern World* (New York: New American Library, 1948), p. 85.

material dealt with. . . ."[7]) are required in the rigorously chaste natural sciences, is it to be wondered that selection of material and use of a principle of ordering are tasks of the learner and of the scholar in every field? This does not mean caprice and arbitrariness, but it does mean that facts and data are not self-explanatory any more than a stimulus is the equivalent of perception. It also means that in more complex subject matters there will be wider ranges of difficulty and of debatability concerning principles of selection and of intelligible organization.

Moving to other subject matter (the object) one realizes that extension of the systematic attempt to reduce the object and to detach the knower from the object can lead to supposed knowledge, because the nature of the object renders knowledge inaccessible to one who is merely a spectator. The realm of values, for example, can be approached empirically and statistically, but can this approach yield knowledge of this which Santayana calls the central human activity? Genuine knowledge of values and of the valuing activity comes out of participation and reflection, out of the reality of moral choices in the greater and lesser crises and relationships in human life. Further, genuine apprehension of the religious life and of the nature of religion is precluded for the objectivist who would remain apart and observe. Paul Tillich maintains that there certainly is a place for objectivity even in religion. "But it touches only the surface. There are objects for which the so-called 'objective' approach is the least objective of all, because it is based on a misunderstanding of the nature of its object. This is especially true of religion. Unconcerned detachment in matters of religion (if it is more than a methodological self-restriction) implies an a priori rejection of the religious demand to be ultimately concerned. It denies the object which it is supposed to approach objectively."[8]

The theoretical inescapability of selection and organization and the problem of adequacy of a method of knowing to a given object (subject matter) make necessary some qualification of claims for a radical objectivity. Practical experience in teaching also bears this out, for even at the level of choosing textbooks, the teacher is exercising duly chosen criteria. And in the textbooks themselves the draped or revealed presuppositions (methodological, selective,

[7]Max Planck, *The Philosophy of Physics* (London: Allen and Unwin, 1936), p. 12.
[8]Paul Tillich, *The Protestant Era* (Chicago: University of Chicago Press, 1948), p. xi.

and interpretative) of the writers indicate the practical impossibility of thoroughgoing objectivity.

Not infrequently, under the guise of perfect impartiality, the presuppositions of a textbook are concealed. Consider, for example, Allport's study of psychology texts currently used in the United States. The two-dimensional character of most volumes is the result of a methodology which reduces the object of study to aspects amenable to the method. A widely used text, Ruch's *Psychology and Life*, "contains no discussion of will, conscience, self, wonder, awe, or worship; nor does it consider conflicts between knowledge and belief, between morality and impulse. . . . One mental function almost universally neglected is prayer. Although the number of people who say their prayers at night is probably greater than the number of people who dream after going to sleep (certainly greater than the number who can report a dream), yet prayer is seldom mentioned, whereas dreams are discussed *in extenso*. Dream activity seems important to psychologists, prayer activity does not. But man's conduct is far more influenced by his prayers than by his dreams."[9]

Convinced that their works are impeccably public and objective, most writers of psychology textbooks do not explicitly state their epistemological and metaphysical presuppositions which to a degree determine their method, selection of material, and interpretation of data. "Most of our authors would be shocked to learn that their texts *have* any metaphysical coloration. Yet it is precisely this shading, of which both author and student are seldom aware, that leaves the most dependable impression upon the mind of the reader. By and large, modern psychological textbooks are marked by four implicit attributes: determinism, mechanism, environmentalism, and antirationalism. These four attributes are not distinct, but are often blended into a single metaphysical atmosphere, the metaphysical atmosphere of psychologism."[10]

This reduction of the object by selection, methodology, and presuppositions is especially noteworthy in a field in which the practitioners strive quite consciously for impartiality and objectivity, a field of which the study of objectivity-subjectivity is a part. The discrepancy between the object as experienced and the conceptualized object as presented by psychology is more strik-

[9]Gordon W. Allport, "Psychology" in *College Reading and Religion* (New Haven: Yale University Press, 1948), p. 83.
[10]*Ibid.*, p. 97.

ing because of the fact that "the very authors who in their private lives are inspired by a purpose, living (as all men must live) by affirmation, loyalty, and a philosophy of life, fail to represent adequately this psychological requirement to their students. Their difficulty lies chiefly, I think, in a certain insufficiency in their own philosophical training which has led them to work with a store of concepts too impoverished to do justice to the full-bodied personality. The law of parsimony is overworked by psychologists."[11]

On the basis of our consideration of the structure of knowing and of the practice within a wide range of subject-matters, our first question (Is objectivity possible?) must be answered negatively—if by objectivity is meant a radical domination of the knower by a self-evident object which discovers itself to the passively receptive beholder. In elemental perception the knower is an active participant and much more so in the organized intellectual disciplines in which selective attentiveness, synthetic ordering of experience, and interpretation are inescapable and are invaluable functions of the knowing subject. In practice we have seen that if this theoretical impossibility of pure objectivity is not kept in mind, the pretense of pure objectivity may unintentionally obscure underlying presuppositions which are obliquely expressed in a methodological reduction of the object, in limiting principles of selection, and in guiding organizational concepts. Objectivity, then, in learning and teaching, is a theoretical ideal subjectively rooted in a passion for intelligibility, which, unscrutinized, through the assumption of its attainability and of its being attained, can result in the subversion of the very aim of the ideal of objectivity itself.

A RE-INTERPRETATION OF OBJECTIVITY

The ideal character of pure objectivity does not destroy its significance for the learner and the teacher. The relevance of an impossible ideal is not eliminated either by theoretical or practical unattainability. Consciousness of the fact that radical objectivity is precluded can be an aid to higher relative attainment of objectivity. Knowing that "the intellect is no dry light" and that no fact stands utterly naked and self-evident is a pre-condition for seeking and using devices and methods whereby a better "hearing for the object" may be obtained. This, however, means a re-interpretation of

---

[11]Allport, *op. cit.*, p. 100.

the meaning of objectivity. It need not and it ought not mean a reduction of the object by a chosen methodology, or the elimination of areas of experience and thought from serious consideration, or the use of claimed objectivity to conceal consciously or unconsciously the underlying presuppositions. This alteration in the concept of objectivity is not a capitulation to scepticism or solipsism or a subjective idealism, but it does assert the polarity of knowing and the inescapability, as Kierkegaard says, of knotting the thread if one is to sew.

Objectivity in this second sense is opposed to obscurantism—willful obscurantism of prohibition as well as the obscurantism of reductionism which by ignoring complexity and mystery claims to have unscrewed the inscrutable. For both learner and teacher objectivity re-interpreted implies an openness, an active willingness to be instructed by the whole object.

For the teacher in relationship to the learner it means an unwillingness to short-circuit the student's wrestling with a problem and coming to his own position. Students may like very much to "buy in" on the instructor's conclusions. But the instructor's openness to the object and his respect for the student should result in a fair hearing for the object, so that the student is not left a spectator observing the instructor and the problem but is rather involved in the task of analysis, comprehension, integration, and judgment.

Nevertheless, without dominating the student, the teacher ought to escape leading or misleading the student into a pseudo-objectivity of indifference and scepticism. This the teacher can best do, without violating the student, if there are implicit in his teaching a tone of respect towards the problem and explicit an indication of the significance of one's coming to terms with the problem. The student ought to come to some conclusions, and the teacher who can best create the atmosphere for significant intellectual inquiry, it seems to me, is one who, while presenting or introducing all relevant view-points, has within his limits come to some standpoint himself. It is not dishonest or unobjective to come to a conclusion—for the student or for the teacher.

A re-interpretation of objectivity also means that the approach will not be confined to teaching and learning data (which are not self-evident and do not stand discretely alone) to the exclusion of values and will not be confined to "knowledge" to the exclusion of wisdom. Value norms can hardly be equated with descriptive averages. Wisdom is not gained by memorizing data and practicing techniques. Oliver C. Carmichael, President of the Carnegie Foundation for the Advancement of Teaching, expressed a rather common view that this problem of values and judgment is the critical problem in higher education today. Quoting Moberly as saying that " 'the university today no longer asks the fundamental question,' " he gives the following analysis:

> Science has usurped the place formerly held by philosophy and science seeks only proximate answers. . . . It is concerned with analysis rather than synthesis, with *search for knowledge* rather than *pursuit of truth*, with the *what* and the *how* rather than the *why;* with the means of making a living rather than the meaning of life.
>
> A basic fallacy in our thinking which may result from this shift to science is illustrated by the inscription frequently found engraved in stone over the doorways to halls of learning: "Know the truth and the truth will make you free." This purported quotation from the Master Teacher is seriously misleading. He said: "If ye be my disciples, ye shall know the truth and the truth will make you free." It is but another way of saying that facts have meaning only when there is a frame of reference, that truth is revealed only to those whose lives are properly oriented. Knowledge is not synonymous with truth and yet the assumption of this scientific age seems to be that it is. Facts may be discovered in the laboratory with test tube and beaker but truth only in the crucible of experience based upon commitment. It is this fact which has been overlooked in our emphasis upon science and the scientific method and in our neglect of philosophy.[12]

If objectivity as open teachability, as respect for both object and student, and as wholeness (non-obscurantism, non-dogmatism, and non-reductionism) is compatible with a teacher's having commitments, objectivity means yet something more—openness concerning presuppositions. Every course ought to include an uncovering of implicit assumptions involved in the method itself, guiding definitions, axioms, and concepts, and its unjustified principles of justification and judgment. Every discipline has them, as does even a scepticism which assumes principles of thought to demonstrate the impossibility of knowledge and assumes the possibility of communication to propound and propagate the sceptical view. Such honesty in discovering presuppositions and aims has been characterized as being "objective about one's subjectivity."

---

[12]Oliver C. Carmichael, "Higher Education—A Review," in *Association of American Colleges Bulletin*, XXXVIII, 4, Dec. 1952, 587.

Finally, objectivity re-interpreted would mean openness to the range of live options. If mathematicians say: "Choose your geometry," how much more should it be made clear that a seeker is confronted by genuine alternatives in spheres closer to the personal center. To grasp and to consider adequately varying basic positions and to lay clear the presuppositions and implications of each is very demanding. It would be easier to reduce the area and the possibilities, still claiming objectivity while leaving one's own position as the fact of the matter. How much more educative for the student and commendable in the teacher is a consideration of alternatives and, if the instructor is explicit about his own position, the presuppositions and criteria which are factors in his reaching his conclusion.

The ideal of objectivity as domination of the learner by the object (the subject matter) and as the teacher's respect for both the student and the object of study remains unquestioned in this re-interpretation of objectivity. Confronted, however, by the theoretical impossibility of radical objectivity in every area and by the comparative undesirability of it in some areas and also by the practice of distortion of the object and the cloaking of presuppositions in the name of objectivity, we have re-interpreted the practice of ideal objectivity in terms of openness: open teachability, openness in relationship to the learner, openness to the whole object, openness of presuppositions and criteria, openness of alternatives, and openness to arriving at conclusions.

THE CHRISTIAN FAITH AND OBJECTIVITY IN TEACHING

If objectivity as re-interpreted were ideally practiced by all teachers, Christian, non-Christian, religious, non-religious, anti-religious, *et al.*, there would be no easily discernible difference between them. Because of all teachers' respect for the whole object and honesty towards presuppositions and principles of selection, description, interpretation, and evaluation, the Christian faith as a historical fact that as an interpretation of nature, man, and ultimate reality would be presented in its relevance to the subject matter at hand by every teacher. But this ideal of objectivity is not universal in practice. Even Christian teachers often approach their subject matters with a closed reductionism, unconsciously or wittingly (in accordance with the theory that religion is a private affair with no relevance to the intellectual world and the common life). In any case the omission of relevant consideration of the religious view of reality and existence is an unwarranted repression of a wholly justifiable part of an objective approach to the object.

For the Christian teacher relevant consideration of the Christian faith within the intellectual world ought to mean expression of the Christian faith as superior in comprehensiveness and in faithfulness to the whole range of thought, experience, and reality. The Christian teacher ought not, in the integrity of his thought and convictions, be guilty of silence or apparent indifference. This does not mean that the class-room is a chapel or the college a church, but it does mean an openness to the whole object and in the presentation of relevant conclusions an openness of alternatives, presuppositions, and criteria. For many Christian teachers the problem of the Christian faith and objectivity in teaching is not one of principle (which it should not be) but one of preparation. Educated in a system characterized by fragmentation and reductionist objectivity, they have not thought through the implications of the faith relevant to their disciplines. Thereby the significance of Christianity in culture and for culture is suppressed by default. Suppression is likely to occur also in the teaching of a positivist, a determinist, an economic or metaphysical materialist, a scientific humanist, *et al.* Insofar as such omission characterizes teaching by the Christian teacher it means abandoning the arena of the human mind and in effect means declaring the faith to be irrelevant to human knowledge and to the human situation. Therefore, the Christian teacher should, as a teacher participating in the ideal of objectivity, consider the relevance of the faith in his subject matter and, as a man of considered convictions, in fair openness give appropriate expression to his conclusions.

This full respect for the whole object should, especially for the Christian teacher, be accompanied by respect for the student as subject, a person, not an object. Objectivity towards students means treatment of them as they are—as persons. Education, then, becomes an intellectual, moral, spiritual task, because men are intellectual, moral, spiritual beings, at least beings whose unique potentiality is to become intellectual, moral, and spiritual.

Just as objectivity towards the whole object implies non-reductionism, objectivity towards the learning subject implies non-reduction of the student as an experiencing, conceptualizing, value-discriminating, aspiring person. Objectivity, then, is double-edged: respect for the whole object involves the learner in a significant pursuit of many-tiered truth and respect for the learning subject as a person precludes truncation of the object. Only a sceptic and cynic can characterize education as casting false pearls before real swine. For the Christian teaching objectively it is rather a corporate quest to become truly human through active participation in the fullest possible knowledge of nature, man and God.

CHAPTER 5

The Administration of the Christian Liberal Arts College

by Sidney A. Rand

The primary purpose and function of the college is the instruction of its students. All other functions and all other purposes are subsequent and related to this one.

In its simplest organizational form the college consists of professors and students doing their work of teaching and learning in whatever way best serves their purposes. The suggestion that a college is a log with the professor at one end and the student at the other expresses not only what some have thought to be the ideal in student-teacher relationships but also the simplest (and many would say best) pattern of college organization. However, this idyllic picture ceases to be real in our day, if indeed it ever was. Few professors, and few students, have been content with their log. Sometimes they have wanted more than one log. And when more than one professor and one student appear on the scene, there arises the problem of how many students per log and per professor. Also, someone must provide the log in the first place.

The attempt to make some of the necessary arrangements for the effective meeting of professors and students has given rise to what we call "college administration." The administration of a college is the sum of those functions which seek to provide the proper personnel, facilities, funds, and general environment in connection with which teaching and learning may take place.

THE PROPER RELATIONSHIP OF FACULTY AND ADMINISTRATION

The functions of the faculty and the functions of the administration of the college are not exclusive of one another for two reasons.

First, in almost every college and perhaps in every one, some of the teaching is done by persons who are chiefly administrators, and there are administrative duties performed by those who are primarily teachers. Presidents, deans, registrars, and even business managers have been known to teach! And teachers, such as chairmen of departments, have responsibilities for the recruitment of faculty and determination of departmental budgets.

This overlap of personnel is of course more common in the small college than in the larger institution for obvious reasons. An advantage of the arrangement is the fact that there is an understanding of the total work of the college by more people because of their personal involvement in more than one of the college's functions. A difficulty, and sometimes an occasion for trouble in the college, is the fact that this dual role of staff members can result in a lack of clarity concerning the proper responsibility of professors and of administration thus leading to personal tensions and disagreements.

The second and more important reason why the functions of the faculty and the administration are not mutually exclusive is because of the nature of the college. At this point it is quite important to understand that the faculty is the indispensable heart of the college. Without teaching there is no college. A separate administrative group is not essential to the operation of the college but is instead a practical means of adaptation to a situation in which it is well to delegate certain responsibilities to those other than the faculty members. A college could be a college without an administration; it would cease to be a college if it had no faculty. It is the faculty in which the continuity and life of the college is to be found. The faculty has the responsibility for and therefore should share in the determination of college policy. One of the sad results of the assignment of policy determination to the administration alone, as is the case in many American colleges, is the relegation of faculty members to the role of hired servants rather than a retention of their proper status as co-proprietors of the college, together with administration and constituency, and thus responsible for college planning and policy-making.

Such matters as the determination of the objectives and goals of the college, the policies by which the college seeks to achieve these goals and even the planning of some of the details involved in this (such as standards for the admission and graduation of students, faculty procurement, faculty rights and responsibilities, and decisions regarding new buildings and future plans) are the joint responsibility of faculty and administration. The administering of policies and decisions thus jointly determined becomes the responsibility of either faculty members, or administration, depending upon whether a teaching or an administrative function is required as a result of the decision jointly made.

In many universities outside the United States administrative functions are to a large measure carried out by teaching personnel in addition to their instructional duties. Such positions as rector, dean, or principal are frequently rotated among faculty members. In the United States, with its tradition of colleges and universities organized on the pattern of business corporations together with our American inclination toward specialization and organization, there has tended to grow up an increasingly complex administrative machinery in higher education. Also, more and more the administrative function has been separated from the teaching function and even set over against it and made superior to it in terms of policy-making and business affairs. Finally the college is "run" by the administration composed of the board of trustees or regents together with the officers of the administration.

It is difficult to avoid this state of affairs. In the United States approximately one half of the higher educational institutions are operated by organizations other than the government. Many of these are church-sponsored or church-related. Such colleges and universities enjoy great freedom before the law with regard to the educational functions of the institution. The state is interested in fixing financial responsibility, establishing clear title to property, and protecting the public from fraud and malpractice. Therefore a college must be a corporate entity which may acquire, hold, and dispose of property and funds, and accept liability for its own action. There must be a board of trustees responsible for the government of the corporation. All these arrangements tend to make of the college a responsible unit in the system of American free enterprise. They do not deal with the essential function of the college, which is education.

Following very naturally upon this legal status of the college is the practice referred to above, the assignment to the college administration of the primary, if not total, responsibility for decisions relating both to the college as a "business" and as an "educational institution."

In the Christian liberal arts college a determined effort must be made to recover for the faculty the responsibility of sharing in determination of college policy. Only then can the college be directed by a program which is essentially educational and liberal.

THE ROLE OF ADMINISTRATION

Though basic policy decisions must be the joint responsibility of faculty and administration, there are specific areas of work in the liberal arts college which belong to the administration. The administration in some form is here to stay and has an important part to play in the proper functioning of the college.

The executive officer of the college is the president (sometimes chancellor or provost). He is the agent of the board of trustees in the administering of their decisions and is the chairman of the faculty. The president, ideally, is the "bridge" between faculty and administration. His office frequently spells the success or failure of the college. It is interesting to note, in connection with what we have said above concerning the American emphasis on the administration of the college, that in this country the president is invariably considered the "chief administrator" and seldom is thought of as the "chief professor." The European terms "rector," "dean" and "principal" convey the latter concept better and ordinarily indicate a different point of view regarding the head of the institution.

Technically the President could be the whole administration. But, because of added specialties of administration and the fact that even college presidents are human, a system of administrative organization and delegation of responsibilities is usually adopted. The common pattern is to divide the administration into two chief areas, business management and academic affairs. A business manager, comptroller, or vice-president for business affairs, heads one area; and a dean or vice-president for academic affairs heads the other. Subdivisions within each of these two major areas vary. Such functions as accounting, property management, purchasing, fund-raising, and management of auxiliary enterprises often become departments within the business administration. Within the area of academic affairs such divisions as instructional program, student records, and student life frequently become separate offices responsible to the dean or vice-president, or directly to the president in smaller colleges.

Such functions as public relations and admissions are newer to the college scene than those mentioned above. They are handled in a variety of ways in college organization, but usually they center in an office or in offices responsible directly to the president. The concept of a "development" office to embrace several functions of the administration is an increasingly popular pattern.

Remembering what we have stated above concerning the joint responsibility of faculty and administration for the determination of college policies and for college planning, we may list the following as functions of the college administration in the area of business management:

a. The preparation of the annual budget and its application to the affairs of the college.
b. The receipt and disbursement of funds and all moneys handled.
c. The acquisition and management of the property and facilities necessary for the proper functioning of the college.
d. The investment and care of all permanent funds of the college, such as endowments and special gifts.
e. The securing of gifts for the college.

Specific responsibilities of the administration in the area of academic affairs include the following:

a. Together with the proper faculty members in the various departments, the recruiting and maintaining of a qualified and effective faculty.
b. The support of the faculty in the work of instruction through the provision of adequate faculty salaries and other benefits.
c. The proper care and use of all academic records.
d. The supervision and direction of student life.

THE CHRISTIAN LIBERAL ARTS COLLEGE

The role of the administration in the Christian liberal arts college has much in common with the administrative work in any other type of college. Administering the affairs of a college of the church differs from that of other schools not so much in the type of organization as in the viewpoint and attitude of those who do the administrative work. In any organization the capable and wise administrator is the one who knows and understands the organization for which he is responsible.

In every college and surely not least in the college of the church such virtues and practices as honesty in the handling of money and in dealing with people, faithfulness in the job to be done, service in terms of directing all energies to the benefit of the student and of the professor in his work of teaching, and care and thrift in the use and maintenance of property, are minimum essentials.

Because the Christian liberal arts college is a certain kind of college there are some ways, however, in which its administration differs from that of another type of college or university. The administration of the Christian liberal arts college needs above all to be in the hands of *educators*. There may be a place in some large universities or even other types of colleges for the specialist administrator who is at home and effective in his area of interest but not especially an educator. There is no room for such a specialist in the Christian liberal arts college. Because of the nature of this kind of college it will most likely always be less than wealthy. For this reason, if for no other, the administration must understand clearly what is essential, what is secondary, and what is unimportant or unnecessary. There will never be money enough even for all that is essential. If the administration does not understand this, the result will be the use of funds for that which is less worthy and even objectionable rather than for the more worthy and truly educational in the college program.

The president of the Christian liberal arts college must often be a money raiser; he is frequently expected to be a "glad-hander"; it is desirable if he is impressive in public; and it goes without saying that he should be a churchman. But none of these nor all of them together can compensate for what is lacking if he is not an educator with a knowledge of and a conviction about the need for the kind of education a Christian liberal arts college offers. He must be a man of sincere Christian faith. He needs to be a man who understands human nature in all of its failings and in all its possibilities. Above all he must be a man who believes that education is a Christian experience when it liberates man to be his best and to realize who and what he is before God in Jesus Christ.

What has been said about the President can be said about the business manager, registrar, dean, and other administrators. The Christian college needs each one well trained for his work, but it needs, even more, men who are sound in their convictions regarding the total program and objective of the college.

Having said this everything else ought to follow automatically. Personnel such as described above following sound administrative practices should insure, as far as is possible, a program of Christian higher education in the best tradition of the church and the liberal arts. Some more things need to be said, however, about how this kind of administration carries on its work.

Internally the college needs unity and a sense of direction. The administration can foster this in several ways.

Staff members (especially instructional personnel) will be carefully selected. Because of the apparent "requirements" of accrediting associations as well as of professional and "trade" organizations, together with the desire to offer the "best" program in certain fields, it is easy for administrators to secure as faculty members learned specialists, each capable in his own field, but also quite oblivious to what education is all about. The end result of this system of staffing a college is its conversion into a conglomeration of heterogeneous departments each knowing little or nothing of what the other does. This, of course, means the college has ceased to be a Christian liberal arts college. In an age of specialization, technical progress and vocationalism it is not easy to secure the type of faculty needed for a Christian liberal arts college. But the difficult is not impossible.

The admission of students and relations with them after matriculation gives rise to special problems and opportunities in the Christian college. Not all high school graduates are suited for college. Not all students suited for college are suited for the liberal arts. An admission program in the hands of those not understanding this but intent on raising enrollments at any cost may prove disastrous. The college can change complexion in a few short years. The present situation in which enrollments are rising without great effort on the part of the admissions departments emphasizes the need for care and constant study in this connection.

Externally the administration faces just as important obligations. The administrative officers and their representatives are the ones most frequently in the public eye. The president, the public relations officers, the admissions representatives, and others are constantly giving the public the information they receive about the college. Depending on what this information is the public will grow to understand the college and its program or will cease to understand the purposes of the college altogether. This is important both because financial support comes most readily when the college is understood and because the college must be understood, especially by those directly responsible for its continuance, if it is to have any meaning at all in church or society.

As stated above, we live in a society which in many ways is indifferent if not hostile to the liberal arts. This is also true, to some extent, with regard to church-sponsored education. It is considered "American" in many quarters to foster only an educational program which is directly tax supported and which is geared to the specialized and occupational needs of the day. This means there are people, even in the church, who look upon the church college as excess baggage. Fortunately this attitude is changing and public opinion is becoming increasingly favorable toward the private liberal arts college. But much of this is based on vague notions and not on real knowledge of this kind of college. Here is where the administration has a task of "selling" and "educating." The argument that "the product sells the college" is only half true. Graduates of our colleges do, in a large measure, "sell" our program wonderfully well. But this is never enough because it is often on a sentimental basis or because of a brand of Christian piety displayed rather than because the graduates are educated Christians. Here is where interpretation is needed and administrators must accept this responsibility.

CENTRAL CONCERNS

There are two fronts: the *Christian* and the *liberal arts* objectives of the college. There are those who are convinced the college is Christian and do not care or know much about liberal arts. There are those who are devotees of the liberal arts tradition who either do not care about the meaning of Christian education or who have concluded it is synonymous with liberal arts. These persons need either to be educated or converted, or both. A college can be what it wants to be, come what may (especially if it has mended all its financial fences). But it cannot grow in its effectiveness and remain a vital force educationally unless it is doing a job which not only the college but its constituency believes needs doing.

There is order to the values in education. This order must be understood by the administrator of the Christian liberal arts college. People matter more than buildings. Christianity is a matter of the whole man and the whole life and not an isolated program of Bible study and organized religion. Nor is it a quiet retreat from life for the purpose of intellectual stimulation and contemplation. Professors and students are essential ingredients of the process and football is of a lesser order. Such convictions must guide the administrator. He will have his sleepless nights because of lack of funds and the misbehavior of students (and faculty members?). But he also should sleep better than otherwise if the money for the college has been honestly obtained and used for the right ends and if the faculty and students who make up the college are devoted to the high purpose for which the Christian liberal arts college is intended.

CHAPTER 6

The Problem of Curriculum

by William H. K. Narum

When Herbert Spencer spoke of the "enormous importance of determining in some rational way what things are really most worth learning," his words apply directly to the problem of planning a curriculum. As Mark van Doren has said so well: "the college is meaningless without a curriculum, but it is more so when it has one that is meaningless."[1] We must agree with Dean Jerald C. Brauer's prophetic call to the Christian college:

> If then the Christian college has the possibility of playing a truly creative role once again in American higher education, it can only do this through a concrete attempt to understand the Christian faith in *relation to the curriculum* and to the totality of college life. . . . the Christian college should take an unambiguous stand with those who contend that a liberal arts education is the basis of all sound education. It should go much further in an attempt to work out an education in the liberal arts that is expressive of the disciplines and insights of the arts and sciences yet in a framework that seeks to understand their constructive significance from the perspective of the Christian faith.[2]

In trying to work out some guiding lines along which the curriculum of a Christian liberal arts college should be constructed, this chapter draws heavily upon the actual curricula of some representative liberal arts colleges and universities, upon various books about liberal education, and upon books and conferences concerned specifically with the Christian college. Before taking up the actual problem, however, let us first examine the last sixty years in American higher education.

THE LAST SIXTY YEARS

The Downfall of the Elective System. There may be some who read this who will assume that the elective system has been a permanent feature of American higher education. To the contrary it

---

[1] *Liberal Education* (New York: Henry Holt & Co., 1943), p. 108.
[2] Brauer, *op. cit.*, pp. 240 f. (Italics not in the original.)

is a phenomenon of the last half century or more, and what it led to might be compared to the man who jumped upon his horse and rode off madly in all directions.

The history of Harvard College in the last sixty years is emblematic of this chaos as it affected a single college. *First,* after the wooden, stipulated curriculum of previous years, the liberal arts ran into the *elective system* that we have mentioned. Pres. C. W. Eliot put all sciences and arts on a democratic level, contrasted to the previous hierarchy of studies with philosophy reigning as queen of the arts and sciences. It was a "let the best art win" sort of curriculum, and although there was diversity of foods offered in this feast of education, students left the banquet table with the notion that they had acquired a liberal education simply because they had eaten something. There were few requirements, teachers' reputations attracted the students hither and yon, and the student did not even have to make out a menu of his own. If he ate enough credits, he left the table with an A.B. and, usually, chronic educational indigestion. *Secondly,* Pres. Lowell inaugurated a "concentration and distribution" program, which permitted an unbalanced diet to correct the evils of the elective system. *Thirdly,* early in the administration of Pres. Conant the faculty took the pith out of "distribution" with the result that the training of specialists became the main emphasis. One "might" specialize under Eliot; one "had to" under Conant. It was dissatisfaction with the state of affairs that produced the so-called Harvard Report, *General Education in a Free Society,* 1945, which sounded the call to *general education.* It was reminiscent of the older system in effect before Eliot, but with considerable differences in detail. There was no integrating center, such as proposed by the former chancellor of the University of Chicago, Robert M. Hutchins, but with the coming of Pres. Nathan Pusey, Harvard experienced a dramatic change of administrative philosophy, for it would seem that Pres. Pusey thinks of religion as the integrating center. This has touched off an intramural warfare at Harvard, which at this writing remains to be settled.

Most church colleges during this series of changes blithely followed in the footsteps of their admired secular cousin instead of standing by their guns or advancing any new ideas of their own.

It is now seen that some kind of order must be found. While the elective system was clearly inadequate, this does not imply that the only alternative would be an entirely prescribed program of studies. There must be both freedom and order—the freedom to choose one's special field of concentration and even other subjects, but the student must be protected from himself by requirements of order, such as prescribed "areas" within which he would choose subjects.

The Trend to Vocationalism. Another trend of the past fifty years or so has been the gradual transformation of the liberal arts college into "service" colleges, "meekly serving," as Norman Foerster said, "the ends of vocational knacks and skills."

Thus in many colleges such studies as the following, which have a professional rather than an educational interest, have been invited into the curriculum and have been tacked on to the liberal studies: business education, journalism, library science, parish education, vocational physical education, vocational music education, home economics, nursing, and the like. These fields are all worthy ones, but they are professional rather than liberal in aim. In accord with the vocationalistic demand of these areas, the colleges have advertised widely how they can prepare students for jobs, not only in these professional areas but in the liberal arts fields as well. A subtle change has thus permeated the philosophy of the colleges—their catalogs point with pride to job-training, or pre-vocational and pre-professional courses. Little suggestion is made, if at all, that the study of the liberal arts might be of *educational* value. Little attempt is made to educate the constituency not to expect the church college to be everything to all men. As a result of this defection from the liberal arts by all liberal arts colleges there arose during the 1940's especially the "general education" movement. Dr. Earl J. McGrath and others, writing in *Toward General Education.*[3], said:

> Liberal arts colleges have been so preoccupied with the training of psychologists, chemists, and musicians, that they have neglected the education of the free man. They have not realized, as Montaigne did, that "the object of education is to make not a scholar, but a man." (p. 11).

Dean Brauer, previously mentioned, scolded the church colleges at their second quadrennial convocation at Des Moines (Summer, 1958) in this way:

> The problem is that the Christian college is still trying to be all things to all men, not in order to witness to the vitality of the faith but in order to keep the doors open. This cannot go on. Why should a student take commerce, secretarial work, or even a teaching certificate in a Christian college when the quality of work (and frequently the services of the campus religious foundation) is of a much higher order in a state or private institution? The answer is quite simple—the Christian college has had to add these things, unexamined, to its curriculum in order to survive. Survive for what, when it is no longer engaged in a distinctive effort? *(Op. cit.,* p. 240.)

The Christian college, then, ought above all colleges to have stood for the education of man as man, but it bowed as easily as others to the winds of vocational and commercial pressure. Some will say that this is because the church college must yield to the vocationalistic pressures of its constituency (at least this is said to be their pressure). In effect such a notion advises that standards of education should be set by the butcher, the baker, and the candlestick maker. It is dubious that the theological seminaries of the same constituency would construct their theological curricula in such a manner. Besides, such a policy would be an abdication by a faculty of its responsibility over against the rest of the church. The church in education is the faculty, and it is responsible for its trust—both to the church and to education.

---

[3]Earl J. McGrath et al., *Toward General Education* (New York: The Macmillan Co., 1948).

As many commentators have pointed out, the cure for the curricular chaos prevalent today *ought to be* found in colleges that have a religious philosophy at their heart. But the sad fact is that these colleges lack the imagination to experiment and venture forth on their own. G. R. Elliott[4] urged that material and professional interests are winning out in the church colleges as elsewhere because "these interests are *believed in* by their promoters more religiously than the college as a whole believes in humanity and wisdom; such is the plain, hard fact." In other words, let the church colleges recover the wisdom of their fathers who founded them!

Giving up their real objectives, the liberal arts colleges have aped professional and vocational institutes. One former professor has warned liberal arts colleges against the two temptations that threaten their mission: (1) the "vocational pull" and (2) the "university ambition."[5] Too often the non-liberal studies claim more and more of the money, the propaganda, and the students in the liberal arts colleges—not so much in private liberal arts colleges as in church colleges—thus detracting from the real task of the college, and misrepresenting the purpose of the college to the public. It is a vicious circle, for soon prospective students will come to assume that vocationalism is the philosophy of the church college. The pragmatists have succeeded only too well! Little did they realize that the church college would so easily fall into their way of thinking. Students brought up in the atmosphere of public education with its job-consciousness notice little difference in the atmosphere of the church college.

The other temptation, the "university ambition," is what leads liberal arts colleges to add on subject after subject, field after field, to the curriculum, in a mistaken imitation of the universities. This is to lose what makes the liberal arts colleges great: their closely-knit, integrated program of studies—with ample choice of subjects, but not a chaos of unrelated ones. If an economic argument is needed to convince people: how much less expensive it would be to operate a college that has adhered to the liberal arts instead of the kind which extends itself in all directions of vocational and professional interest!

PLANNING A CURRICULUM

A curriculum is, simply speaking, a course. It is like a track down which one runs to the goal. Thus it is a "course of courses." For a

---

[4]G. R. Elliott, *Church, College and Nation* (Louisville: The Cloister Press, 1945), p. 52.
[5]Hoyt Hudson, *Educating Liberally* (Stanford University, Calif.: Stanford University Press, 1945), last chapter.

Christian college it should be set up with the aim of Christian liberal education as its guide, and it should have some kind of structure. No curriculum will ever be ideal, and thus every college must
constantly criticize and evaluate its own curriculum. Furthermore,
a curriculum requires teachers who know how to teach, and students who are there to study—if it is to succeed. Since these are
such variables, one cannot evaluate a curriculum by what actually
happens in a college—a poor curriculum may have superb teachers,
and thus seem quite successful, and vice versa. What a church
college should endeavor to do is to map out a curriculum that expresses its unique mission in the educational world.

A Course to the Goal. The first principle is that the curriculum
must be planned in accord with the philosophy and nature of the
Christian liberal arts college. Our problem is one of implementation
of this philosophy in planning the curriculum itself.

No doubt many suspect that the norm for inclusion of subject matter in
the liberal arts college is how little useful a subject is, or whether it makes
the gentleman. This was credible in the Nineteenth century, but the notion of
the leisured gentleman is purely accidental to the notion of liberal arts, for the
liberal arts tradition dates back as far as ancient Greece.

But if this is no norm, no more should the selection and formulation of
the curriculum be dependent upon adult activities. By "adult activities" is
meant adult jobs, adult life as citizens, etc. Such an "ad hoc" conception implies that the curriculum should train rather than educate. This does not mean
that the curriculum should be divorced from life. It is difficult for people to
see how practical it is to grasp life and experience intellectually if they have
not undergone the process themselves.

A third misconception of the norms for liberal arts is the view that the college must help its students "adjust to the environment." As Bernard Iddings
Bell has said against the Deweyite educationalists who use this term, that
perhaps a university "might become a breeding place of rebels, a sender forth
of graduates who, unadjusted and unadjustable, would try to turn the world
upside down."[6]

Too often in the past the norms for constructing a curriculum have
been those of expediency: keeping the college doors open by adding
vocational courses, departmental pressures, the demands of professional groups, and the like. In so doing a Christian college can easily
lose sight of its goal. What is the aim of Christian liberal education?
As we have argued before: *it is to educate the total person, and this
principally by the formation of his mind.* Unquestionably the total

---

[6]Bernard Iddings Bell, *Crisis in Education* (New York: Whittlesey House, 1949), p. 158.

person is more than the mind, but a *curriculum* is limited in what it can do. By forming the mind it prepares the student for a more total and personal growth, and aids this whole by stimulating students to grasp life and experience intellectually. What makes the Christian college curriculum distinctive is that the integrating centre of this formation is to be found in the Christian faith and the philosophy of education springing from this faith. Because it has this integrating centre, the Christian college curriculum cooperates *indirectly in the formation of character.* The curriculum, after all, is taught by a faculty, and in a Christian college the concept of man held by the faculty will never permit it to be interested in producing men of mere intelligence, possessing only an impersonal knowledge and skill, perhaps even men of endless doubts, "induced only to be ever learning and never coming to the knowledge of the truth (2 Tim. 3:7), and thus acquiring a certain laxity of character."[7] Theology will provide the curriculum with its center in truth, but a deeply evangelical theology will also set the mind free for truth as pursued in open, competent inquiry. The impact of such a curriculum combined with the impact of Christian personalities who are its teachers can indirectly aid the campus —which has even greater possibilities through chapel, social fellowship, and the Christian climate of the entire college—in producing men and women of energetic will as well as formed judgment. With all this said, it remains true that the curriculum's goal is primarily an intellectual one:

1. *To form the judgment:* by means of the four basic skills, as T. M. Greene has called them: the logical-linguistic, factual, normative, and synoptic . . . thus:
   a. To think as clearly as possible
   b. To achieve competence in one's mother tongue and one or more of the other major "languages"
   c. To become competent in accurate factual inquiry about nature and society
   d. To acquire greater sensitivity to moral, esthetic, and religious values
   e. To see relationships between things

2. *To understand fundamental truths concerning nature, man, and God.* Issuing from these basic skills, and in accord with the nature of knowledge, there are the four basic areas of human knowledge:

---

[7]H. L. Martensen, *Christian Ethics*, Vol. III (Edinburgh: T. & T. Clark, 1899), p. 303.

a. Formal knowledge
   (1) Formal thought—logic and mathematics
   (2) Linguistic—languages, semantics, linguistics
b. Empirical knowledge
   (1) Natural sciences
   (2) Social sciences
c. Normative knowledge
   (1) The arts
   (2) Art criticism
   (3) Normative disciplines: ethics, esthetics, aspects of the study of religion
d. Synoptic knowledge
   (1) History
   (2) Philosophy
   (3) Theology

To form the judgment and to disseminate truth (or at least to encourage the pursuit of it) have to do directly with an intellectual grasp on life and experience—and such is the aim of the curriculum. And if we believe that the human judgment cannot be fully formed without a religious basis, and if we believe that truth is only a half-truth without reference to God as Truth, then the Christian college has a most strategic position in education—for it can truly provide a *universal* education.

To have such a goal in mind does not mean that the student himself is forgotten. It is his welfare that a planned curriculum has in mind. The intellectual goals of the curriculum—mental health, vigor, and vision on the one hand, and a body of truth on the other—have direct relevance to a man's tasks in society. If liberal education aims to free the mind, then a Christian college, with its concern for spiritual and moral truth both in the curriculum and on campus, should be able to fulfill this aim in an eminent degree. Whether it does so or not depends on many factors along with the curriculum, but few will deny the importance of carefully planning the curriculum.

What Should be the Order of Studies? Nothing has been said so far about specific courses, or the order in which they should be studied. What follows now will say very little about specific courses. Each college will have to decide for itself what specific courses can meet the goals of the curriculum. But the question is sure to arise whether there is any order in the curriculum, or don't all roads lead to Rome? Since the latter is merely another expression for the elective system, we must believe that there is an order, that the curriculum singular for all students must have some structure. The search for this order, as Mark van Doren comments, must be a search for a narrow formula, with only three or four headings at the most. In this connection he cites Whitehead's witty comment that the average list of subjects currently taught "is a rapid table of contents which a deity might run over in his mind while he was thinking of creating a world, and had not yet determined how to put it together."[8] We must determine in some rational way what is of more importance and what of lesser importance for *all* students. This "judgment of importance," as Whitehead calls it, cannot be escaped by anyone who denies the elective system. To cite van Doren again: "A curriculum creates a world. It is important then that it have a center and an order of parts. Some studies are surely secondary to others, as some rest on others as a base."[9] As the Danish Lutheran theologian of the Nineteenth century, H. L. Martensen, remarked:

From of old . . . the deepest thinkers have always perceived that not the physical, but the ethical world is the higher, and that the central point of human inquiry and the enigma of human life, is man himself.[10]

Christianity emancipated men from the limitations peculiar to the ancient world, and penetrated all knowledge like a leaven. Not only so, but Christianity itself brought forth a new science—theology. Without any apologies the church college regards this subject as the very core of its curriculum and the central point of integration.

A clear statement of this centrality in recent literature is given by Nels Ferré.[11] It goes without question that the assertion of theology as central and most important for all students does not mean that the teachers of theology are the most important faculty on campus. The Christian doctrine of vocation applied to the academic life should clear the air of such notions. A Stanford professor has remarked:

To treat every actuality of the environment as standing on the same level as any other . . . lead(s) us into insuperable difficulties and gross absurdities. . . . Plainly we need to find, or to assume, some center of relevance. . . . I find history and philosophy to stand at the central core of relevance which must determine the content of a liberal education. (H. Hudson, *Educating Liberally*, pp. 77-80).

---

[8]Quoted in van Doren, *op. cit.*, pp. 113 f.
[9]*Ibid.*, p. 114.
[10]*Op. cit.*, p. 273.
[11]Nels F. S. Ferré, *Christian Faith and Higher Education* (New York: Harpers, 1954).

Himself a teacher of literature, Prof. Hudson was not defending a departmental prejudice, but arguing from the nature of learning—that both these areas "methodize" the curriculum. History, said Hudson, represents experience, what has happened or comes into existence, whereas philosophy represents the mind's work of ordering, interpreting, and evaluating experience. Every subject is "methodized" by these two areas—that is, each can be taught both historically and philosophically.

Alexander Meiklejohn was an educator who emphasized the need for order and structure in the curriculum. He called the belief that all parts of knowledge are equally good for a liberal education the "fallacy of the scholar." As he said,[12] if this point of view is shared by any teachers, it is an announcement that they have no guiding principles in their educational practice, no genuine grasp on the relationship between knowledge and life, persons lost in their own specialties. He also commented that there are many college teachers who believe the unity of knowledge to be a myth. They know the related subjects of the same group, or subjects in relation to practical application (knowledge in order to control). And thus such educators will gladly talk about students being "well-rounded" by taking a little of this and a little of that in addition to their major. Meiklejohn believed that natural science has particularly contributed to this view, for natural science invites division. Not a theologian, he argued that a liberal course of study must be a study in philosophy. "I know I am saying this—but one must say it because it is the truth."[13] If the teachers are merely devotees of "subjects," then no wonder the students gain no philosophy. Students should learn in wholes, and teachers must teach in wholes.[14]

Of course the more Aristotelian-minded educators, such as Robert Hutchins or Jacques Maritain, argue for the necessity of order in the intellectual realm. It would be a mistake, however, to think this is a viewpoint peculiar to Aristotelians. It is a view shared by idealists and realists, and denied by pragmatists and other naturalists.

From this center, and with the idea that the human and the ethical studies are of most vital concern to every human being, the order of studies proceeds from this center to the outer circle, or from top to base (synoptic, normative, empirical, to formal). But where should one begin in the curriculum? At the center or top, or at the base? This raises the question of the distinction between the logical and temporal order of knowledge.

The temporal order of acquiring knowledge. Perhaps the seven ages of man have much in common, but studies should honor the normal process of human growth. Plato argued that youngsters should be educated in gymnastic and music (all arts)—thus that

---

[12]Alexander Meiklejohn, *Freedom and the College* (New York: The Century Co., 1923), pp. 175 f.
[13]*Ibid.*, p. 202.
[14]*Ibid., passim*, pp. 193-203.

the physical and the emotional-imaginative precede the rational. Likewise in higher education the acquisition of tools—such as logic, language, and mathematics—precedes their use. In each subject matter the "grammar" of each must be mastered in order to be able to handle greater complexities. Regarding the synoptic disciplines, history should be preferably a lower division occupation of students, whereas by their junior and senior year they should be ready for a more philosophical approach to knowledge. However, in keeping with its position of centrality, theology should perhaps be taught throughout the student's career in college.

In planning a curriculum, then, consideration ought to be given, first, to the psychological or temporal order of learning. The logical-linguistic disciplines are thus basic, and the most important in the temporal order.

Linguistic disciplines. The traditional course in Freshman English, however much it may be modified and retitled, is quite naturally basic to college study, for it occupies those powers proper to the attainment and expression of further knowledge, and this chiefly by increasing skill in reading and writing (and speech as well), although it would include some initial approaches to the study of literature. Knowledge of language enables a man to say what he means and even more important, to say how he feels he means. Language expresses reason, and the person behind the reason—both. This is true of both written and spoken rhetoric.

The study of foreign languages, besides enabling a student to read and study in another tongue, is of immeasurable benefit in understanding his own tongue. It is unfortunate that the learning of the grammar of another language (at least) is not taught in the lower grades, so that college study could be spent entirely on the literature of a foreign tongue. Despite the value of translation courses in the various literatures, it remains impossible to translate poetry and perhaps other literature from one language to another without serious distortion.

Each subject matter has its own "language" too, which must be mastered in order to carry on effective thinking and understanding in these fields, not to speak of communication. Specialized vocabularies especially must be learned.

Formal disciplines. Every student should learn as soon as possible to think clearly and consistently, and thus the understanding of logic and mathematics especially is crucial to several areas of the curriculum. This does not mean that logic's role is merely one of art, or that it can guarantee that it will teach a person "how to think." The will is involved in thinking as well as the intellect's self-consciousness of the rules of valid thought. Logic has been called the "chief liberal art" because it is the formal constituent of all thought and knowledge whatsoever. It is closely connected with the linguistic disciplines. Too often, however, logic is taught as rules, rhetoric as tricks, and grammar as data—as van Doren has said. They should work together, and perhaps someone may someday devise a course which would combine them effectively, apart from departmental concerns. Actually logic has developed so much in the modern era that it could almost be a department in itself, analogous to mathematics. As a preparatory course it should be a course in functional logic, the expression of arguments and analysis of them in ordinary language, rather than symbolic logic. Sir Richard Livingstone, the British educator, has commented: "It is strange that geometry and algebra should be regarded as an essential part of education but that logic should not."[15] Logic could easily be taught in the secondary schools. Mathematics, of course, is one of the mother tongues of knowledge, and Plato advised all students entering his Academy to have a knowledge of it before entering. Certainly it is essential for all students, for it is essential to the understanding of the empirical sciences, without which a liberal education is impossible. But mathematics, like logic, is a science in its own right as well. As a preparatory course, it trains the mind in formal thought as logic does, but primarily in terms of abstract quantity.

The logical order of knowledge. There is an ordered connectedness between the elements of knowledge, and possibly all knowledge is one subject in the end. It is simply a fact that the human mind, being finite, has to move gradually and carefully through the elements of the structure. If Christian theology is the integrating centre of the curriculum, and if philosophy and history are the two other synoptic studies which "methodize" all subjects of the curriculum, then these three disciplines should permeate the entire curriculum. Martin Buber says,

Man's threefold living relation is, first, his relation to the world and to things, second, his relation to man—both to individuals and to the many—third, his relation to the mystery of being—which is dimly apparent through all this but infinitely transcends it—which the philosopher calls the Absolute and the believer calls God, and which cannot in fact be eliminated from the situation even by a man who rejects both designations.[16]

Ethico-religious decisions and attitudes are the central concerns of human beings, and that is why worship and theology stand at the central core of relevance for campus and curriculum respectively. But closely allied to theology in the curriculum are philosophy and history. Emil Brunner speaks of the Christian philosopher who "philosophizes from that point at which God's revelation sets him."[17] And he points to the centrality of philosophy next to theology by saying,

We need Christian specialists in all spheres of life; hence we need a

---

[15]*Some Tasks for Education* (London: Oxford University Press, 1946), p. 94.
[16]*Between Man and Man* (tr. R. G. Smith, London: Kegan Paul, 1947), p. 177.
[17]*Revelation and Reason* (tr. Olive Wyon, Philadelphia: Westminster, 1946), p. 393.

Christian philosophy, which, from the standpoint of the Christian faith, can penetrate into the region which the theologian does not enter, because he also is only a specialist in a particular sphere of knowledge, namely, in that of reflection upon the divine revelation. The co-ordination of the various spheres of life is the task, not of the theologian, but of the philosopher.[18]

Both Richard Kroner and Paul Tillich argue that philosophy is the true link between the sciences and theology.[19] But theology, because it deals with God and ultimate truth, remains the center. History is sometimes called a social science, and in that connection Kroner states: "history is of all sciences we have analyzed the nearest to religious knowledge; so near indeed that the philosopher who inquires in their essence may be tempted to take historical for religious knowledge. . . ."[20] The "sciences" referred to by Kroner are the natural and social sciences. Since Christianity emphasizes historical revelation, that is why history is so close to religion.

What has been said should not be misconstrued as arguing that these three synoptic areas will suffice for a liberal education. They would be empty apart from the other three great areas: the normative, the empirical, and the formal. Thus the normative studies point to the fact that all students are and will be making value judgments all the time. The normative studies are, therefore, of immense importance for all students. There are first, studies of norms themselves—religion (theological ethics, for example), philosophy (ethics and esthetics primarily); then, the several areas of artistic and literary criticism; and finally literature and the other arts. In terms of temporal order certainly literature and actual art *experience* would come first. Criticism and esthetics must build upon it. In regard to his experience, it is essential that the college will surround the student with exemplifications of the finest art—opportunities to hear the best music, art exhibits of all kinds, dramatic productions, and the like. In this way the students will learn to distinguish the good from the bad by actual experience, besides the study of criticism or of esthetics which could

[18]*Ibid.*, p. 395.
[19]In *Culture and Faith* (Chicago: University of Chicago Press, 1951), p. 8 and in *Systematic Theology*, Vol. I (Chicago: University of Chicago Press, 1951), p. 23. In the latter Tillich says: "The theologian has no direct relation to the scientist (including the historian, sociologist, psychologist). He deals with him only in so far as philosophical implications are at stake." (p. 23).
[20]*How Do We Know God?* (New York: Harpers, 1943), p. 29.

only come later in their study. The imagination is sensitized and taste developed by the reading of literature and experience of the other arts. Included in such experience would be actual participation in writing, creating, or performing in the various arts.

But all these areas would be vacuous and irrelevant without factual considerations, and thus every student needs to learn facts too —a great many facts about himself, and about his environment, whether physical, social, or cosmic. The empirical sciences not only seek to describe (or interpret) facts, but to train the student to make factual judgments, to learn how observation and reflection are carried on, and thus how facts are established.[21] In a real sense they are part of the humanities, for science is a triumph of the human mind just as literature and art are. The creative power from which great discoveries in science have been made and will be made is akin to creating in the humanities. But it remains true, as a chemist writes, "that the truth secured by science is proximate truth and not ultimate truth."[22] The pursuit of the latter he leaves to philosophy, art, history, and theology.

And finally we could not think in any of the foregoing areas, nor could we express ourselves without learning how to think correctly and how to use language accurately. This "conjoint logical-linguistic skill" is basic to the other studies. It is a kind of grammatical skill: the grammar of thought (logic), the grammar of empirical science (mathematics), the grammar of language, and the grammar of the arts as well.

As we look back over the entire structure, we can see that the synoptic and normative areas are the more centrally human concerns, and consequently, the most important for man as man. If this sounds like the prejudice of a humanist, let a well-known scientist speak:

In terms of their importance to each of us as human beings, I think the very subjects which fall outside of my definition of accumulative knowledge far outrank the others. . . . A dictator wishing to mold the thoughts and actions of a literate people might be able to afford to leave the

---

[21]*Vide* T. M. Greene, "A Liberal Christian Idealist Philosophy of Education," Chap. IV of *Modern Philosophies of Education* (The Fifty-fourth Yearbook of the National Society for the Study of Education, Part I), ed. by Nelson B. Henry (Chicago: University of Chicago Press, 1955), p. 122.
[22]Hugh Taylor, "Physical Sciences," in *Religious Perspectives in College Teaching*, ed. Hoxie N. Fairchild (New York: Ronald Press, 1952), p. 223.

scientists and scholars alone, but he must win over to his side or destroy the philosophers, the writers, and the artists.[23]

In Conant's terms, then, what we have called the formal and empirical sciences, he would call "accumulative knowledge" and ahead of them would place poetry and philosophy. Yet the formal and empirical sciences are quite basic to these other areas, and there is mutual interrelation and independence both. All the facts in the world will not produce a value, but conversely, values cannot produce facts either. But in its curriculum the church college will recognize the centrality of the synoptic and normative areas, for these areas encompass the primary concerns of all human beings in whatever occupation they are. Even the fact that special equipment, laboratories, and special techniques are required by the empirical sciences make them a more restricted concern of human activity—the province of specialists, whereas the concerns treated of in the synoptic and normative sciences are universal, requiring little if any special equipment.

The distinction is the age-old one between *sapientia* (wisdom) and *scientia* (knowledge as information about). Men need both, but the genius of liberal education compared to mere technical training lies in its emphasis on the importance and centrality of *sapientia.*

How to run the course? How shall a college structure its curriculum so that this order of knowledge can be achieved? Since the preceding discussion has talked of areas, not departments, each college will see different ways of meeting its needs. Usually colleges have attempted to establish some order in the curriculum by establishing requirements for both *distribution* (general college requirements) and *concentration* (the "major"). The preceding discussion has not raised the question of what subjects should have majors and which should not, or what students should major in. It has spoken only of distribution, and the argument has been that a college must have some notion of the logical order of studies in order to have any principles whereby to set up distribution requirements. Otherwise the college should logically advocate the elective system, which means its faculty recognizes no order of studies.

<hr>

[23]James B. Conant, *Science and Common Sense* (New Haven: Yale University Press, 1951), pp. 38 f.

But another problem besides distribution-concentration is that of integration and interrelation. Here too, without any principle of order, the college must hold to the absolute autonomy of all disciplines—the philosophy behind the elective system. It should be clear that we are now speaking of integration with respect to the disciplines—not integration of the personality of the student. How the disciplines shall be systematically interrelated is a question which, again, each college (not accepting the elective system) must solve for itself in terms of departmental or cross-departmental offerings. Some will feel general education courses, core courses, and the like, will meet the need. Others will disagree. What we have tried to argue is that there is a logical order implicit in knowledge itself, without suggesting the actual departmental studies.

There has been increasing interest in this question during the 1950's. In the 1958 Convocation of Christian Colleges already referred to there were several references to the need for integration of studies. Dean Brauer said: " . . . the Christian college cannot rest content with the fragmentation in education and the total lack of inter-relationship between many disciplines. . . . It seems to me that the Christian college has a positive contribution to make at this point."[24] Brauer mentioned specifically the St. Olaf College Ford Foundation study,[25] as a "genuinely creative attempt."

Prof. Bernard Loomer of Chicago also commented: "The Christian college has long had as a stated aim a concern for the wholeness of the individual student. But this concern for wholeness has not always seen the necessity for *systematic* inter-relations between the several disciplines of the academic curriculum."[26] To achieve this end, Loomer suggested that colleges would have to appoint faculty with an intellectual concern for inter-relatedness as well as those with specialized competence.

No curriculum actually established can be effectively enacted unless it has faculty who can teach. Liberal education forms a man by exposing him to the authority and demands of masters—both the actual teachers of the curriculum and the worthy men whose written expressions are studied. It is no secret to any college that the problem of faculty is really its most important curriculum problem. Whitehead once commented that moral education is impossible without "the habitual vision of greatness." This could be extended to all education. Sir Richard Livingstone, the British educator,

---

[24]Jerald Brauer, *op. cit.*, p. 238.
[25]*Integration in the Christian Liberal Arts College* (Northfield, Minn.: St. Olaf College Press, 1956), edited by Howard Hong.
[26]*Ibid.*, p. 284.

echoed this notion when he spoke of "excellence" as the great teacher. This means "excellence" of instruction as well as "excellence" of what is studied.

And before we speak of some methods of implementing a curriculum, we should remember not to expect everything from education. It is not life; man as experienced is not man in existence. Students overawed by their educational experience sometimes think nothing of importance occurs in the family or in the school aside from studies. The curriculum is limited, however—it aims to form the judgment and to search for truth, even if this is not the whole of life. But, of course, it is a worthy task, a necessary one, and not a small one. To accomplish its task the curriculum will need time, and must proceed gradually through the course it follows.

What follows now will be discussion of some of the ways whereby this task might be accomplished.

Distribution. The discussion of the logical order of studies gave some idea of the relative importance of areas, but it did not suggest which courses would meet the need, or what kind of courses. What we shall discuss here is not specific courses, but *kinds* of courses. Shall survey courses be used? Their danger, we are told, is superficiality. Mark van Doren cites Newman's comment about a "spurious philosophism" that advocates a sort of "viewiness" of things—brilliant general views about all things. The antidote to this, says van Doren, should be solid work in each subject matter rather than survey courses. But others would argue that while survey courses would be superficial, departmental courses would be too narrow. Thus they would suggest "core courses," or "general education" courses. Here any college would have to experiment possibly in order to determine workability in its curriculum.

But distribution also includes integration and interrelation. How shall this be achieved within the complex or departmental offerings? It would be a mistake to assume that the synoptic studies are the only means to this end. Obviously they must be important means to it, but integration ought to be wrought into the very structure of the entire curriculum. This might be done by a planned series of courses, but it should also be done in the teaching. Each teacher in a Christian college should be expected to teach within a religio-philosophical context. If Christian faculty in non-church colleges are much concerned about this problem, certainly church college faculty should be as well.[27] There should be mutual interchange of ideas between the college theologians and other faculty. Perhaps the teachers in other fields besides theology are inadequately prepared in theology to carry out such integration, and therefore some kind of theological instruction ought to be provided for. Yet each department would have to work out the inner details of such integration for itself, for it is not merely a theological or philosophical problem. The integrity of each field must be preserved too. Perhaps some colleges might experiment with "Christianity and—" courses, either in each subject, or each division, or over the entire curriculum. Thus at the end of the curriculum, church colleges might well experiment with courses similar to the University of Chicago's "Observation, Interpretation, and Integration" course. The rationale for such a course, so the Chicago plan argues, is that students "needed a treatment of intellectual problems, of both practical and theoretical importance, which could not be considered adequately in the courses restricted to particular ranges of learning."[28]

Concentration. No college can educate liberally unless a student is brought, with respect to at least one subject, to an experience of concrete knowledge. This is called "concentration," or the field in which a student "majors." Besides the horizontal distribution of courses, a vertical exploration of at least one field is necessary. This means not merely factual mastery, but a total contemplation of the subject addressed. Premature specialization should be avoided, however, lest the student turn into a departmental pedant instead of becoming a liberally educated man.

Several institutions, such as Princeton University, have found it wiser to allot more time to the major but also confine the major more specifically to the upper division. Under this plan a student in the lower division would not actually declare a major in a subject: he "majors" in a division during his sophomore year, and in nothing his freshman year. This is modified slightly for natural science majors, and in the natural course of events, the student

[27]Compare the already cited *Religious Perspective in College Teaching* and also the periodical *The Christian Scholar.*
[28]*The Idea and Practice of General Education* (Chicago: University of Chicago Press, 1950), p. 233.

easily secures at least one prerequisite course (a year course) for the major he eventually studies. The point of such a plan is to draw the line more sharply between lower and upper division, so that promotion to the upper division is regarded as a distinct accomplishment.

In this connection Meiklejohn recommends a sharper line for the two divisions by insisting that the lower division be spent in the general apprehension of the culture of one's race, whereas the upper division should be chiefly concerned with the actual process of mind by which that culture is made. He recommends that the general sense of an examination to be given all sophomores be the following questions:

(1) Can he and does he read books?
(2) Can he express his own thoughts in writing?
(3) Can he speak clearly and accurately?
(4) Can he listen to and understand another's speech?
(5) Can he derive an implication, draw an inference?
(6) Has he a sense of fact?
(7) Has he a sense of values?

Meiklejohn believes that if a student proves he has these qualities, then he is on the way to a liberal education, and in the upper division he should have actual contact with working minds whereby knowledge is made.[29]

Concentration is essential to enable the student to learn for himself what it is to gain knowledge, how exacting and laborious a process it is. He must go forward to a point which might be termed scholarship. Colleges should be aware of the possibility of "area majors" in addition to "departmental majors." Some area majors now being offered in many colleges are history and literature, mathematics and physics, philosophy and art, physics and philosophy, and the like. There are also the so-called "area studies," such as American studies, social studies, Far Eastern studies, and the like.

Manner of Approach. As to manner of approach, or what is colloquially called the "slant," the church college should hold firm to the notion of an integrated, interrelated curriculum for each student, one that at the same time permits ample room for concentration. The whole college then is an enterprise which believes in the unity of knowledge, and exemplifies it in its curriculum.[30]

There arises the question of how courses should be approached

[29]*Freedom and the College,* pp. 207-31.
[30]As Meiklejohn says (*op. cit.,* pp. 193-203), there are many who believe the unity of knowledge to be a myth. As to his strictures against this, *vide supra,* p. 95.

on the two levels. Some have recommended that the lower division levels be taught "historically" and the upper division ones "philosophically." As an example, courses in literature" on the lower division level would be "history of literature" courses, whereas upper division courses would be less historical than systematic, such as the literature of one author, or literary criticism, or the nature of poetry, and the like. Others suggest that introductory courses should lead the student not so much by content as by method, not by answer but by problem, not by an external list of studies but by the dialectic of a mode of thought which seeks and finds the content it feeds upon.[31] A factor to be considered, of course, is the intrinsic nature of each division. Thus, the humanities naturally permit more of an historical and evaluative approach, whereas the social and natural sciences are less historical, and more empirical. Nevertheless, there are educators who recommend a historical approach to science, at least to show how the present state of a given science has come about. And certainly in the later stages of any science there should be an attempt somewhere to relate the field to the whole of knowledge and faith.

We should remind ourselves at this point that we are Westerners, that the cultural context of all these studies of the curriculum is both Hebrew-Christian and Graeco-Roman. In this respect the courses in religion (or theology) of the Christian college, besides explicating theological content, also spell out the Hebrew-Christian background. Some colleges make the Graeco-Roman background the subject of a required area of distribution. Perhaps the Christian Church is not irrevocably bound up with Western Civilization, but the latter is the cultural context for us. Along the same lines the Church is not identical with democracy either, but there are, nevertheless, permanent values which democracy embodies or seeks to embody. In its emphasis on eternal values, the Church college cannot forget what is of relative value—its graduates are citizens of both the eternal and the temporal.

The specific philosophy of the Christian college, then, is taught both in specific courses (however they are planned, departmentally or more broadly) and in all courses.

How much should be required? As we have already mentioned, the elective system was rather hit-and-miss. A professor might ad-

[31]*Ibid.*, p. 201.

vise his students to "round out" their education with subjects from other fields, but the assumption was that it did not matter what the student took. A sort of double standard prevailed: order and progression within one's concentration, anarchy and chaos in distribution. We have already attempted to show that there must be order within the entire curriculum as well as in each field of concentration. Distribution cannot possibly be a matter of indiscriminate choice. By requirements the college sees to it that the student does not miss any important part of a total education. Exactly how such requirements shall be articulated is another question. It is not necessary to prescribe courses, for example. One might prescribe "areas"—and within such areas several elective courses. And, of course, students will still be free to choose their "major" field of study for concentration. But this is a choice made within the total order of studies as found in a liberal arts college. The rhythm of freedom and order is thereby preserved—not everything is prescribed, but not everything is allowed either. Colleges will have to determine for themselves, perhaps by creative experimentation, how much to prescribe and whether to prescribe areas with electives, or combine this with certain prescribed departmental courses, and the like. It is essential, in order to attain this goal of ordered education, that the faculty think and act together as members of the one college, instead of thinking and acting merely as professional defenders of departmental prerogatives.

What of general education? There is much confusion as to the meaning of general as over against liberal education. Are they the same or not? The McGrath report (already cited) recommended general education because liberal arts colleges have become too occupied with specialized, vocational training. Man is first of all a responsible human being before he is a doctor, chemist, or teacher. Is this not the same thing as liberal education, then? However, others choose to regard general education as *part* of liberal education, not as identical with it. It is then used to denote the wider divisions of knowledge (such as the typical triumvirate of the humanities, social sciences, and natural sciences), rather than specific departments. On this reading, a liberal education would include both general education, and other subjects. Requirements for distribution would include general education courses and departmental courses both.

The so-called Harvard Report (see p. 88) uses the terms "general education" and "liberal education" almost synonymously. But it becomes clear that the former term refers to the general side of liberal education. According to one writer, the defect of the Harvard plan is that no priority is given to any subject, the centralizing idea appearing to him to be the promotion of business and industrial efficiency.[32] The argument of *Toward General Education* (McGrath et al.) is that liberal arts colleges have sold out to vocationalism, and general education aims to prepare youth "for the common life of their time and their kind." The University of Chicago Report[33] more consistently identifies general and liberal education than any other plan. The main distinction is between general and specialized education, the former not to be thought of as vague generalities in comparison to the rigor and precision of the latter. Clarence H. Faust argued in this report for basic divisional courses (natural sciences, social sciences, and humanities). These would not be survey courses, like a survey of world literature. The approach is "methodological"—students are led to consider fundamental problems in each division of method, interpretation, and the like, by reading and discussing well-argued approaches to problems in the social and natural sciences, and studying and discussing great books in the humanities. The lecture system is restricted, and emphasis is placed on the discussion method. Faust argues against introductory courses in each department for the purpose of general education, for they are usually first steps toward specialization and students cannot possibly have time to take introductory courses in each department. The Chicago plan has three years devoted to divisional courses, progressing each year within each division, with the fourth year primarily devoted to integration.

Two men who have been liberal arts college presidents, Donald Cowling (Carleton) and Carter Davidson (Hamilton),[34] argue that general education is a part of liberal education, but not the whole. General education, they argued, is never completed; it goes on at all levels of growth. It is the education common to our "genus," a mastery of common tools, ready use of numbers, general psychology for self-analysis and self-realization, self-expression through speech and writing. Besides these tool subjects are the social and natural sciences, and history. "Upon this four-sided frame of general education, liberal education . . . will select the threads and weave the manifold permutations and combinations that constitute personality" (p. 47). Liberal education places greater emphasis upon the higher mental powers, say the two educators. General education may be attained through observation, association, memory—tested objectively; liberal education is much more difficult and requires logical reasoning and creative imagination. It should begin as soon as general education, for the two are complementary. The so-called "three R's" are general education: readin', 'ritin', and 'rithmetic,' but the "three R's" of liberal education are Reason, Resourcefulness, and Responsibility. Liberal education prepares for all occupations, but does afford special training to those occupations emphasizing the higher mental activities, such as teaching. Liberal education is thus more personal than general education is.

[32]Oliver Martin, *Two Educators: Hutchins and Conant* (Hinsdale, Ill.: Regnery, 1948).
[33]*Vide supra*, p. 103.
[34]*Colleges for Freedom* (New York: Harpers, 1947).

A Roman Catholic educator, John E. Wise, in *The Nature of the Liberal Arts,* agreed that general education aims more at information than formation, is more utilitarian and social than liberal education, the distinguishing mark of which is mental training and breadth of vision.

The upshot appears to be that general education is really a part of, not the whole of, liberal education. It crosses departmental lines, and often general education courses are equivalent to divisional courses, although they need not be.

Whether the notion of general education as delineated by the institutions most closely associated with it is accepted by Church colleges or not, certainly the Church college must have something like it. It seems impossible, at least, to meet the needs by departmental offerings alone. But how is a general education program to be implemented? Opinions differ widely on this point. Some argue that it is sufficient to have students take introductory courses in the various departments during their first two years—samplings it will be, but add them together and it comes out general education. Others will prefer the traditional survey course, but not many. More will prefer divisional-type courses, whether they are called "core" courses or "general education in" whatever division it may be. There are even some institutions who will try the great books as a means of general education. Here again the experimental venturesomeness of each college is called upon.

In the *Report of the Conference on Curriculum in General Education of the Church-Related School* (1949) there is a good summary of the various types of general education. This report felt that the *distributive-requirement* system, enabling students to sample work in many fields, is inadequate. The introductory courses are usually the first steps to specialization, and the whole program leads to departmental fragmentation, and can only be profitable if the whole faculty is alert to the opportunity and is exploiting it in a systematic way. The *survey-type course* of the traditional type is also criticized as confusing students by trying to cover all data in truncated form, the result being superficial and frustrating to the student. The *general course* plan, like Chicago's, was approved, especially if it helps the student to make meaningful generalizations and to appreciate the inter-relatedness of knowledge. The *Great Books* plan of St. John's (Annapolis, Md.) was felt to be too unsure a device—an unusually able faculty would be needed.

General education, then, is one way of meeting the problem of appropriation of the requirements for distribution. Perhaps it is not the best way, but it deserves attention and possible use. In the Christian college, of course, religion and ethics are actually general education requirements. But general education does pose some problems. One of its major problems is that of faculty, for it will need a strong faculty. Each teacher ought to have departmental affiliation, perhaps, but the aim and method of general education will differ from the typical courses offered by a professor. There is even the problem of the initial expense necessary when a general education program is inaugurated.

Should the general education program be concentrated in the first two years, or should it be spread out through four years? The latter seems most feasible. For one thing, major course requirements, in most instances at least, reach into the first two years. If a plan similar to Princeton's were adopted, concentrating the major in the last two years, then the general education requirements could be the first two years. Another problem is that of foreign language, for learning one will eat into the time required for general education. The major portion of general education might well be given the first two years in order to give undecided students a better opportunity of finding their own interests. But by allowing general education to permeate the entire four years, one will insure that the student will not take on the mistaken attitude that once he is in his specialty he can let the rest of knowledge and reading go hang. Compartmentalized thinking, narrowness, and lack of integration in one's education would be likely results of such a one-sided training.

IMPLEMENTATION

Having now explored the planning of a curriculum on the basis of a Christian view of liberal education, we shall next discuss possible ways of implementing this, both in the curriculum and in regard to the faculty and students.

Methods. First of all, let us look at methods—that is, methods of instruction in relation to the curriculum. The class technique has much to do with the success of the curriculum, and no one method will work for all types of study. In the methods discussed below, the use of the laboratory in the natural sciences is not mentioned, but it is assumed that this is most likely the basic method of teaching in that area.

The *lecture* has been widely condemned in recent years, but it remains one of the more valuable of teaching methods, and indispensable for certain purposes. Its defects are that the students remain passive, that they assume the lectures are all they have to know to pass the course (too often true), that it is too impersonal. Its advantages are that it permits the teacher to keep pace with the subject in his classroom teaching, that it is the only way of handling certain problems of teaching, and that it can be a great stimulus to the student.

The *class discussion* is a valuable method if the number of students involved is not too great, for wisely handled, it obliges the student to engage actively in the learning process by formulating his position on a problem, giving his reasons for it, and defending them against objection.

The *seminar* is especially useful for advanced courses, substituting for the lecture a round-table discussion of project reports prepared by individual students and presented orally to the class. It is individualized, and thus more expensive, but extremely valuable.

The *independent reading course* is valuable for advanced work too, in which the student takes a list of books in a field, reads them at his own convenience, and reports on them to his instructor. This is inexpensive, and very worthwhile.

The *thesis course* is another device for advanced work, and is individualized work at its best, requiring the preparation of a research paper on the part of the student, with frequent consultation with the instructor. This sort of course should be the goal of every student of ability.

The *comprehensive examination* in the major study is another method which ought to come into use more and more. Some colleges insist on both a written and an oral final, which is desirable when possible. The evaluation varies: some require the student who fails to take it again, but postpone graduation; others use it to determine graduation honors; and a few grant credit for it.

The *tutorial method*, similar to the thesis course, has the student work intimately with his major professor upon a topic, or as used in some colleges, it is for freshmen. Faculty members to be used as tutors are relieved of one-third of their normal load, and assigned about twelve freshmen. The student meets twice a week with his instructor, discussing books assigned for reading, papers written by the student, work done in other courses, and general personal and vocational problems. This will perhaps be too expensive an operation for the Christian college.

The Student. The curriculum cannot work wonders of itself, and requires the active cooperation of both student and faculty. We cannot discuss personality attitudes and moral obligations of learning at this point, although we cannot deny their importance, but there are several more tangible elements of the student's work in relation to the curriculum that can be dealt with here.

The college year, divided into two semesters or three quarters is the normal pattern of college study in the United States. In convenience the semester system requires less mechanics, and is more leisurely in its program of study. The quarter system, however, permits greater concentration of hours for a given course, and thus fewer courses per term. There are advantages both ways.

Residence. Each student should be in residence for four years to gain full benefit from the curriculum. The example of Northwestern University ought to be followed: residence is not counted in terms of credits but in terms of four regular college years. To emphasize accumulation of credits encourages a hurried learning, whereas the purpose of college education is to deepen the educational experience by giving the student time in which to reflect and mature his ideas. Besides this the student who accelerates his program in an institution organized on a four-year basis misses many other things—he is out of step with the valuable routine of the institution, and misses out on many intangible values of college life. If the curriculum is "one course," then a student should be advised when he enters that the college is a four-year college; that the student who intends to drop out or transfer after two years is likely to incur unfavorable results in his educational experience.

Quality of work. The "honor point" system is a method devised to provide a standard for quality of work done. Some institutions place a higher requirement of quality for courses in the major; some even reduce credit requirements for students accumulating surplus quality points, a dubious procedure. More emphasis might be placed upon "promotion" from year to year, especially from lower division to upper division, by some composite of time, credits, and quality.

Honor students. Superior students deserve the special concern of the college, and this means that honor courses should be developed in every area of the curriculum for such students. These courses are designed to allow the individual to move ahead as quickly as possible. The essentials for such courses are: selection of the best students, a more rigorous course of study than in the regular curriculum, and the greatest possible freedom of work consistent with adequate supervision. (Cf. Wise, *op. cit.*)

Average load of hours. The usual load in most colleges is from 15-17 hours per semester (or quarter), and from 120-128 semester credits for graduation. If one considers two hours of preparation for each credit hour, this means a work-week of from 45-51 hours. Better students will not require this amount of time, and possibly ought to be assigned extra work. English universities distinguish a pass degree from an honors degree, and we might consider the same policy. The Christian colleges, with religion requirements a vital part of the curriculum, will probably have to require more hours than usual for graduation (the normal being 120). But it could be argued that students now take too many courses (which the semester system practically requires).

Vocational courses. The pressure of vocational preparation has caused many colleges to add vocational courses. None is required for the degree usually. The colleges would probably be much happier if such courses could be eliminated, but this is an unforeseen eventuality. Courses in military, naval, and air science receive credit from ROTC institutions; nursing programs usually receive credit; and state laws concerning certification of teachers have practically forced colleges to credit professional training courses in educational methods and practice teaching. Some institutions, (in desperation, or by policy), are adding a fifth year for prospective teachers, requiring the student to finish his liberal arts course first, then take his professional courses the fifth year. Liberal education, it might be noted, is not anti- or non-vocational, but it makes no apology regarding humanity as man's first vocation, and the liberal arts the best preparation for any field. No education is more useful, or vocational, than liberal education.

The Teacher. The kind of teaching will determine the quality of the curriculum to a remarkable degree. As we mentioned before, good teaching can even make a poor curriculum seem like a good one. Again here we must omit reference to personality traits and moral obligations, and thus will concentrate on a few points of direct relationship to the curriculum as a whole.

(1) *All courses should be taught liberally.* It is not enough that a subject matter is a liberal art. Any art can be taught illiberally—as a technical specialty, for example. This happened to the teaching of the classics in the past, and the danger is uppermost in the teaching of the sciences today. Several educators point to the fact that the natural sciences are being taught frequently as "professional 'specialties'" rather than liberating arts. The object is to train physicists, chemists, professional scientists, and the professor points to the successful graduate careers of a half-dozen out of a hundred students as evidence of the success of his course. This attitude ignores the vast majority who have no intention of becoming professional scientists, and who must (along with the "majors") sell their souls to this professional objective. As J. H. Randall, Jr., has written: "In our liberal arts colleges the scientists have become notoriously the most traditional and hidebound members of the faculty, the least able to understand and sympathize with a program of liberated education. Fortunately they remain the allies of those interested in education, against the cookbook science of the engineers"[35] The result is that students who want a liberal education today hate the sciences, Randall writes, as a generation ago they hated the classics, and for much the same reason. But the same can be said for the languages and humanities, and/or when a false idea of "scientific study" or professionalism creeps in. *How can one teach liberally?* First, by recognizing one's subject as being one among many in the universe of knowledge, not as being a specialty isolated and unrelated. It is not enough for a professor in a liberal arts college to know his own subject. There is a central task of the institution to which he must be committed also. *Second,* by teaching one's subject both historically and philosophically. William James once said that you can give humanistic value to anything by teaching it historically. Conant advises this method even for the sciences. It is perhaps best to teach subjects "historically" to lower division students, and to teach them "philosophically" to upperclassmen. To teach courses philosophically means "in a spirit critically aware of their assumptions and

---

[35]"Which are the Liberating Arts?" *American Scholar* (April, 1944), p. 145.

methods, and of their place in the whole of knowledge, and their function in our culture."³⁶ To pursue a study for its human significance is to gain a liberal understanding of it.

(2) *All courses should be taught Christianly.* It is not enough that a course is given in a Christian college, or that the instructor is a professing Christian. It is necessary for the instructor to become aware of the implications of Christianity for his study, and to teach this relationship. This implies on his part a Christian philosophy of his own art or science, along with an understanding of his own Christian vocation in it—all within a Christian world-view. Each study must discover these implications for itself, and all Christian scholars are called upon to explore them. Today students complain that they are not led to see the relevance of their major study as such to Christianity. They can hardly do this if the professor in charge is proud of teaching his subject just as "they" teach it in the secular college or university, and when he uses a textbook indiscriminately, as if anyone can escape a point of view (which all too often is at odds with the Christian world-view). Some Christian educators have proposed an upper-level course in each division, to be entitled "Christianity and—" or "Christian Philosophy of—" as a means of pulling together the threads of one's work in that division. A final, comprehensive course in the Christian philosophy of life has even been recommended. To approach a course from a Christian perspective in no way robs it of its scholarship—in fact the Christian insights may enrich it. The Christian college teacher is first of all a Christian, then a liberal artist, before he professes his particular art or science.

(3) *All courses should be taught exactingly.* A good curriculum will be defeated if students find that studying the liberal arts means taking life easy. Actually there are no arts more exacting than the liberal arts—if they are taught according to their nature. Students can and ought to be made to work in order to master these arts. "Only a good teacher is capable of instilling technical accuracy as well as cultural taste and historical judgment, but it can be done with hard work. The present humanistic courses in college, including philosophy, need more calories and more calisthenics."³⁷ To

³⁶Randall, *ibid.*, p. 147.
³⁷Wise, *op. cit.*, p. 177.

insist on exactness does not entail a resorting to pedantic devices, such as constant quizzing and examining, with the illusion that these make the subject matter itself exacting. There is an intellectual precision involved in teaching and learning any liberal art, and this precision (with its corresponding discipline) ought to arise from the study itself without resorting to examinations as a club over students' heads.

The aim of all of these recommendations is that college professors may not merely instruct, but that they may educate.

The Curriculum Itself. We have already said that no curriculum is ideal, and the curriculum listed below will only be a suggested list of constituents rather than a detailed presentation. The reader can come to his own conclusions.

On the basis of about twenty courses of a year's duration (twenty are necessary because of the religion requirements of church colleges), the following is an outline of some of the basic constituents of a curriculum:

A. *Basic Courses*
1. English Composition (exemption upon examination?)
2-3. Modern Foreign Language (same?)
4. Formal Thinking (Mathematics/a. Logic, b. Introduction/ Ethics)

B. *Distribution*
5. Natural Science
6. Social Science
7. Literature (both classical and modern?)
8. History
9. a. Fine Arts, b. Philosophy

—— or ——

General Education Distribution
5. Elementary Natural Science
6. Elementary Social Science
7. Elementary Humanities
8. Advanced Natural Science
9. Advanced Social Science
10. Advanced Humanities

C. *Concentration*

    10. Departmental Course
    11. Departmental Course
    12. Departmental Course
    13. Departmental Course
    14. Departmental Course (including departmental thesis)

D. *Religion*

    15. Freshman-Sophomore Religion
    16. Junior-Senior Religion

E. *Electives*

17-20. (Possibly a final semester of a Capstone-integration course)

If one gives 6-hour equivalents to each year course, it will be seen that it adds up to 120 hours. Some colleges actually require 128 credits with religion, which could easily be done, simply by adding another elective. Note that the major is 30 hours, and that credit is given for preparation of thesis.

The Extra-Curriculum. Just as in one's life work there is time for play and recreation, so in the college the student has ample time outside of his classroom work and study. It is the unusual student who uses this free time wisely, such as filling in gaps in his education (as in music, for example). It is natural for a student to spend some of this free time in recreation—conversation, games, listening to the radio or TV, "dates," movies, daydreaming—but these should not be his only interests.

One of the problems of extra-curricular activities is so arranging their use and number for the individual student that they do not run competition with scholarship, and thus defeat the purpose of the institution. Most students will probably need as much advising about the extra-curriculum as about the curriculum.

Student self-government can be highly educative, especially if real responsibilities are given the students. A student-faculty council, composed of the principal student officers and the executive committee of the faculty, might discuss matters of general campus interest. Discipline of students can be left with student judiciary committees (such as honor councils, etc.).

Religious activities ought to be a natural part of the life of the Christian campus, and here the student congregation idea ought to be carefully considered. Various organizations, such as LSA, men's and women's organizations, and the like, along with chapel services and dormitory devotions—all develop a sense of responsibility for social and religious life that no course in ethics can achieve. The Christian understanding of vocation, however, ought to be a preventive against any idea that these activities are the essential religious life of the college—the classroom is also a religious activity in the deeper sense, as is the total community life of the college.

A major activity for many students is *recreational sports* and *intercollegiate athletics*. The intramural program ought to be expanded, especially in variety, so that all students will be able to participate in some form of athletic activity. The learning of individual sports is particularly valuable. This does not mean dropping the intercollegiate sports program. Observers of the college scene have pointed out that the college community loses a major cohesive force if this is done, and the male population loses in manliness. All this is hard to document, but it is not hard to see that this happens. Many colleges that have dropped intercollegiate sports soon have reinstated it, and for these reasons. The intellectual goal of the college is actually better served when students are not merely intellectual.

The *college theater* is a laboratory for the speech student, besides a recreational and educational activity for any student who likes to act or apply his artistic talents to play production.

College *musical organizations,* though not professional in purpose, often achieve high standards in many colleges. Many music departments require participation as part of the curricular program. Usually, however, musical activities are a way to general musical appreciation and enjoyment.

Public speaking activities of all sorts, debate, oratory, radio broadcasting, plus the parliamentary procedure of the departmental and social club are valuable for all students, who ought to be learning to speak effectively in public. Future lawyers, teachers and ministers will find this training of extreme usefulness.

Writing for the college paper, literary magazine, humor magazine, or yearbook can be a valuable adjunct to the courses in writing, as well as an effective means for actual literary effort, future journalistic work, and any career requiring writing.

Departmental clubs of all types can be good laboratories of discussion for interested students, and are of social value as well, frequently enabling the student to come to know his professors better.

Social clubs run into the difficulty of promoting caste, and many colleges prefer a highly developed dormitory system. There is value to a smaller group, however, so that both all-college social activities and smaller group activities should be encouraged as opportunities for all students to become socially mature.

Every campus usually has an *artist and lecture series* that can be of high educative value, and should be selected for the students, not the townspeople. For some events attendance might even be required.

If such activities are intelligently organized and supervised they supplement the curriculum and may well be called "co-curricular activities." Besides all such organized activities, however, the student ought to be acquiring the habit of leisure reading of "great books." In general, the atmosphere of the entire campus ought to be such as to be conducive to study, for the essence of the college is that it is a "community of scholars," whether they be faculty or students.

CONCLUSION

The foregoing has been an attempt to discuss the Christian philosophy of higher education in terms of its curricular expression. It has not been an attempt to lay down a blueprint so much as to point to certain goals and to suggest general directions to these goals. The specific details of courses, and the like, when they have been mentioned, were intended merely to give examples of possibilities. But the author stubbornly holds to the general picture he has painted in the preceding pages, and hopes that his readers, even when they disagree, will have had their own ideas aroused into greater clarity and distinctness because of the discussion.

Part Three

Implementation

CHAPTER 7

Religion

by Harold H. Ditmanson

Since the Second World War religion in America has entered upon prosperous times following a period of "depression." The soaring statistics of church membership indicate that religion has become socially acceptable. An increasingly favorable climate towards religion within the university world indicates that it has become academically acceptable. A battery of experts would be needed to account for the many and subtle causes of this "boom" in religion. Among the factors which have made for increased sympathy towards and interest in the academic role of religion is a series of important books: *Religious Perspectives in College Teaching*, edited by H. N. Fairchild; *The Teaching of Religion in American Higher Education*, edited by C. Gauss; *Liberal Learning and Religion*, edited by A. N. Wilder; *College Teaching and Christian Values*, edited by Paul M. Limbert; *Toward a Christian Philosophy of Higher Education*, edited by J. P. von Grueningen; *The Christian Idea of Education*, edited by Edmund Fuller. In these and other worthy books of this sort the case for including religious ideas, values, and practices within the curriculum and life of the university has been impressively argued. These writers have also been able to record the steady trend towards the establishment of Departments of Religion and officially recognized religious foundations at state and private schools.

THE CHRISTIAN COLLEGE AND THE MISSION OF THE CHURCH

In this essay, however, we are not primarily concerned with the problem of "religion in higher education." Our immediate perspective is confined to the place and function of the Department of Religion in the Christian or church-related college. Therefore, our point of departure must be the very existence of the Christian church. The organized fellowship of believers exists as a distinctive community within a family of human communities. To a certain extent the church shares the membership and interests of these other communities. But it is unlike them in important respects. It has always been conscious of having been called into being by its Lord for the purpose of bearing witness in thought, word, and deed to the Kingdom of God. The church is in the world but not of it. It is deeply involved in the social milieu, yet has a transcendent dimension which puts it beyond the reach of exhaustive scientific analysis or manipulation by political and economic forces.

Within western history the Christian church has seized the opportunity and achieved the right to promote its cause. This cause is associated in the realm of idea with belief in a creative and redemptive God, who gives meaning to the natural and moral orders, and was "in Christ reconciling the world to himself." This cause is associated in the realm of action with deeds of neighbor-centered love. It is the conviction of the church that it has a peculiar and indispensable contribution to make to the temporal and eternal welfare of mankind.

From the days of its origin the church has fulfilled its missionary charge not only within the context of the ancient worshipping communities of man but also within the context of the equally ancient educational enterprise. The church inevitably offered a more or less systematic understanding of nature, man, and God as an alternative to the dominant intellectual schemes of antiquity and it has continued to confront rival systems throughout its history. It has always been the special function of the college and the university to be a community of rational inquiry within which facts, implications, and perspectives can be discovered and evaluated. Knowledge has been pursued for its own sake and control for the sake of human welfare. The church has entered quite deliberately into this forum of research and discussion and has found its special role to consist in a careful and never-ending exploration of the relevance of Christian faith to all fields of inquiry and all aspects of life. This has meant bringing to bear upon the concerns of the world of the university the intellectual and moral implications of the experience of redemption by the grace of God through Jesus Christ.

The Christian college exists to give tangible expression to a Christian philosophy of education. Christian scholars may differ as to the elaboration of such a philosophy, but they will agree that in general it means to see the life of man in the light of God's self-disclosure in Jesus Christ and the events which created the Christian community. The very experience of redemption creates a sense of obligation to engage in this effort and within a democratic and pluralistic society the church-in-education has a right to set forth its distinctive understanding of life. Quite plainly, then, the Christian college must make available to its students an adequate knowledge of the Christian religion.

THE COMMUNICATION OF RELIGIOUS KNOWLEDGE THROUGHOUT THE CURRICULUM

There is general agreement that despite the way men actually practice it, religion cannot properly exist as a marginal, part-time, superficial affair. All this smacks of religious ignorance and insincerity. The very nature of God, of adoration, of faith, and of devout work implies that religion is all-embracing or it is nothing. If religion is peripheral rather than central it is insignificant. Consequently, the student must not encounter religion only in a Bible course or a chapel service. The Christian perspective is relevant at every point in the curriculum. In certain subjects basic Christian doctrines such as Creation, Revelation, Redemption, Incarnation, Atonement, Sin, Justification, Sanctification, and Eschatology will have a plainer and more immediate relevance than in others. It is no simple matter to work out in detail the specific religious implications of the several disciplines and no uniform interpretations have gained wide acceptance. But among Christian scholars the discussion goes on. It is agreed that religion should not be dragged into a subject except insofar as it is a legitimate part of the full treatment of that subject. Since every human enterprise has its religious aspects, it is up to Christian scholars in history, philosophy, literature, art, the natural sciences, and the social sciences to discover, explore, and expound these aspects. Much important work has already been done along this line and tentative conclusions have been set forth in many books and magazines well known to the readers of these pages.

That the discussion continues year after year is proof of the fact that the Christian outlook is not a collection of logically demonstrable and rigidly enforceable particular answers to particular questions, to be handed down intact from one generation to another. It is rather a commitment to a certain point of departure in the basic affirmations which transcribe the creative acts of God upon which the Christian community is founded, plus a refusal to oversimplify any problem by evading the difficulties created by the consideration of these basic affirmations. The Christian intellectual outlook is not like the answers in the back of an arithmetic book. It is more like a constant quest pursued by like-minded men who share a fundamental experience of God's grace and are loyal to certain fixed points of conviction. They find the experience and its associated convictions to be liberating and illuminating rather than stultifying and restrictive. But the illumination does not yield obvious conclusions. Mystery remains as a permanent ingredient of man's knowledge of God, of the world, and of himself. Therefore, as these scholars inspect the fascinating and puzzling realms of nature and history, they agree to disagree with respect to detailed answers.

It is clear that students can gain a knowledge of Christianity as Christian teachers in every discipline will make explicit the doctrinal and moral insights which are legitimately involved in the study of Gothic architecture, the causes of the Reformation, the poetry of Milton, the novels of Faulkner, the observed regularities of nature, the handling of guilt and frustration, the roots of prejudice, the problem of knowledge, the nature of justice and the good society and so on. To point to such connections, where they can be seen to exist, does not violate the integrity or infringe upon the freedom of the Christian teacher because he really believes that everything that does exist, exists because God existed first and is constantly and graciously present in and with everything He has created. Nor does the act of calling attention to points of Christian relevance upon the basis of the prior assumption of the existence and providential activity of God in any way reduce the scope of one's inquiry, diminish one's respect for accuracy, or prescribe the conclusions at which one will arrive, except insofar as such conclusions would wipe out one's prior assumption. In such a case, the teacher could no longer espouse a *Christian* philosophy of education and it is unlikely that he would find a church-related college an attractive or appropriate platform for his career as a teacher. (Lest the foregoing remark sound unduly harsh, it should be added that while the Christian man must make certain basic and limiting decisions about the meaning of life, it is understood that doubt has a proper place within the life of faith. Moreover, in the case of a given individual God may be so vividly encountered as the negation of all finitude that the traditional categories of public religion must be reformulated. Radical and significant denials have often given rise to a renewal of Christian faith and love. Consequently, if one is led by thought and research to conclusions which cause uneasiness with respect to one's ultimate presuppositions, one should be patient with himself and others should be patient with him. It is not unusual for the Christian scholar to find himself periodically looking into the Abyss and sufficient time should be allowed for one to assess fully the significance of such a vision.)

THE CASE FOR A DEPARTMENT OF RELIGION

If religious beliefs and values can enter the curriculum by way of the several disciplines, why should a college establish a separate Department of Religion? Such departments do exist in most of the colleges and universities of the country. This fact suggests that an adequate knowledge of religion can be gained only if separate courses in religion are used to supplement the religious implications included in other studies. Religion can and should be taught in separate courses because it is a distinguishable body of experience and knowledge. Certainly in Western culture religion takes on the form of a systematic whole both in life and thought and it cannot be understood properly apart from a systematic study of its distinctive features.

The story of religion is wider than that of the Bible and of the Christian church. The fact that Christians ascribe finality to their faith and tend to speak of it as "a religion to end all religions" or as "the redemption of religion," should not prevent us from acknowledging that the great family of human religions, including Christianity, can be described in terms of a common pattern. Religion always marks off for special treatment a particular segment or aspect of the world. This special area is known as the sacred or the holy and it is set apart from the rest of reality by various forms of special regard. Religion functions as the caretaker of sacred places, objects, writings, and persons. These sacred things are given special treatment because they are thought to have a particularly close relation to the supernatural, the more-than-natural power or goodness with which man seeks to make contact. Man's awareness of the sacred is thought to be a reaction produced within him by the self-communication of the supernatural to chosen individuals or groups. Man senses a contrast between the greatness and perfection of the Uncreated and the smallness and imperfection of the creature. In his mood of humility, awe, wonder, and reverence man seeks through religious practices to make beneficial contact with the supernatural. Since it is held that man is in some kind of trouble from which he needs rescue or deliverance, these organized techniques of approach to the supernatural constitute ways of salvation. Religion as a universal phenomenon is probably rooted in man's general and irreducible sense of awe and dependence in the presence of the incalculable and more-than-human aliveness of the world. Out of this raw material the specific features of religion are elaborated, namely, forms of worship, prescribed modes of conduct, fellowship with the faithful, and a creed or body of doctrines.

Clearly religion is preoccupied with totality. Any definition of religion must make room for its emotional, volitional, intellectual, and communal components. Its fundamental goal is to make a total personal response to the most ultimate reality in the universe. Religion is not the only pattern by means of which man organizes his efforts, loyalties, and purposes. There are also the other great patterns represented by the natural and social sciences, philosophy, and art. But religion is that distinguishable form of the spiritual life which is centrally concerned with the orientation of the totality of man's being and life towards the totality of the universe. Religion is interested in salvation. It is a very practical sort of communion. But since it involves the whole man it is associated with intellectual, moral, and esthetic impulses. Yet, worship within a community of faith and conduct is the characteristic response of the religious man. This response sets him apart from other men or from himself as scientific, philosophical, or artistic man.

Considered merely as a social phenomenon within history, religion is worthy of careful study. It has been so potent a factor in the shaping of civilizations that to be ignorant of its influence is to have one's view of his world distorted. Full education requires an understanding of the place of religion in life. Such an understanding can best be provided in separate courses within a Department of Religion. But it is only for the sake of analysis that we can speak of religion "as such" or religion "in general." Religion does not exist "in general." It always takes the concrete form of believing persons and worshipping communities. Consequently, a very practical motivation for the careful study of religion is felt by a specific religious group which has the right and the duty to transmit its heritage in every age to new recruits. This transmission is necessary for the continuity of the group and also for the enhancement of the individual's appreciation of religion's benefits. The Christian church in its effort to bear the most effective witness to its faith finds it particularly necessary to practice such transmission in the form of academic study as a means of overcoming the imbalance which generally exists between the young person's knowledge of religion and his knowledge of the humanities, arts, and sciences. A sophisticated knowledge of some technical field such as physics frequently coexists with a most immature understanding of religion. Such an imbalance is productive of distorted concepts of religion, of an inadequate understanding of the religious aspects of other subjects, and of severe personal tensions within the individual as he struggles with seemingly opaque "religious questions" to which the religious tradition, maturely understood, has fairly clear answers. If this imbalance can be overcome, both the individual and the group will profit. It would appear that the very nature of religion and the nature of the benefits associated with a mature understanding of it call for the presentation of Christianity in separate courses as well as in a more diffused form throughout the curriculum.

The contention that a Department of Religion is a necessary part of the college organization may be supported by a second line of argument. The time has come in this essay, and may indeed be overdue, to draw a distinction between religion and theology. We are interested in the problem of making available to students in the church-related college an adequate knowledge of the Christian religion. We have seen that religion is a very practical sort of communion with God, indefeasibly personal and inescapably social, which involves beliefs, rituals, codes of conduct, and a fellowship. These elements combine to form a dynamic life pattern. But how can such a reality be studied in the classroom, discussion group, or library? The classroom cannot be a place to which people go in order to practice believing, or to worship, or to love one another, or to bask in the glow of "togetherness." In other words, one cannot *study* religion because for the religious man religion is the very form his life takes. One can only study *about* religion. Religion *is* man's relationship to God. But like other fundamental experiences, religious experience tends to make statements about itself. When such statements are made they are put in grammatical form, they respect the rules of logic and of all meaningful communication, and are presented as intelligible propositions. Theology is, therefore, an intellectual procedure which is appropriate to the mood of investigation and analysis which must prevail in the classroom. When the student studies religion he is actually studying theology, or what we say about our religion. Christian people have said a great deal about God, about man's nature and destiny, about the significance and proper use of the physical universe, about Jesus Christ and redemption, about faith and knowledge, about the good life, about worship, and about the nature and task of the church. All this is theology in its biblical, historical, systematic, and practical aspects. Theology in one form or another is the subject-matter of every course taught in a Department of Religion.

It is the claim of the church-related college, and of an increasing number of private and state schools, that theology as the systematic study of religious phenomena should take its place in the curriculum alongside the other special disciplines, each of which studies its own appropriate set of phenomena. Theology qualifies for this position not only because of the massive importance of religion in human history but also because theology is a genuinely intellectual procedure. It is important to note that theology did not find its way into the educational pattern due to the operation of purely speculative or esthetic interests. Theology arose out of the very practical needs of the early church as it sought to put its beliefs into teachable form for the sake of the instruction of new converts, the refutation of heresies, and the persuasion of outsiders. Yet, from its earliest days the church has laid undeniable stress upon interpretation, understanding, words, argumentation, and propositions. While man's relationship to God must involve vivid emotional reactions and acts of will, the very conceptions of revelation and faith point to the indispensable role played by man's rational capacities in religious experience. Jesus said, "I am the Truth" and the New Testament sets forth the significance of Jesus by calling Him the "Word" of God. The place of the written Scriptures within the life of the church implies that God has chosen to communicate with man through the medium of words, the means of intercourse between rational beings. God, the "Fount of Truth," addresses Himself to that in man which can apprehend truth and respond to meaning.

It is true that many outside the church think of theology as the enemy of truth and freedom and that many inside the church regard faith as an affair of the heart rather than of the head. Yet, it is a cold fact that almost from the beginning there has been a strong strain of conscious rationalism in the leaders and scholars of the church. From the first Christianity was faced with rival religions, and had to argue its case. As it came into full contact with the

Greek culture that dominated the West into which St. Paul had penetrated, the Christian faith had to be rethought so that its basic ideas could be clarified and linked together in a rational order. From the second century Christian scholars saw quite clearly that the Christian faith is a way of life that is grounded on a view of the nature of the universe and that it must present itself to the world not only as a gospel but as a theology or philosophy, an argued system of theoretical truth. Besides defining her doctrine in creeds, the church encouraged her thinkers to put the doctrine into the shape of grand theological systems. The works of Origen, Irenaeus, Augustine, Anselm, Abelard, Aquinas, Luther, Calvin, the Protestant scholastics, Schleiermacher, Ritschl, Barth, Brunner, Temple, and Tillich, as well as the official confessional documents of the various divisions of Christendom, support the contention that a considerable degree of rationalism is orthodox in all the larger Christian churches. Associated with this intellectual tradition of the church is the church's spectacular record as a founder of schools and universities. The great procession of scholars who have pursued intellectual interests in both sacred and secular studies have found that the faith that gives substance to Christian discipleship is not intellectually destructive but is intellectually suggestive. Their effort has been motivated by religious considerations, for the obligation to be intelligent is a moral obligation and the love of truth is one aspect of the love of God. Faith inevitably seeks understanding.

This may be the appropriate point at which to observe that the Christian teacher, whether in the Department of Religion or in any other department, is conscious of a double commitment. He is committed both to the gospel and to the intellectual tradition of the church and of the society in which he lives. Obviously the Christian college must be *Christian*. But it must also be a *college*. As a college it shares intellectual methods, ideals, and goals with the general educational enterprise. A brief review of the joint goals accepted by Christian and secular education is an important part of any argument on behalf of the collegiate study of theology.

The scholars who carry on the work of the educational community manifest, first of all, a basic respect for truth. Any scholar worthy of the name refuses to entertain false beliefs willingly. He affirms that truth can be sought and is worth seeking. This basic commitment is quite distinct from commitment to any particular set of opinions. It is rather a respect for the only condition on which one can ever know anything at all. It is loyalty to one's own commitment to the search for truth. It is not only distinct from any particular set of opinions but it is compatible with varying degrees of scepticism and agnosticism. It takes faith to doubt. One must be sufficiently sure of his basic commitment to truth and his belief that truth is worth seeking to be prepared to lose or hold in suspense certain cherished opinions.

The usefulness of a school depends upon its conviction that the things of the mind are worth pursuing. Without this conviction teachers become a sort of academic civil service and fail to feel or to communicate the spark of intellectual passion. This passion cannot be legislated. We can only provide the conditions under which it can come alive. One such condition is a rather intensive inner concentration. Teachers should avoid letting many "interests" become a distraction, choking intellectual passion. Moreover, the school as such has a responsibility to society to function as a *school*. Schools of many kinds will choose to "serve" the public by training workers in various fields and developing the technical skills of the community. But the school has a primary responsibility to be a place where the criticism and evaluation of ideas is being continually carried forward and where the intellectual virtues are being fostered and transmitted. This is its unique function and opportunity. If the school fails to focus the *intellectual* conscience of the community, there is no other agency to take its place.

Secondly, the genuine scholar is loyal to the obligation embodied in the biblical phrase, "Prove all things." He resolves to beg no questions. Of course, we are all conditioned by circumstances of time, place, and personal history. But we are not wholly prisoners. If a theory of social conditioning were to be accepted as an exhaustive explanation of human thought and action, it is difficult to see how one could be aware of himself *as conditioned*. Any theory of truth must be able to account for the fact that it can itself be regarded as true. The scholar can allow for a great measure of arbitrariness in life and still hold that it is intrinsically right for him to start from the beginning, to examine his presuppositions, to subject to a radical questioning any assumptions that are neither self-evident nor supported by cogent reasoning. Here it may be said that theology is unusually self-conscious about the problem of method. It is painfully aware that it begins with the fundamental conviction that it has encountered the truth. It is eager to discuss with all other disciplines the logic of the procedure by means of which one moves from a primordial judgment of importance to empirical observation to rational hypotheses to conclusions. With respect to self-examination theology is far more honest and radical than many other disciplines.

The obligation to "prove all things" implies, of course, that one will exercise the discipline of accuracy in dealing with evidence. The Christian who believes that all truth is God's truth and that genuine knowledge about a contingent world can be gained not by a priori notions but only through the most painstaking observation and deduction, could not possibly be interested in anything less than the strictest accuracy. The scholar will manifest a sense of justice and fair-mindedness not only in the assessment of evidence but also in trying to appreciate what others are after. One who is committed to radical honesty and accuracy in intellectual procedure could not tolerate for a moment the misrepresentation of an opponent's position. What conceivable interest could one who trusts God and loves truth have in displaying anything but the utmost fairness both in assessment and in controversy? This loyalty to accuracy and justice makes possible an agreement in attitude between people who may differ widely on schemes of interpretation.

The third intellectual commitment shared by theology with the other disciplines is a desire to work within the widest possible context. Stated negatively it may be described as a resolve to suppress no information. Respect for truth and a refusal to beg questions imply that one should be able to think critically and have a wide range of truth to interpret. To suppress any information would be a betrayal of one's commitment to the search for truth. One must regard all data as relevant to his search. This requires a catholicity of interest. There will be many things beyond the competence of the Christian scholar but there can be nothing about which he is not curious. Herbert Farmer states the point well:

"If by 'God' we mean that final reality of righteousness and love from which all things, including ourselves, depend for their existence, their nature, their coherence, their unfolding history, and final outcome, then the whole meaning of our existence is at stake in him, and nothing less than the whole breadth of our experience could be the appropriate and sufficient context for thinking about him."[1]

The resolve to suppress no information carries with it a resolve

[1]Herbert H. Farmer, *God and Men* (Nashville: Abingdon-Cokesbury Press, 1947), pp. 23-24.

to ignore no point of view. Thus the college must acknowledge freedom of mind as a condition for productive thought. Toleration is not indifference but a belief that truth is too great to be grasped by any one school of thought. Such toleration and humility should not prevent a school from endorsing a certain perspective nor should it prevent the individual from making up his mind and speaking about it. But he is obligated to state his position, tell why he holds it, and discuss its relation to alternative positions. Freedom and toleration can exist only in association with discipline and responsibility. Genuine thinking is responsible. It is not a mere rationalizing of one's own prejudices but is disciplined by a serious desire to find out what one ought to think and to stand by the result. A school should tolerate unconventional thinkers if they are fairminded and responsible. The alternative to toleration of differing emphases is the imposition of "loyalty oaths" or detailed theological tests. This would have the effect of preserving pure doctrine at the cost of seriously narrowing the context within which the fullest breadth of God's creativity may be appreciated. Moreover, turning the school into a platform for the presentation of a few rigidly selected and authorized positions would condemn the church to cultural isolation and irrelevance. Serious and vital Christian thought has nothing to fear, if it is true, from a careful and openminded inspection of the many "isms" of our day. Such an inspection is a possibility within a community of scholars whose primal assumption is that God exists and has revealed Himself in Jesus Christ as Sovereign Love.

THE ORGANIZATION OF THE RELIGION CURRICULUM

The foregoing argument suggests that certain ideals and methods of scholarship are the goals jointly of secular and of Christian education, and it is clear that the central place of theology in the intellectual tradition of the church qualifies it for a position in the curriculum alongside the other major disciplines of thought. But what particular courses should be taught in the Department of Religion? A brief statement of what theology tries to do for the church and the university world will help us answer this question. Christian theology began as reflection upon data, the data being provided by the experienced relationship with God. The revelation of God in Christ "under Pontius Pilate" gave rise to great religious convictions which are first found in the New Testament, then in the creeds of the church, and then in the varied testimony of Christian thinkers through the centuries. It is the task of theology to give systematic and adequate expression to these convictions. They must be given systematic expression because we are concerned with a subject which is not a mere collection of unrelated truths, standing side by side independent of one another, but an organic whole every part of which is in vital connection with every other part. It is the conviction that the revelation of God came to a climax in the ministry of Jesus Christ which provides the central organizing principle of this body of knowledge.

The church has used theology, in the first place, for the transmission of its message. From the pulpit and in the instruction class the implications and applications of the gospel have been set forth. The church points to the saving deeds of God in Christ. This proclamation of the gospel aims at persuasion, conversion, and nurture. In order to accomplish this task the pastor or teacher must draw on a wide range of knowledge, but his chief and indispensable resource will be a profound understanding of the Bible and of the human condition.

In the second place, theology performs the function of clarification. Since the church is made up of forgiven sinners whose finitude and continued betrayal of God prevent them from receiving without admixture of error the illumination of the "Spirit of truth," it is necessary that the message of the church be subjected to constant and critical examination. Superstition tends to proliferate in the atmosphere of adoration and surrender. Therefore the church must always talk to itself in order to keep straight on its own message. It is plain that an institution may in the course of its history diverge considerably from the intentions of its founders. Our Lord warned against adding the "traditions of men" to the Word of God. This is the temptation which the church faces in every age. We may add to the essence of the gospel, which proclaims the evangelical mystery of salvation, our own elaborations and explanations and then consider these additions as being equal to the gospel in authority and importance. Men have often imposed upon the gospel psychological, sociological, political, and economic forms and then with good intentions have transformed these into theological principles to which loyalty has been demanded in the name of "the faith of the fathers." Christians may find themselves manifesting loyalty to a great body of theological and moral opinions which arise more from personal prejudices and social customs than from the gospel. Since, then, we are all too fallible, we must in all seriousness submit our theological and moral apparatus to constant review in the light of the regnant and normative concepts of the earliest church. Only by so doing can we have any assurance that there really is a continuity between the church of the first century and the church of the twentieth century. To refuse to submit to such review is arrogance and idolatry. It would be to claim finality not only for the Truth of God but also for our formulation of that Truth and for our personal participation in that Truth and Love. Therefore, the church must with God's help essay the difficult task of reflecting upon its own belief and practice in order to guard against distortions from within. In short, the church must talk to itself.

The third function of theology is to engage in conversation. The church must enter into each new age not only with continuity but also with mobility. It must be able to speak to those outside the church, to enter into the questions of the unbeliever, to meet the spirit of the times. This dialogue may be carried on in the mood of criticism, that is, the intellectual discussion of the Christian faith in the light of contemporary ideologies which are opposed to it. Here the theologian takes the offensive and seeks to show that attacks on Christianity are irrelevant, contrary to sound reason, involved in self-contradiction, or based upon misunderstandings. Origen, Augustine, Aquinas, Pascal, Schleiermacher, Kierkegaard, and Reinhold Niebuhr have provided models of discussion with the educated unbeliever.

This conversation with the spirit of the times must also be carried on in a constructive mood. The negative attack simply removes hindrances or creates some space within which the Christian message can operate. But bearing witness can be a sterile effort unless the Christian position can be integrated with the truth which the listener already possesses. The constructive theologian, interested in conversation across the boundary lines, will take as his subject matter not merely biblical knowledge, church history, ethics, liturgy, history of doctrine, and so on. But for him the subject matter of theology is life itself, the life of the universe and the life of man, considered in their relation to the will of the Creator and the coherence of all things in Jesus Christ. Theology in this sense is what Matthew Arnold said literature should be, a criticism of life. The constructive theologian must enter the forum of cultural synthesis and attempt to issue from time to time, not a final summation, but a trial balance which may give to both church and society a fresh and creative possibility of seeing the total meaning of the life of man under God.

Transmission, clarification, conversation—these are the functions performed by theology in the service of the church's total mission. How should these theological concerns operate within the collegiate community? First, a disclaimer should be entered. It is said that our modern liberal democratic culture has suffered from general confusion ever since it revolted against the coerced and authoritarian unity of medieval culture. Since the Renaissance, education has explored the various realms of interest and enlarged the scope of man's activities. But it has gained and exploited departmental independence at the cost of a sense of wholeness in the meaning of life. Widespread distress is felt with respect to the fragmentation and lack of cohesiveness which marks contemporary education. There are many Christian scholars who argue that it is now the major function of theology to provide a unifying point of view for the modern curriculum. They urge that theology should again play the role of the "Queen of the sciences." Despite what has been said about the constructive task of theology, it is very doubtful whether in the present state of knowledge it is possible or desirable for theology to try to overcome the atomization of knowledge into specialisms by the construction of a new comprehensive synthesis in the style of a *Summa*. We are at the stage in which such an external unity in the pattern of knowledge could be achieved only by the imposition of an ideology, that is, an oversimplified unity of outlook gained by the domination of one particular interest or type of thinking over others. Thus, natural science might dictate to ethics or philosophy, or theology might dictate to natural science, politics, or economics. Without a commonly accepted metaphysical structure such a synthesis is impossible and we must resolve to live out our lives within a relativistic or pluralistic context. A humility as over against human limitations should prevent any discipline, including theology, from making imperialistic claims. But while we respect the relative neutrality and independence of each discipline, our assumption that truth is a unity should stimulate the most eager and fruitful experiments in inter-departmental discussions of general and special problems.

Although theology cannot be expected to collate the findings in every field and to issue a synthesis, it can operate in such a way as to make the Christian faith a live and significant option for the faculty and students. It must represent the Christian faith in the collegiate community. Theology will pursue the study of religious phenomena and will insist that in the construction of a world-view the significant data and categories of theological research should not be left out of account. In this age of fantastically rapid departmental expansion and preoccupation with specialized studies, it may be that a peculiarly important function of theology within the curriculum is to stand guard against any oversimplified reading of reality on the part of the other disciplines. Its unusual interest in wholeness and comprehensiveness should make it the inveterate foe of all reductionisms. Theology protests in the name of the Ultimate against the absolutization of partial perspectives and against the idolatrous pretensions of scholars in all fields, including theology itself. Because both theology and philosophy claim the entire field of human experience as their legitimate province, the work of sentinel is done by a borderline discipline known as philosophical theology or Christian metaphysics.

As it engages in give and take with the other disciplines, theology will not only insist that its findings be given careful consideration, but it will also open its methods and categories to rigorous criticism. Theology will be immeasurably assisted in the self-critical operation to which reference has been made earlier if it can examine itself for illusions, distortions, and irrelevancies at the very center of the responsible intellectual life of society.

How can all these needs and interests be structured within the course offerings of the Department of Religion? Departments of Religion probably agree about as much as do other departments as to the basic courses to be offered. But as to the sequence of the courses there is little agreement. Perhaps there is no single best way of organizing the religion curriculum. But the indispensable subjects may be enumerated. The church's interest in continuity and transmission practically dictates a course in Biblical study. Certainly the Bible is the heart of the Christian heritage and for the Protestant possesses a peculiar authority. While the student should be encouraged to think critically and independently about religious issues, he must have a thorough understanding of some factual material before he begins his independent reflection. The Bible should be studied exegetically, historically, and theologically. A first-hand scrutiny of the text is required. Since God reveals Himself in and through historical events, the history of the people of God must be seen within the context of ancient Mediterranean history and culture. But unless the Bible is understood theologically it cannot bear coherent meaning. The aim of Biblical instruction is to equip the church member and potential scholar to continue the intelligent study of the Bible on his own. This is in harmony with the Protestant principle of the priesthood of all believers. It is not easy to know just how much acquaintance the college student ought to have with the findings of Biblical criticism. Certainly the emphasis in such a course should not be on the problems and details of historical criticism. Yet, some of the critical problems are inescapable and many of the findings of historical and textual scholarship are of great help in elucidating the meaning of the Bible. Moreover, it should be remembered that many of the students who study the Bible in college as though there were no such thing as Biblical criticism will some day, either in graduate school or through their own reading, confront such problems and feel that they have been cheated by teachers who knew nothing about Biblical criticism or were afraid to speak about it. But the vast majority of religion teachers rejoice in the fact that during the past thirty years Biblical criticism, based on the same scientific methods as have wrought great changes in other fields of human life during the same period, has been largely domesticated in the household of the church.

In addition to a thorough knowledge of the Old and New Testaments, the student should have a broad knowledge of the historical experience of the community whose origin is described in the Biblical documents. The study of church history or of the Hebrew-Christian tradition continues the story told in the Bible about God's creative, redemptive, and providential action. The student who has information about the dynamic interrelationship between the church and the world in which it is set, about the various patterns of witness and survival which the church has devised, and about the development of the church's teaching, worship, ethics, organization, and expansion, will find his faith strengthened and his understanding of the meaning of history deepened. Moreover, such a historical perspective should deliver the scholar from many provincialisms of time and place.

To the Biblical and historical studies should be joined a systematic study of Christian doctrine and ethics. With constant reference to the Biblical and historical background, one will examine the contemporary relevance of basic Christian doctrines and of basic Christian principles and areas of ethical responsibility. Doctrine and ethics are usually taught as upper division courses. They presuppose a certain accumulation of knowledge, maturity of judgment, and capacity for abstract thought. In these courses theology is concerned to transmit and clarify, but its conversational or constructive function is likely to play a larger part than in the study of the Bible or church history. In the teaching of doctrine and ethics it is exceedingly important to give careful and honest attention to problems of methodology, to operate within the widest possible scope of investigation, to confront all significant alternatives, and to suggest a consistent pattern of thought and action.

With these basic courses in Bible, church history, doctrine, and ethics, there is generally associated a course in comparative religion. Such a course enables a student to understand the religious concerns which are common to men in all cultures. The non-Christian religions must be presented as fairly and fully as possible. The Christian scholar who trusts in the God of all truth could have no motive for misrepresentation or special pleading. The significance of such a course for the development of cultural breadth and a deeper understanding of the place of religion in one's own culture and personal life needs no comment.

The five courses enumerated above are generally accepted as the essential courses of religious instruction. Beyond these foundation courses many other types of study can be offered depending upon the size and resources of the institution. Advanced courses in Bible, the expression of Christian ideas in literary classics, problems of religious thought, and the theology of culture constitute worthy areas of study. Also of great importance are the philosophy of religion, the psychology of religion, and the sociology of religion, although the tendency is to offer these courses in the departments of philosophy, psychology, and sociology. A Department of Religion is pleased to have other departments share its interest in religious phenomena and apply to them their own specialized methods of research.

Church-related colleges quite generally require of the student a certain amount of religious instruction. The amount required varies, however, from two to four years or from eight to fourteen hours. One method of organizing this requirement is to prescribe all or most of the courses to be studied. A typical core curriculum might embrace Bible in the first year, church history in the second year, and doctrine and ethics in the third or fourth year, with comparative religion or some other course as an alternative to doctrine or ethics. A variation of this pattern is to prescribe not such general courses as Bible, church history, and doctrine-ethics but subdivisions of these Biblical, historical, and systematic studies. The method of prescribing specific courses has the advantage of guaranteeing spread over the whole range of theological knowledge. It can set up a logical sequence, with the hope that the student will carry with him to his advanced courses the information he has learned in his earlier studies. It must be accepted, however, that such a pattern cannot allow fully for the pursuit of special interests by either teachers or students, because it will rule out elective courses. The teacher cannot specialize because he is involved in very comprehensive preparations in every field of theology. This may prevent a teacher from acquiring expert knowledge of anything and encourage him to a dilettantish specialization in generalities. Furthermore, this pattern of organization assumes that every teacher is equally capable of teaching every subject. This assumption is almost certainly unrealistic and fails to utilize special abilities.

For these and other reasons some colleges prefer to require not specified courses but a specified number of hours in prescribed areas of study, leaving it to the student to choose from the several possibilities in the Biblical, historical, and systematic areas. This method allows for the satisfaction of special interests, offers somewhat less assurance of spread over the entire theological curriculum, and suffers from the chief disadvantage that it may require a larger staff to provide electives for a sizeable number of students taking two to four years of religion than the college can afford. However the religion requirement is organized, the very fact that the requirement exists at all implies that the religion courses bear a heavy obligation to be broadly educational in their impact since they take up time which the student would otherwise give to the humanities, sciences, and arts.

The introductory or first-year course in religion presents a special problem. Perhaps most colleges use the course in Bible for this purpose. But it may be questioned whether the standard course in Biblical history and literature is the most fruitful point of departure for religious instruction. Certainly these Bible courses take the students at a point where they have very little intrinsic interest in the Bible as such and where their general knowledge of the Christian faith and general outlook of their own denomination is very scanty indeed. Moreover, it is perfectly obvious to any teacher of religion that the going really gets lively in the Bible course when *theological* questions come to the fore. Freshmen seem to feel that they have just now come to a forum where they can ask the radical and far-ranging questions which they have been afraid to ask previously, or to which they have failed to receive helpful answers. Watch the light come into a freshman's eyes when the discussion veers away from Rehoboam and Jeroboam to predestination, baptism, or purgatory! A strong case can be made out for the contention that the introductory course in religion should be *problem centered* and that systematic inspection and interpretation of the Biblical documents should be delayed until the junior or senior year. The unique importance of the introductory course lies in the fact that strong positive or negative attitudes toward religion are created by this initial encounter. Furthermore, in the case of the many students who drop out or transfer this introductory course may be their only exposure to college-level religious instruction.

Materials and methods of instruction lie outside the scope of this essay, but a few remarks about the "ideal" teacher of religion may be consistent with its purpose. The teacher would, of course, be deeply committed as a theologian to the joint-goals of Christian and secular education which we have discussed earlier. He would exhibit a profound respect for truth. He would exercise the discipline of accuracy and fairness in both assessment and controversy. He would manifest an insatiable curiosity. These ideals imply certain qualities of mind and spirit. The teacher must have the makings of a scholar. He must be a man devoted to reading and thinking and have sufficient intellectual passion and competence to master a field of knowledge. Students have a right to expect that a teacher will be a learned man. No amount of friendliness and enthusiasm can take the place of hard intellectual work.

The teacher of religion must plainly be a man of deep personal faith. He cannot be indifferent to the students' response to religion and he will make every effort consistent with the ideals of theology as an intellectual discipline to present his subject persuasively. He will be able, however, to distinguish between personal religious loyalty and the obligation to be fair-minded in showing more than one side of a controversial issue. In short, he will hold in balance commitment and critical thought.

The teacher of religion should be a free man, psychologically and intellectually. Productive work can hardly be done by one who is so tied up by inner conflicts that he is abnormally touchy, easily offended, and out to prove something about himself. Inner freedom makes for balance, self-confidence and the ability to enter sympathetically and creatively into another's experience. The free man can be objective enough about himself to take another person seriously, even though the other person may be asking naive questions or intruding his concerns into a tight schedule. The good teacher cannot be a stuffed shirt asking for any dignity and authority beyond what the quality of his mind and the plausibility of his point of view can command. The teacher must also be a free man intellectually and not a pattern-thinker, dominated by stereotypes. He must be sure enough of his basic commitment to truth to suspend judgment and to study an unfamiliar idea without being hostile or shocked.

One of the most delicate and exacting tasks he will face is that of dealing considerately with the misinformation about religion which the student has picked up from diverse sources. Teachers in every department must deal with ignorance, but the teacher of religion has a peculiar problem in that his students have already read the Bible in some fashion and hold to relatively fixed notions about religion. His students have not too little knowledge but too much knowledge. As Nietzsche put it, "At least every man considers himself an expert in morality." As a result of the interacting influences of home, school, church, and private speculation the students often bring with them to college the strangest medley of unsupported and unorganized notions about God, sin, salvation, the Bible, and so on. Yet, these ideas are all they have and they seem to them to have come from authorized sources. Some teachers prefer to launch a frontal assault against this confusion so they can level the walls and build anew. But others feel the wiser course is to deal gently with the student, validating those of his convictions which are sound, clarifying the meaning of the terms and concepts which have led him astray, and presenting a solid and authentic position so positively that the student will be led to grow in his understanding by the intrinsic pressure of truth itself.

Required courses in religion can be justified by several lines of argument. But any such justification must lead to the recognition that the heavy claim of the Department of Religion upon the students' attention implies an unparalleled opportunity to be and to do something significant within the context of Christian higher education.

CHAPTER 8

Philosophy

by Stanley L. Olsen

Even a cursory glance at the histories of philosophy and religion reveals the fact that these two disciplines have always been closely associated. The reason is partly because each in its own way provides a broad, overall intellectual orientation towards the totality of existence, but also because they both concern themselves with practical ways of living. Such basic concerns as the quest for certainty, the yearning for security, the aspiration for some imperishable good, the groping for larger meaning—these human concerns, and not just the pursuit of knowledge for its own sake, have compelled philosophy to deliver something more than a theoretical view of existence. While some philosophers would disparage this value emphasis as being detrimental to a candid approach to truth, the fact remains that man is a valuing creature, and is willy-nilly compelled to attach values even to the most supposedly disinterested account of the truth. At the same time, it is also true that philosophers have not been sufficiently alert to these value elements in their motives, nor have they been sufficiently candid in confessing their addiction to them. Herein lies a subtle kind of deception that can insinuate itself even into the clearest minds. Complete disinterestedness is a hypocritical illusion, and should be so labeled.

Because philosophy and religion relate to basic human concerns, it is the thesis of this paper that we must find some way to relate them to each other for their mutual advantage. Setting them against each other can only lead ultimately to their mutual impoverishment. This is not to say that they deal with basic human concerns in the same way or that they provide the same satisfactions to basic human needs. The writer hopes that this will become evident as we proceed. But it does mean that in the final outcome, philosophy and religion need each other in any educational philosophy worthy of the task of developing mature and intelligent Christians.

The present situation in philosophy and religion presents us with a very confused picture and taxes, to the point of despair sometimes, the efforts of any teacher who tries to embrace both areas. We are witnessing in our day studied efforts to separate them in such a way as to make any attempt at relating them appear suspect at the very start. For example, much contemporary philosophy leans over backwards to declare itself independent of religion, and reveals an attitude of cynicism, if not downright hostility towards religious faith. On the other hand, contemporary religion, through some of its ablest representatives, has insisted that it will have no truck with rational "speculations" of the philosophers, and that religion pursues a method and concerns itself with objects that are intrinsically religious. Again, philosophy will often repudiate with base ingratitude the religious tradition that gave it birth and that now provides it with much of its impetus and sustaining social medium; while religion on its side with the same ingratitude will repudiate the philosophical tradition that helped religion to forge its concepts and to give it relevance to the cultural setting. To add to the confusion, philosophers and theologians are now discussing the problem of language and are suggesting the view that there are two distinct language systems involved in religion and philosophy, and that there are no significant interchangeable terms that can make clear communication possible. Were this shown to be the case, the rift between philosophy and religion would be complete. Philosophers and theologians would be moving in separate universes of discourse, not being able to understand each other's language. Fruitful interaction would then be reduced to the vanishing point. But the present writer is in agreement with the position set forth by Robert L. Calhoun:

High religion and intellectual enterprise belong together. Each gains from close association with the other. The two in conjunction, but neither by itself, can move with hope toward a more effective conquest, of the chaos that now and again threatens to engulf all human living.[1]

PHILOSOPHY IN THE LUTHERAN TRADITION

One does not need to labor the point that the teaching of philosophy in our colleges is not regarded as having the degree of importance it once assumed in the liberal arts tradition. It suffers by comparison when viewed in relation to other areas in the curric-

[1]Robert L. Calhoun, *The Place of Religion in Higher Education* (New Haven: The Edward W. Hazen Foundation, 1949), p. 10.

ulum. Perhaps some of the reasons for this are practical ones. Most of our colleges do not require it for graduation, and students can usually round out their majors without it. Students can teach; they can go on to graduate school in most areas (even some seminaries list no pre-theological requirement in philosophy); they can assume responsible positions in church and society and be completely ignorant of the sort of problems philosophy raises as well as of possible solutions to them. In this matter, our colleges appear simply to have drifted along with secular education generally. A good case in point is the more or less general tendency on the part of education departments to make short shrift of the great philosophical tradition in the history of education. Merely to call the roll of great educators in the past—Plato, Aristotle, Aquinas, Kant, Herbart, Froebel, James and Dewey—reminds one that great educators have also been great philosophers. One wonders what justification there can be for turning out teachers as we do without a better orientation toward, and a more informed appreciation of, the great philosophical tradition in which they stand.

But one suspects the neglect of philosophy has deeper roots. Intimately connected as we are with the Lutheran church, our schools naturally reflect the attitude of the church toward the whole philosophical enterprise. Luther's strictures on philosophy are well known, and in the light of the situation he faced in the academic world of his time, his wholesale condemnation of scholasticism can be understood, if not forgiven. Philosophy in his day had little room for a dynamic and existential confrontation with the revelation. By reducing the Gospel to so many intellectual formulations of the "truths" of the Bible, scholasticism had obscured, if not destroyed, the evangelical basis for an assured faith. Nor did it help when the study of ethics was pursued, not on an evangelical basis, but on the basis of Aristotle—something that led Luther to think that Aristotle had displaced Christ and the Bible. Melanchthon, however, thought better of philosophy and insisted that it be preserved in the curriculum at Wittenberg.

Though many of the continental philosophers since Luther's time had Lutheran backgrounds and give evidence of being deeply influenced by that fact, they shared in general the skepticism of the enlightenment relative to the traditional interpretations of the Christian faith. (Leibniz, Kant, Fichte, and Hegel come to mind). Certainly the Lutheran church would find it hard to give positive approval to the religious views of such men. With the exception of

Sören Kierkegaard, it is a fact that no great philosophers have arisen from the ranks of the Lutheran church comparable to those who have come out of the Roman Catholic tradition. No wonder Lutherans are sceptical of philosophy when the whole philosophic enterprise from the reformation on has received its motivation from non-Lutheran sources.

Thus, the problem of giving positive emphasis to the study of philosophy in our church colleges is faced with a backlog of historical hindrances. One is often led to feel that too easily Lutherans give way to a mood of despair relative to the intellectual aspects of our cultural setting, and that consequently it has tended to assume only a negative attitude towards any genuinely philosophical interest. One wonders whether Lutheranism which historically has assumed a positive (though dialectical) relation to culture is true to its genius in this respect. However this may be, the following discussion is designed to deal with the problem under three general heads: (1) the need that religion has for philosophy; (2) the need of philosophy for religion; and (3) suggestions as to areas in the curriculum and in specific courses where the two can be fruitfully interrelated.

THE NEED OF RELIGION FOR PHILOSOPHY

For one thing, philosophy can do much to stimulate in students some critical thought relative to their faith. Most students come to college with either vacant or dogmatic minds on matters of faith. Both illiteracy and dogmatism are certainly contrary to the whole spirit and purpose of liberal arts education. Philosophy may not do much for the religiously illiterate except perhaps to uncover the abysmal ignorance students reveal, and to shame them into doing something about it. But on the score of dogmatism philosophy has much to say. If by dogmas one means certain basic presuppositions of belief, then philosophy no less than religion has its dogmas. The philosopher's faith in the powers of reason or in the intelligibility of the universe are basic presuppositions of belief, and certainly assume the appearance of dogmas to those who see fit to question them. But *dogmatisms* are something else again. The philosopher cannot afford to be dogmatic about his beliefs. He must be willing to expose them to criticism. And should it not be the responsibility of the student of religion to do the same for the basic presuppositions of his faith? The principle of self-criticism, so ardently advocated and espoused as being a basic condition for *moral* growth, needs equally to be advocated and espoused for *intellectual* growth. It was Spinoza who said that religion is a refuge for ignorance, precisely because the religion he encountered in his day discouraged this sort of criticism. And lest it appear that this kind of criticism is injurious to faith, one need only be reminded of the Socratic dictum that only in this way does one come to a proper appreciation of one's ignorance, and only in this way does one come to know something of intellectual humility. Dogmatism may really turn out to be a kind of intellectual stubbornness or arrogance obstructing the road to genuine Christian humility.

The tension that exists between philosophy and religion, stemming as it does from the fact that philosophy assumes a more objective and detached attitude to objects of belief and that religion fosters the attitude of commitment and surrender towards them, can be a wholesome one. It is a tension that should be construed as taking place *within* the religious sphere, for the good of faith itself. Granted, the tension may lead to surrendering points of view too complacently held, or too benignly sheltered to stand the strain. But in the long run no great religious commitment need be destroyed by the tension. Its positive values can be great, not least the gain of knowing what beliefs are really worthy of wholehearted commitment. When a religious commitment is made to untenable scientific views (or even tenable ones) it is well to be reminded that such commitments may rest on attempts at absolutizing the relative, and thus may contribute to a kind of pious idolatry. Too simple and too naive views of the Scriptures may lead to the same sort of thing. To forget that the Bible has a human side all too easily leads to absolutizing the letter and to recourse to fantastic apologetic expedients to secure a letter-perfect revelation. The problem becomes more difficult when philosophy deals with questions of ontology, as does religion, for they both deal with the problem of the unconditioned and involve very directly a religious concern. But even here, the tension may be wholesome, for it is the tension that compels a choice, a "leap of faith" so necessary for genuine religious commitment.

Again, religion needs philosophy to make the faith relevant to the society in which it lives. Faith has a tendency to outrun and outlive its intellectual expressions, and when it does, it loses its relevance as far as the intellectual milieu is concerned. Philosophy can be called upon to forge the concepts, the language of communication with which the faith can find significant expression. This is a time-honored function of philosophy from the very beginning of the Christian era. Early theologians like Clement, Origen and Augustine were great philosophers as well as theologians thoroughly steeped in the philosophy of their day. So much so that it is hard to say where theology ends and philosophy begins. In doing this, the Christian faith succeeds in avoiding a kind of monastic isolation from the surrounding culture and at the same time succeeds in making it meaningful and relevant.

Perhaps it is in this area that philosophy can make its greatest contribution to religion. As noted earlier, the problem of communication is becoming increasingly difficult. This situation is complicated by recent trends in theology which would set faith off in a context, the thought structure of which is so *sui generis* in nature that any real communication with the "going" thought trends of the day is doomed to failure. Consider, for example, the strictures placed on philosophy by Bishop Aulén when he says: ". . . faith has nothing to do with metaphysics." Or consider the following: "Christian faith in God is something else than a rational explanation of the universe." No doubt it is, if by "something else" he means only "something more." But such statements, coming from a leading figure in ecumenical Lutheranism would certainly discourage any effort to relate the faith to contemporary thought. Granted, the danger is great when concepts drawn from philosophy are used to give expression to the Christian faith, still the risk must be taken lest faith lose its relevance and become reduced to clichés that have largely lost their meaning to modern minds. The danger, though great, is not any greater than that experienced by missionaries in making the faith relevant in non-Christian cultures. Having to use words, concepts and ideas that have currency in non-Christian contexts, they make use of them by pouring into them meanings and connotations that are definitely and specifically Christian. Such words, concepts and ideas must certainly be reconstructed if they are to convey the meaning of the faith but in time they become naturalized and normal modes of expression. So much so that the Christian missionary no longer feels strange or fearful about using them.

A good case in point is the doctrine of the Logos which assumed a leading role in ancient philosophy. This doctrine had gone through a long development in Greek philosophy, dating back to the time of Heraclitus, and came to occupy a quite central place in Stoicism and Neo-Platonism when Christian theology appeared on the scene. For a Christian theologian to have said that the Christian faith was to have "nothing to do" with such Greek metaphysics would certainly have appeared strange, for early Christian theology (and even the New Testament itself) bears eloquent witness to the use of the term, making it as central in theology as it was in philosophy. True, the doctrine came to be reconstructed and re-interpreted in the context of revelation, but its basic idea of mediation continued to be the central core of its meaning. Today, the Logos doctrine has become so naturalized that no one raises any questions as to the legitimacy of its use.

Should philosophy be taught in such a way as to provide an apologetic for the faith? This too has been a time-honored function of philosophy, though it is questionable whether philosophy as taught on the college campuses should be put to such use. Paul Tillich warns that when philosophy is put to such use, it stands to lose its peculiar "eros." By this he means it ceases to be free to pursue its task, motivated by uncommitted reason, which is the very heart of the philosophic enterprise. For those who teach in a Christian college there is a perennial danger that philosophy be not permitted to speak for itself, and that it be loaded with theological prejudice or restrictions. Certainly one ought to grant that certain philosophical doctrines are more congenial to the Christian faith than others; that a philosophy that moves in an "open universe" is apt to make more room for faith than one that does not. But when a teacher seeks to use the study of philosophy to impress students with such values, he should be honest enough to confess that he is doing so out of a prior commitment to the faith, and not necessarily as a philosopher. It is because he happens to be a theologian as well as a philosopher that philosophy can be put to such uses. The history of philosophy makes it abundantly clear that philosophy can be put to destructive as well as constructive uses as far as the faith is concerned. One wonders whether the dubious values that religion can achieve in this way adequately compensate for other values that tend to be lost when philosophy is put to apologetic uses. For example, the value that accrues from actually having to face alternatives that appear equally plausible; or the value of having to suspend judgment on important matters over a longer period of time before making a commitment; or the value of judging a philosophy *on its own terms;* or the value of appraising a philosophy in terms of the specific objectives that a given philosophy seeks to achieve—all of these values and many others are jeopardized when the scales are loaded in advance. It may well be that the best sort of apologetic for the faith, at least on the college level, is not any direct support that philosophy can give but rather the indirect support of leading students to think for themselves and to make significant choices, with the Christian faith as one possible alternative. The danger students face is not that of rejecting Christianity but of ignoring it; of not seeing any live alternative to it. In the last analysis, the Christian faith is chosen and embraced, not when philosophy speaks in its favor but when the faith is permitted to speak for itself.

THE NEED OF PHILOSOPHY FOR RELIGION

It is a matter of historical fact that the study of philosophy has often served to lay bare a certain hunger for solutions that only faith can give. Augustine's conversion to Christianity was certainly aided and abetted by his failure to find solutions to his problems on the basis of philosophy. Insofar as *any* conversion involves an intellectual search as an essential ingredient in coming to faith, philosophy may help to shape and formulate the questions, the answers to which can never be found in philosophy. The late William Temple in his book *Nature, Man and God* speaks of the "hunger of natural theology." Philosophy seeks a kind of knowledge of its objects that will lead to personal commitment. Only such a philosophy will in the end prove satisfying. Philosophy seeks a faith. Perhaps this roots in the fact that basically man is a believing creature despite his rational proclivities; that no matter how thoroughly committed he may be to a rational solution of his problems, such solutions do not and cannot evoke full commitment or sustain him in such commitment. He cannot rest his ultimate destiny upon a manufactured article of faith, however fool-proof it may seem to his reason. It must ultimately rest upon a *given* element, which when properly responded to, becomes the lodestar of his faith and the "master light of all his seeing." If the teacher has succeeded in teaching in such a way that these faith-demanding problems receive their clarification and thus create a hunger for faith, it may well be that he has achieved his highest role as a teacher of philosophy.

COURSES EMBRACING RELIGION AND PHILOSOPHY

No doubt every discipline has its philosophical side. So every teacher touches upon some philosophical problems in connection with his field. Some courses, like those in literature and history, offer many opportunities for relating the study of philosophy and religion. Courses offered in philosophy departments in our church colleges should make a special point of indicating such interactions and thus enrich the student's appreciation and understanding of areas other than philosophy proper. The two courses I have found most closely related to this problem are those of comparative religion and philosophy of religion. In comparative religion, it soon becomes evident that any religion when it matures begins to take on intellectual structures, and sometimes develops full-blown philosophies. This is especially true of the older religions of the Orient. Students who have taken such a course are more open to the view that the Christian religion is no exception to this tendency. They begin to see that not only has Christianity developed a variety of forms of theology, but it has shaped a variety of philosophies as well. They are able to see how philosophy and theology have interacted in the past and how they have both become reconstructed in such interaction. The trends of theological thought cannot possibly be understood apart from the trends in philosophy. It may be that the best sort of course in philosophy of religion as it bears on the Christian tradition is a course in the history of the philosophies of religion, showing how the Christian faith has made its impact upon and come to terms with widely different points of view. In this way, students need not be committed to any particular philosophy of religion, but rather develop a background from which they may make intelligent choices of their own.

It would be inappropriate to outline in any further detail the specific strategy teachers in philosophy should follow. It is important that our colleges give more concentrated attention to the possibilities that the teaching of philosophy may have in the program of developing enriched, alert, and mature students and thus make possible more effective servants for church and society.

CHAPTER 9

Literature

by Arthur C. Paulson

The place of literature in the liberal arts college was never a question before the turn of the century—and only a minor one up to the end of World War I. Literature was an intimate and integral part of every college curriculum; no student doubted its value or its validity. He had come to college from schools which exposed their students to literary masterpieces and literary backgrounds from the first grade on. Their elementary readers (1-8) were filled with choice selections from English and American literature. Before he entered high school even, a student read bits of Shakespeare, Tennyson, Browning and Lowell, and was steeped in Whittier and Longfellow. He became acquainted with the Greek gods and heroes, and with Norse mythology and legend. He lived in a world of imagination with King Arthur, Robin Hood, Robinson Crusoe, and Sinbad the Sailor. He formed nodding acquaintanceships with George Eliot's Maggie, Scott's Marmion, and Kingsley's Amyas Leigh. He soaked up a mass of great truths, great non-truths, moral precepts, and stock platitudes from little excerpts of prose and poetry divorced from their contexts—and he could quote many of them verbatim. Moreover, he had excellent magazines to read if he wished: *Youths' Companion, St. Nicholas, John Martin's Book, The American Boy.* All these were filled with ideals and adventure, told by writers who understood both young people and the art of writing. It was all very exciting. Moreover, the young people who later were to enter Christian liberal arts colleges usually acquired a good background of Biblical knowledge and a thorough indoctrination in Christian fundamentals. And all this before they entered high school.

In high school this training was continued in four years of English studies, backed by three years of American, English, and world history. It was a more formal study of backgrounds and masterpieces than his grade school expeditions into literature had been. Longer selections were read—the author's purpose was pointed out and discussed. Of course, there were any number of poor teachers

151

in those days, too, but a student usually found in his four years of high school one or two inspiring teachers who knew what they were doing.

But it was not only his English studies that added to his knowledge of literature. The high schools in those days required foreign language study—four years of Latin, two years of German, and in some of the schools a year or two of Greek. While it must be admitted that these studies often degenerated into disciplinary drills in vocabulary and grammar, the students were exposed to some of the world's best literature and to a knowledge of backgrounds that was thought essential for every educated person. The student, therefore, came to college with some understanding of literature, some appreciation of literature, and the tools for further understanding and appreciation. And in college the study of literature was an intimate and integral part of his education.

In the elementary school of today, all this is changed. The older type readers are gone. Instead of reading literature, the pupils now read to become better socially adjusted. They become acquainted with the activities of their community; they interview the milkman and the corner grocer, and go out in the country to see all the little lambs and pigs and chickens on McKewen's farm. It is rather interesting to note that these readers deal with things and animals and processes rather than with people. The way the milk gets into the bottles and is distributed to the customers is much more important than the milkman as a person. The animals on the farm are much more interesting than the farmer, and the machines and mechanical devices are much more significant than the persons who operate them. For their knowledge of human nature and human adventure the students go outside the school—to television and the comic books. And in school and out, their lives are so filled with supervised activities that it is a wonder they have time for anything else.

Fortunately, this stress on social adjustment comes to a minor close in the sixth grade.

In the junior and senior high school, at least theoretically, the position of literature is better. Here as a part of his English studies —which includes reading, writing, listening, and speaking—a student is inducted into a planned study of the literatures of both England and America. Often it is "integrated" with a study of community life—a continuation of the social adjustment idea—but despite methods, the literature itself is there, and under some teachers the results are good. On the other hand, there are a number of things that stand in the way of good results. One of these is the enormous increase in the number and complexity of high school activities. Another is the "terminal" program, which sets up a *practical* course of studies for those who are not planning to go to college, but who often change their minds. The third is a rather derisive attitude toward literature itself. Because it is taught mostly by women, literature becomes a "sissy" subject, in contrast to the sciences, taught by men. To the many students who are eager to get into their life work it is a waste of time. And to many, for no reason at all except that they don't like it, it is "junk" or a worse word.

And so it goes. Too many of our high school students today are ignorant, not only of literature but of the tools of literature as well. Few of them, now that Latin is no longer a required subject, know anything about Greek mythology and legend. They have never heard of the Norse gods or the Germanic heroes. Fairy stories, animal epics like *Reynard the Fox,* and the great adventure tales are a closed book to them. King Arthur, Robin Hood, Ali Baba are mere names. They have missed almost entirely the whole world of allusion; words like "Trojan horse," "Open Sesame" and "Round Table" bring no response.

There remains one bright spot, however; students coming to our Christian liberal arts colleges still have a background of Biblical knowledge—but this comes from private instruction, not from the public schools.

This introduction is long, but it is necessary to have this background in order to realize what we are up against today in trying to determine the place of literature in the Christian liberal arts colleges.

The first thing we must realize is that we can take nothing for granted. Some of the high school seniors come to college with a fund of literary knowledge and literary backgrounds; they know the values of literary studies. But the majority are either refreshingly ignorant of things pertaining to literature, or definitely skeptical of its value. Consequently, we must start from scratch. The second thing is that a great many students come to college determined to avoid literature as much as possible. Many of the reasons given are good ones—the pressure of other interests, other requirements—but often the real reason is pure antipathy or the lack of understanding. As one of my students in English said to me at our first conference: "I hate English. It is the most useless, uninteresting junk I know of." He was speaking of the literature he was exposed to in high school. And he had the highest college aptitude rating in his high school class. The third thing is that the amount of required literary study in college is woefully small. At some colleges students are required to take six hours of English and fourteen hours of a foreign language or its equivalent in English translation. But the teachers of English 1-2 can devote only a part of their time to literature, and the teachers of beginning language courses even less. Only in the translation courses is it possible to devote the whole time to literature.

Taking college students as they are, the instructor in literature discovers that his first task is to demonstrate through literature that literature actually has a place in the Christian liberal arts college. For a student who defines literature as "junk," he must draw out a new definition; to one who thinks it is useless, he must show its practical value; to one who thinks it uninteresting, even boring, he must make literature the most fascinating subject in the curriculum. And to reach all the students, he must do this through one of the required subjects, usually freshman English.

AN APPROACH TO THE APPRECIATION OF LITERATURE

This first step is the same in all liberal arts colleges—Christian or otherwise—though the selection of material may be somewhat different. To show that it can be done, I shall give an account of what we have done in our freshman English classes at St. Olaf through the years. The approach has varied, but the general plan has been the same. During the first semester, we co-ordinate it with our training in reading and writing. From the point of view of literature, we try to bring about a redefinition of literature for those who need it. One method is to tell the student at the beginning of his course that we want to know something about him, and ask him as his first assignment—due in two weeks—to write a short autobiography. This usually floors some of the students; they do not know how to begin; besides, there is nothing to write about—nothing has ever happened to them. And so we read autobiographies— well chosen ones, college level, modern, with incidents and actions rather closely approximating the experiences of college freshmen. What usually happens is that even the most indifferent student responds. He discovers that the lives of others are not so different from his own; that he has had the same experiences as the writer, thought the same thoughts and had the same doubts. He reads Hudson's *The Death of an Old Dog* and recalls his own first experience with death—the fear, the mystery, the promise. He reads *The Secret Drawer* by Kenneth Grahame, and he too clasps hands with the boy, dead for a hundred years, who also collected treasures—bird's eggs, stones, and what not—and hid them in a secret hiding place. He reads *Hardscrabble Hellas* and catches the author's enthusiasm for works of literature he has never heard of. As he reads he begins to realize and appreciate the importance of words; that if he can put his ideas, his experiences, in words that will reproduce the idea, the experience, exactly as it occurred— make the reader see it and feel it and understand its significance exactly as he did—his autobiography will be as interesting and significant to others as the autobiographies he has read were to him. At the same time he discovers that the language, especially in the selections he has read, is *his* language; that the language of literature is not the stilted, ornate, many syllabled stuff he imagined it was. He has caught a glimpse in autobiography of literature as a study of human life in all its complexity. As a result, his theme, when it is finally written, shows evidence of this discovery; the details are more carefully chosen, the language is better, and the organization as a whole has purpose. All this from the study of autobiography.

The change in attitude toward literature, begun with autobiography, is continued in logical sequence if not in time, with biography. Here in the lives of actual people, studied objectively, the student adds to his knowledge of the complexity and mystery of human life. He discovers that two authors, writing about the same person, using the same sources, and trying to be as objective as possible, come to conclusions entirely different. Both evaluations are works of literature; the writing in both is excellent, the facts are all well established, and the conclusions are well grounded. But are the two authors speaking about the same person? And if they are, just who is the *real* person? These questions confront the student as he is asked to write a theme about some well known character. The climax of this part of the study comes in reading a biography like Strachey's *Queen Victoria*. The students enjoy it immensely. They get great pleasure in Strachey's using Queen Victoria's words to further his own slanting. They like his sense of humor, his perception of the ludicrous in human nature, his bit-ing satire. But out of it comes the picture of Queen Victoria from the cradle to the grave, a real human being, not a superwoman or a puppet, surrounded by very-much-alive human beings. Whether it is a true picture or not—I rather doubt it; in spite of his complexity, it is over-simplified—is not the issue. It fills the need that freshmen have of discovering that literature furthers the study of human nature—of man as man—and as such has a place in the liberal arts curriculum.

The next logical step—it comes chronologically in the second semester—is the study of fiction. Now autobiography and biography are literature, but all things being equal, they are of a lower order than fiction. In the former, the characters are real people, and as such are circumscribed by the things they actually did, by the words they actually said, by the environment in which they actually moved. Viewing his subject objectively, the biographer, for instance, seldom dares to bring out the hidden motives, the secret desires, the deadening frustrations, the whole fabric of intangibles that, unknown to anyone have dominated the whole life of the person under consideration. The known, the observable, are dominant in every part of the biography. The biographer cannot infer anything that cannot be substantiated by evidence. In fiction it is different. The author is a creator—he actually creates his characters and creates them with a purpose. He also creates the environment and the particular situations in which to place his characters. The characters, the environment, the situation, all resemble those we are familiar with in actual life—but they are not. For, though no character in fiction is ever as completely complex as the most simple human being, the character in fiction is more complex within a very restricted area than any human being could be in any part of the larger area. It is this concentration in a very limited area that enables the reader to know the characters, the environment, the situations better than his closest friends, his most observable environment, the everyday situations of his own normal life. For there is less to know. We have before us all there is to know about Hamlet, because Hamlet does not exist outside the pages of a book. Neither does Scarlett O'Hara. But because there are no hidden secrets in their lives, we can learn more about human nature from Hamlet and Scarlett O'Hara than from any living person, because within the restricted area of their lives they have plunged deeper than any living being could possibly go.

"What a strange company it is," writes C. Alphonso Smith, "these men and women who were not born but made. They are not ghosts, for they never wore flesh. They are alive, actively and increasingly alive. Try them by the tests of real life: Do they not influence others? Are they not talked about and written about and thought about? . . . Have they not become a part of the very consciousness of men? Do not some of them keep alive the memory of nations otherwise forgotten? . . . Have they not linked man to man, and nation to nation, and century to century by furnishing a common theme of thought and common center of association?"[1]

We have too little time in freshman English to go very deep in the study of human nature through the study of fiction. But we do introduce them to three of the great works of fiction: Homer's *Odyssey* in Rieu's excellent translation, Shakespeare's *Othello*, and Hardy's *Return of the Native*. And the usual thing happens: the students enjoy these works immensely. They discover that all three are good stories just as stories. But it goes deeper than this. Most of them are rather amazed to find that human nature has been pretty much the same throughout the centuries—that people as people were just as interesting in 1000 B.C. as they are today— that they had the same joys and sorrows, hates and loves, triumphs and frustrations that we see all about us in our time. They discover that each person in fiction is an individual. T. E. Shaw speaks of "the sly cattish wife; that cold-blooded egoist Odysseus, and the priggish son who yet met his master prig in Menelaus." The students make their own judgments. They are especially taken with Nausicaa; they think she would have made a very good student at St. Olaf. They almost hate Shakespeare for what he does to Desdemona, and they take sides for and against Eustacia Vye. They have a hard time seeing Odysseus as "the noble Odysseus" and they absolutely refuse to accept him as a model husband.

The students learn other things in fiction too. For many of them the reading of Homer is their first introduction to Greek mythology and legend. In the *Return of the Native* they are made aware of the tremendous influence of environment. And they study rather carefully the technical set-up of the epic, the novel and the play.

So much for the approach to literature through autobiography, biography and fiction. In this detailed account I have tried to point out one of our methods of demonstrating to our freshmen that literature does have a place in our college educational pro-

[1]C. Alphonso Smith, *What Can Literature Do For Me,* (New York: Doubleday, Page and Company, 1925), pp. 73-74.

gram. In this particular approach the student is not merely told—
he learns for himself that literature can give him a wider and
deeper understanding of human nature; that in reading literature
he is gaining knowledge and wisdom in the vicarious experience of
the lives of others. He is introduced to new points of view, new
insights, a wider horizon of understanding.

But this approach is only one of many. We shall mention some
of the others but not go into detail. Since freshman English is
primarily concerned with writing techniques, we try to show our
students how the study of literature can improve their writing
skills. While not encouraging them too strongly to play "the sedu-
lous ape," we do point out to them the perfect spatial arrangement
of Victor Hugo's description of the battle of Waterloo, the effectiveness of the analogy of the stagecoach in Bellamy's *Looking Backward,* and the ease and simplicity of the modern informal style in
contemporary English and American essays.

The third approach demonstrates that literature can add to the
students' storehouse of knowledge and understanding. For a student whose major interest is history, a term paper comparing Shaw's
Saint Joan with a good historical account of Joan of Arc may leave
him with the impression that literature may expound certain historical truths quicker and better than history itself. William Beebe,
who in addition to being a great scientist is one of the best writers
in America today, has made biology live for people who otherwise
would never have bothered their heads about biological science.
The same is true of G. K. Chesterton and C. S. Lewis in religion,
Stephen Leacock in social criticism, and Joad in philosophy.

The fourth approach is one of the most important. It makes the
student aware of the fact that literature presents the vision of the
ideal. This truth is admirably expressed by James A. Michener in
his article, *Fire on the Hearth of Humanity,* reprinted in one of our
freshman texts.

Today I believe—considering how the school curriculum is disposed—
that the future decency of the world rests largely in the hands of English
teachers. By a process of elimination, English has been left with the
principal job of modern education. Literature must keep alive the sparks
of idealism, human decency, hope, belief in a better world, and dedica-
tion to the goodness of mankind. By a process of elimination, teachers
of literature have become the ministers who must see the world through
its dark night of failing idealism. . . .
I believe this without any *ifs* or *buts.* I honestly believe that a nation

remains strong only so long as it remains idealist. I believe that brightness of vision is better than brightness of rifle barrels; and I believe
without question that young people must be instructed in the principles
of idealism. I cannot admit that I am a sentimentalist about this. In the
hard facts of national existence, idealism pays.[2]

He then goes on to urge, among other things, the study of poetry.
Of poetry he says:

The conscience of a race lies in its poems, and it is the conscience of
mankind for which we are struggling, in our quiet ways. . . . Poetry is
the best part of a thinking and feeling life, and a remarkable proportion
of our students are eager to think and to experience deep emotion if we
have the good sense to encourage them.[3]

These then are the four approaches that we use in our freshman English classes to demonstrate through literature that literature really has a place in the college curriculum. (There is a fifth
approach, the study of literary forms, but we do this in conjunction
with the other approaches.) We feel that we succeed fairly well.
We have no trouble with lack of interest. The students are convinced, I believe, that literature is not such a bad thing after all.
Of course, not all the students go on to further studies in literature
—far from it. But all of them go into the sophomore year with a
kindlier feeling toward literature. The antipathy is gone; they no
longer sneer; they may even read one of the literary masterpieces
on their own and enjoy it. On the other hand, many students who
had no intentions of continuing in literature, give it another try,
and a few even make it one of their major studies. And some of
the students taking the foreign language requirement find their
work more interesting because of their freshman introduction to
literature.

The only thing that could possibly set our freshman English
courses apart from those of any other liberal arts college is that our
instructors and our students are Christians. This means that we
do not shy away from matters of religion or the Christian point
of view. If man, as someone has said, is incurably religious, then
religion is an integral part of literature. We, therefore, give it its
proper emphasis. On the other hand we do not try to drag religion
in by the tail. We do not insist that in our literary studies, the

[2]James A. Michener, "Fire on the Hearth of Humanity," as quoted in *Current Thinking
and Writing*, second series, ed. Joseph M. Bachelor, Ralph L. Henry, and Rachel Salisbury
(New York: Appleton-Century-Crofts, 1951), pp. 25-26.
[3]*Ibid.*, p. 27.

author or any of his characters be Christian. We do not insist that they be good people. But we evaluate literature and this evaluation is tempered by our Christian point of view. What we do insist is that what we read be good literature from the accepted standards of good literature. The rest can take care of itself.

LITERATURE AS A REFLECTION OF LIFE

Beyond the freshman course we are faced with a new situation in the teaching of literature. The students electing literature more or less take it for granted that the study of literature has both pleasure and value. The question now becomes, What shall we stress? and What shall we offer in the way of literature? The answer to the second question is dependent on the answer to the first.

What shall we stress? It depends on our concept of literature. We must stress form and we do—in all our classes. The form is the pattern of words in prose and poetry that most nearly approximates the perfect medium for the content. Our task in the study of form is to find, if we can, that perfect medium for the content. But we stress content more. The content of literature is the study of human nature in all its variant complexities; it is the focusing of the quintessence of life—best illustrated in short poems like Tennyson's *Flower in a Crannied Wall*, Browning's *Prospice*, or Blake's stanza beginning "To see the world in a grain of sand" from *Auguries of Innocence*. In other words, literature tries to throw some light on the question *What is man? What is this thing called life? What is the purpose of life?* And these are the questions we stress.

A ten year old understands life perfectly; he has seen it in the movies. It is the life of adventure in the Wild West, where the Lone Ranger drops an outlaw with every shot, and he shoots often. The adolescent also understands life perfectly; he has experienced it. Life is love, the perfect union of two adolescent hearts. But the college sophomore does not understand life; he has been mistaken too often. He is willing to learn.

And so we show him life as portrayed in the best literature of Greece, Rome, Germany, France, Norway, England and America. We ask him to listen to what the authors and their characters have to say. The very first poem in his sophomore survey of English literature *(Deor,* written about 700 A.D.) tells him that life is suffering, endurance, hope. The next, the epic *Beowulf,* tells him that it is obligation to kinfolk, loyalty to one's lord, and the duty of revenge. As he reads on, he is introduced to Chaucer, Milton, Wordsworth, Tennyson, Browning and a host of lesser lights, poets all, who try to give him their interpretation of life. He meets the dramatists, ancient and modern, who use a different method to tell him many of the same things that the poets do! He hobnobs with the great essayists, speculates with the philosophers, experiments with the scientists. And all of them are asking *What is man? What is this thing called life? What is the purpose of life?*

In all this study there is constant evaluation. Neither the instructor nor the student will accept an author's interpretation of life or its purpose without questioning it. They swamp him with questions, and if he cannot answer them, they cast him aside. They play one author against another, one character against another, one age against another. They go into other fields—philosophy, history, science—for questions to throw at those who think they can interpret life. And finally out of the welter of conflicting interpretations comes the answer:

Human nature does not change; fundamentally, man is the same today as he was a thousand years ago, two thousand, three thousand. Every person since the fall of man from grace has been born with the same potentialities, some good, some evil, but with the potentialities for evil predominant. Man's natural self, therefore, is involved in contradiction, and though he may strive for the good, he finds it difficult to rise above himself. It is only when he discovers something outside himself, greater than himself, that he can transcend himself. If he cannot find something outside himself greater than himself he is a lost creature.

This is the answer that literature gives. And the student suddenly discovers that all the time he has been looking at his own portrait. In literature, then, a person learns to know himself through the vicarious experiences of others. This is the primary reason why literature has a place in every liberal arts college.

But what about the Christian liberal arts college? Is there a special reason for the study of literature here? I believe there is, because literature and the teachings of Christianity come to the same conclusion: *Man is a child of God, created by God, and apart from God he is nothing.* Since the fall, his potentialities for evil have been greater than his potentialities for good. (There is no better illustration of the fact of original sin than that found in some of our contemporary naturalistic novels.) It is only by the grace of God through Jesus Christ that he can rise above his sinful self. And this applies to all of us.

This is the answer that literature should give in a Christian liberal arts college.

CHAPTER 10

Language Studies

by Loring D. Knecht

Stated in its broadest terms, the general organizational objective of the curriculum of the Christian liberal arts college must be the grouping of the various disciplines around a common governing center. Again stated broadly, this center must be the proper study of man, his activities and his relation to his fellow man, to his God and to the world in which he lives. The question then quite naturally arises as to what the positions of the various disciplines will be in relation to this center and in relation to one another. We are then faced with the problem of ascertaining whether or not there is any hierarchy among the various academic disciplines, whether there are one or two that tie all the others to the common governing center.

Even if one rejects the idea that theology and philosophy have any right imperialistically to impose themselves upon other disciplines through artificial comprehensive syntheses, it must be admitted that they ought to play a key role in the integration of the curriculum because of the fact that they do propose a "world view" or "world views." But, granted the key role of theology and philosophy, we can only protest against their sometimes arrogant attitude which seems to presuppose a strictly hierarchical view of the academic disciplines. Their frequent scorn of so-called "tool" disciplines (among these, language study) is like that of a house that would belittle the building blocks of its foundation. Philosophy and theology do not exist without language. In fact, man does not reason or speculate on any subject without some kind of language. For the scientist this language is often mathematics, but language nonetheless. The theologian or philosopher can no more scorn language with impunity than he can scorn a fundamentally sound knowledge of history, cultural anthropology, or creative literature. It would be easy to multiply the illustrations of the fact that language suggests concepts or that literature not only gives dramatic impact to theological and philosophical concepts, but that it actually anticipates them.

163

Theology and philosophy have always presented comprehensive views of man and his predicament and have proposed solutions. These solutions are not, however, always accepted; indeed they are, as often as not, misunderstood. This is perhaps not due to man's more obvious sins, but rather to a fundamental sin of pride which prevents the theologian or philosopher from making a real attempt "to talk the other fellow's language" (both figuratively and literally).

What we have said up to this point would apply to the mode of expression and the linguistic attitude of the philosopher or theologian in his own culture. But he can and should go much further. If he takes the pains, he can even penetrate a foreign culture by being forced into its very own psychological patterns through that most personal and intimate psychological activity, *language*. Once he has penetrated a foreign culture in this way, he will have moved one step closer to that perspective and unity which is the dream of theology and philosophy—not an artificial unity imposed from without, but rather the recognition of a basic unity running like a golden thread through the marvelous varicolored pattern of diversity.

Language (and of course the foreign language) is no mere "fact of knowledge" on which concepts are built, the mere raw material which, dead, is fashioned into meaningful patterns wholly from the outside. It is a living complex of expressions and habits reflecting the deepest psychology of a people. As such it has its own effect on the very concepts to which it gives expression. Man not only creates his tools, but the very tools he creates show him new possibilities of creation which he had not suspected previously. Would you truly know your neighbor, learn his tongue. Would you evolve a concept, you must find the right language through which to express it. If you would appeal to all men, then present your idea to each individually *from the inside,* expressed in his own personal and intimate idiom. Language is *created.* True. But it also *creates.* Understanding this, we see it as a revitalizing force in mending the discontinuity of our cultural heritage which leads to "misunderstanding between people and between peoples." There is no more human activity than language, nor more powerful unifying force, but when no attempt is made to move from one language to another, it can be just as formidable a barrier as it might otherwise be a highroad.

But is there, can there be, a religious point of view toward foreign language study? Are we not repeating what might be said by someone belonging to any non-religious cultural group? We can start by recalling an old Norwegian grandfather who thought that God spoke only Norwegian, or the oft heard phrase in old France, *Dieu parle français*, by recalling the vital centripetal force of Hebrew among the Jews, the holy position of Arabic in Islam. A modern French poet, Charles Péguy, has even identified God with the "chosen" language of a "chosen" people, only this time it is the French.

Is the attitude of religion toward language (and more particularly the attitude of Christianity) fated to be an exclusive, divisive one? Is the notion that God speaks only Norwegian, or French, or German an inevitable outgrowth of the Tower of Babel or can something be done to change it?[1] We must remember that the Tower of Babel is a most effective symbol for the sin of pride. He who would conquer the sin of pride might well start by penetrating exclusive and divisive idioms. The process of exclusivity must be reversed, not necessarily by instituting a universal second language, nor certainly not through the imposition of a *lingua franca* as a result of political domination. (We might not mind this, of course, if the language were English, but how would we feel if it were Russian or Chinese?) No, the linguistic answer is to tear down the tower of pride and make an honest effort at understanding by speaking with our brothers, or still more with our enemies, in their own language.

Missionaries are acutely aware that they must not carry the gospel to the heathen in a foreign tongue, that they must learn the local idiom. Only recently we have seen two women and a small child succeed in gaining access to the Auca Indians of Ecuador where five grown men failed dramatically, paying for this failure with their lives. The difference? A very rudimentary knowledge of the Auca language.

There is all too often in many of our Christian liberal arts colleges a kind of cultural isolation which is not hard to understand, but which is nonetheless undesirable. I am referring to a certain overemphasis of one linguistic and cultural tradition to the exclusion of all others. The varying national and linguistic origins of

---

[1] One would be tempted to answer in the affirmative pointing to the recent tendency toward merger of synods separated heretofore primarily by national origin and linguistic difference. However, attesting to the power of linguistic difference, we must admit that the reunion of the linguistically divided Lutheran Church is coming about in this country only now that a new linguistic unity in English has become a fact.

the different synods and bodies from which these institutions have sprung, make a certain emphasis inevitable, even desirable. But it is vital that we do not neglect the study of other foreign languages representing extremely important lines of development in our western tradition.

If we are not to be self-centered in other ways, how can we be self-centered linguistically, even imperialistic in this regard? Such linguistic imperialism is just as distasteful as philosophical, theological, or political imperialism. A *lingua franca* would be a marvelous instrument in helping us to further understanding among peoples and among disciplines, provided it was the result of a natural evolution. But even if such a *lingua franca* did exist, it would not be wise to forego the opportunity of learning about and penetrating foreign cultures through their own local idioms. At the very least it would be neither courteous nor politic.

Linguistic imperialism is certainly not justifiable on the grounds of the inherent superiority of any particular idiom. We can disdain no foreign tongue on the grounds that it is primitive. There is, as a matter of fact, good reason for stating that there is no such thing as a primitive language. Even the exclusively spoken languages of certain primitive tribes are not themselves primitive. Many such languages are complex and subtle structurally, sometimes even more so than the great cultural languages. Even though they may appear to suffer from a poverty of vocabulary in terms of our own culture, in terms of their own culture such tongues are almost invariably extremely rich in nuances of vocabulary touching on the objects, problems, and facets of life which are closest to them. We ought not disdain any foreign idiom.

Foreign language study attains to high level integration because it attempts to learn to communicate *directly* with another culture *in that culture's own terms and following its own psychology.* This is indeed a friendly, a complimentary concession—and no mean achievement no matter how one views it. Ideally, it is a most rewarding one and even no more than a partial attainment of this objective is of great value in terms of the effort one has made to get out of one's own skin and into that of a foreign brother. If for no other reason, it is of great value in that it brings with it a charitable flexibility of outlook which is absolutely essential to greater peace and understanding in this imperfect world. Here is one of the most effective shortcuts to the elimination of cultural isolation, of bad feeling against minorities, of the kind of overweaning self-pride on a national scale that may subtly lead to super-race theories and attitudes.

What is the "basic teachable matter" in foreign language study? Why, the foreign language itself—especially the *foreign* language, for we know next to nothing of it when we start. This may sound over-obvious, but, because we are advancing many and varied reasons for the study of a foreign language, it must be made clear that we must strive first of all not to learn *about* the foreign language, but to learn the foreign language itself.[2] The psychological, disciplinary, and cultural advantages will naturally follow if the student arrives at the point where he really has a reasonable mastery of the language. Of course, in addition to mastering the language in question, most students develop a flexibility of outlook, of speech, tone, and linguistic form from their contact with the first foreign language, all attitudes and skills which become a habit of mind and constitute a predisposition to think of things foreign not as something stupidly strange, but as merely temporarily different. From there to the mastery of a second foreign language is but a step, for the student then looks on the second language as presenting only a temporary obstacle. This broader, more supple turn of mind (for one does learn to twist it this way and that in studying a foreign language) is invaluable in other disciplines as well. It becomes easier to fathom the history of other lands and peoples, the *foreign* seeming less forbidding. The same would of course apply to foreign music, literature, art, and other fields of liberal inquiry and artistic endeavor.

The study of a foreign language not only offers many quite obvious integrative cultural advantages. It also requires of the student in the process of learning that he discipline himself in a way that cannot fail to help him form more general good habits whose essential quality is integrative. It commands definite respect for excellence of performance as there is an obvious standard by which one is measured.[3] It demands logical thinking and careful concentration as well as a realization of the necessity of assuming responsibility for what one does or does not accomplish. More than many disciplines it requires assiduous attendance and daily dili-

---

[2] One can not help wondering how we can achieve this goal when so many foreign language teachers in elementary and secondary schools do not really possess the language they supposedly teach, but do have an abundance of credit hours in methods courses.

[3] If this is not always the case in college foreign language studies, it is because we have set our sights too low and are completely unrealistic as to the amount of study needed for mastery.

gence. The student must follow closely and regularly or he finds himself almost hopelessly lost. This is a lesson which must be learned for life and not merely for the classroom. But what better place is there to start if one has not done so already?

The goal of foreign language study should of course be to possess the language *well enough to really use it*. This is unfortunately very rarely the goal of our undergraduate students. Our requirements are at least partly at fault in the development of this attitude. Once it becomes obvious to the beginning student that the sophomores have not mastered the language after two years study, he assumes, consciously or unconsciously, that, such being the formal requirement, the college is really not aiming at the goal of mastery. From that moment on he is just "taking a course" or "taking two years of a language." With this attitude firmly entrenched in the minds of most of our foreign language students it is not at all surprising that the language more often than not "takes them" instead of their "taking it." *Veni, vidi, victus sum.*

The integrative value of foreign language study increases in direct proportion to the standard of proficiency reached. Any rational program of foreign language study will not fail to introduce the language *at the earliest possible age* so that the very real rewards that come with proficiency may be reaped in advanced language courses on the college level.[4] The priceless integrative values of foreign language study will not really become evident until such a logical sequence of courses is followed. Some of the rewards of foreign language study as well as the desirability of an early start are aptly illustrated by Montaigne in a passage from his essay "On Education":

Acquaintance with the world is of very great use and travel into foreign countries of singular advantage, not merely to bring back (in the manner of our French nobility) an account of how many paces Santa Rotonda is in circuit, or of the richness of Signora Livia's drawers, or, like some others, how much Nero's face in a statue in some old ruin is

---

[4]Unfortunately many colleges now exempt students from further study of a foreign language if they offer at least four years' study of one language at the secondary level. This is a clear reflection of what Conant has called the giving of mere lip service to the cause of foreign language study. If the goal really were proficiency, then the student with such a background should be required to continue in advanced courses in the same language. He has just arrived at the point where his foreign language study will begin to bring him rich rewards—if he continues with it. This is the only rational end of all his earlier hard work and precious investment in time. But what do we do? We give him the false impression that he has "arrived." He has *not* yet arrived but he is on the threshold and then we tell him not to cross over.

longer and broader than that on some equally old medal; but chiefly
to return with knowledge of the nature and customs of those nations,
and to whet and sharpen our wits by rubbing them upon those of others.
I would that a boy should be sent abroad very young and, in order to
kill two birds with one stone, first into those neighboring nations whose
language differs most from our own and to which, if it be not formed
early, the tongue cannot be bent.

The importance of the early start can not be over-emphasized.
At the same time we must stress the absolute necessity of continuing foreign language study over a longer period of time if anything
approaching mastery is to be attained.

There is nothing basically wrong with the *way* foreign languages
are taught in most of our colleges. Some work on methodology is
in order, but the experienced foreign language teacher generally
knows which method works best for him without taking part in
elaborately contrived methodological experiments which are usually far from being rigidly controlled and are therefore well nigh
worthless and are certainly far from scientific. The variables and
imponderables are so considerable in such undertakings that any
real attempt to control them rigorously is apt to consume a disproportionate amount of the teacher's time. The ironic result:
teaching usually suffers. It would seem that, even though there is
probably a place for some such methodological experimentation,
it should most likely not be done in the liberal arts college but in
some place where the staff can afford to work full time on such
statistical and psychological problems. The good teacher of foreign languages will do well with any method which he finds suits
him and the poor teacher will not do well with any method. It is
not a lack of adequate methods that has made the teaching of foreign languages such an irrational and uncertain undertaking in
the United States. The basic problem can rather be succinctly
summed up in the old saw "too little too late." For some inexplicable reason the foreign language teacher is expected to achieve
results in two years that the piano teacher is happy to achieve in
ten. And yet there is definitely a skill factor in foreign language
teaching that makes this comparison apt.

The prevailing "lick and a promise" approach to the study of
foreign languages in this country is no doubt partly the reason why
so many educators are antagonistic toward it. They have been
brought up and educated in a system which has paid only lip

service to this study. Consequently they have never *learned* a foreign language themselves (although they may have *studied* one), and never having learned one themselves, they are loathe to admit that it has any real value. It is undoubtedly significant that those who have really learned and mastered a foreign language are not those who deny its usefulness. On the contrary such privileged individuals are invariably enthusiastic about its value.

There is great value to the serious student in knowing one of the great cultural foreign languages well enough to consult source material directly in that language. Unfortunately few of our college students ever get the thrill that comes from using a foreign language in a research project involving some other field. But, if we were to have a rational program of language study throughout our educational system, this would be a necessary goal on the upper division level of college work.[5] This is possible even now with certain superior students although they have unfortunately been delayed in starting their foreign language instruction until the age of seventeen or eighteen. They are very much the exception.

The familiar "Area Study" is in fact a whole integrated program actually built around the language or languages of the area as the basic cementing force, not only psychologically, but often, and ideally, as the very medium in which the studies are carried on. The foreign language is not only the mortar binding the bricks together, but is to a considerable extent the very clay of which the bricks are formed. Such programs, when skillfully laid out and imaginatively carried through, serve as concrete examples of a very real kind of integration.

In an ideal situation, the liberal arts college would be, in a sense, one large "Area Study" in which the proper preoccupation with the study of man and his activities, his relation to his God, the world and the universe, would constitute the "area" itself and the fundamental governing principle or center. The need for communication and integration between the components of this "area" is obvious. It has been suggested that, in order to make the unity of this "area" real, one must "go beyond language" or "below language." One might, I think, rightfully question whether such a thing is possible, language being in fact inseparable from the concept. At any rate, before one could even attempt to "go beyond language" one must already possess language as a tool or skill and

---

[5]This would of course presuppose a logical sequence of courses in the same language on a lower level.

this possession must be both physical and psychological. There are distressing signs that too many of our students become inflated with vague, inchoate metaphysical impressions which they "feel" but can not express. They all too often look on language as "merely a tool." This in itself can be disputed, but at least they should know that the workman does not disdain his tools. How often we see these budding philosophers doing "somersaults in the wild blue yonder," thinking they are going "beyond language" when they have not yet even arrived at true possession of their own language, not to mention the mastery of a foreign language.

In this larger "area" which is that of our liberal studies, an "area" as wide as the joys and sufferings of humanity, as high as man's longing for knowledge and understanding, as deep as his longing for God—in this "area" concepts *are* of prime importance, but the vehicle for these concepts must not, can not be neglected if any cohesion is to remain. If our "area" is as vast as we believe it to be, cultural and linguistic snobbery can be a definite contributing factor, not only in lowering a veil before the eyes of man in his search for truth, but even in setting man against man.

CHAPTER 11

History

by Richard W. Solberg

In the contest of our time between liberal and pragmatic education no one seriously questions the propriety of including courses in history in the curriculum. Events of the past fifty years have conspired to thrust the teaching of history into far greater prominence than ever before. Increased contacts with foreign lands have promoted a desire to know more about world history, and simultaneously, the strong emphasis upon national patriotism and loyalty which has accompanied three wars has tended to stress the teaching of American history both in secondary and higher institutions of learning.

If one is only concerned about defending the "place" of history in our present-day curricula, he will find little to fear. History has its secure niche. But if one takes the next step and demands that the "purpose" of the history course also be examined, he may find greater cause for concern. History taught simply for the purpose of glorifying the national tradition may well become a direct threat to the aims and values of the liberal arts, or even a danger to a peaceful world society. History courses taught as easy substitutes for the modest intellectual exercise of reading *Newsweek* or *Time,* or simply for the purpose of getting a teaching job are not pursuing substantially different aims from courses in basket-weaving and salesmanship. The more emphasis there is upon the so-called "practical uses" of the history courses, the less expectation there is that they will serve the aims of the liberal arts.

TEACHING HISTORY SIGNIFICANTLY

There is no doubt that it is possible to teach a course in any field, even in such traditional liberal arts areas as the Humanities, without any sensitivity to human values, ideals, and aspirations. It is possible to count the commas in *Hamlet* or to analyze a poem

172

to death without ever finding its human soul. Quite apart from the question of excluding purely "skill" courses from the curriculum, one of the very real educational problems of our church colleges is the cultivation of liberal arts attitudes in the so-called liberal arts areas. It is our purpose here to inquire whether the study and teaching of history has a valid claim to inclusion within these areas, and whether there is any particular way in which history may help to express the liberal arts tradition within the Christian framework.

It would be a very difficult task to convince a college student who had just completed a course in World History by writing an examination in which he had been called upon to list the names and dates of the fifty most important battles since the fall of the Roman Empire that history was a vital subject, thrillingly relevant to all of the great issues of life. Because history has been so often taught on the secondary level in just this fashion, it is a very difficult task to commend a true study of history to freshman and sophomore classes in college. The notion that history is "a thing of the past," which only recounts the dull details of politics and wars, dies hard.

In its broadest sense, of course, history includes everything in the realms of politics, economics, society, or religion—the architecture of the Hittites, the diet of the Yankton Sioux Indians, or the explosion of the atomic bomb. It doesn't deal only with generals and presidents and kings, but with ordinary people of every age, what they said, what they thought, what they read, and how they worshipped.

Obviously, it is impossible to rediscover all of these past events and customs, to reconstruct the dying words of Ghengis Khan or Pontius Pilate. Even if it were possible, not everything would be of value to us. But through investigation of available sources certain events in the past can be discovered, reconstructed, and made known to us. This is called recorded history, and is, for our purposes, the only kind of history which we can intelligently discuss.

Recorded history, however, can never be simply a factual relation of what happened in the past. It is an attempt to reconstruct events, and this immediately enters the realm of interpretation, if only in the selection of the events to be reconstructed and the particular materials to be used for the reconstruction. But if it is impossible to avoid interpretation even in answering the simple questions, What? Who? and Where? the historian who wishes to place two or more facts or events in relation to each other is thrust into the very midst of the interpretive realm. He must face the question: Why *did* these things happen? and ultimately the greater question: Why *DO* things happen as they do? If he seeks to avoid this question, if, in fact, he does not boldly embrace it and grapple with it, he is not truly an historian, but an animated filing case for pieces of irrelevant information. His place is on a quiz program, and not in a classroom or on a public lecture platform. However, the historian need not feel that his inability to answer the Great Question with finality is a failure. In fact, anyone presumptuous enough to claim for his little answer the authority of the last word, merely exhibits unseemly pride and immaturity. It is in this realm of honest and sincere effort to answer the Great Question that history ultimately makes its most significant contribution to the liberal arts.

THE COMMITMENT OF THE CHRISTIAN HISTORIAN

From the earliest times widely-varying patterns have been discerned in the events of history, and these patterns have been understood as giving coherence and meaning to the stream of human life. Some have found special significance in the rise of great men at periods of crisis. Some have regarded the quest for the satisfaction of physical needs as determinative in history. Others have stressed politics. Some have seen in history the operation of biological laws, with mankind traveling a steady upward road to ultimate perfection. World history has frequently been rewritten for the purpose of elevating and glorifying a particular ideology or national tradition. In the midst of this variety, it would be strange indeed if the historian were not at least stimulated to interpretive thinking. He might pardonably exercise restraint in either committing himself wholly to any theory or in too quickly adding his own interpretation to the existing multiplicity, but eventually he must make his commitment. I use the word commitment advisedly, believing that complete objectivity in the examination and presentation of historical material is impossible.

If, as Oliver Carmichael suggests to the Carnegie Foundation for the Advancement of Teaching, "Commitment to certain basic assumptions is a necessary starting point in the quest for truth"[1]

---

[1]"Report of the President," in *Forty-seventh Annual Report of the Carnegie Foundation for the Advancement of Teaching* (1951-52), 18.

in any field, it is at least possible that the Christian commitment might afford to the liberal arts historian a point of departure in his effort to use his historical materials in answering the Great Question. It is of considerable significance that the presidential address delivered in 1948 before as representative a professional organization as the American Historical Association dealt with the subject, "The Christian Understanding of History."[2]

CHRISTIAN DOCTRINE AND THE LIBERAL ARTS TRADITION

It has been asserted that the modern liberal arts tradition is essentially the product of Greek concepts of man and the universe, and that historic Lutheran theology, "built on the doctrine of the corrupt nature of man and his complete dependence on the grace of God," is incompatible with the liberal traditions of free inquiry and independent judgment. According to this view, the only possibility of a Lutheran liberal arts would lie in the reinterpretation of Lutheran theology in closer affinity with the classical humanism of Melanchthon and Erasmus.

It is unfortunately true that certain types of Lutheran preaching have presented the world as a wholly evil place, from which the Christian should flee as from the plague. In such a context Christian education has been furthered primarily as a means of equipping the soul to stay as aloof as possible from this world until God snatches it mercifully out of temptation. The scriptural truth that every Christian is under an obligation of love to use all his strength and power to serve the Lord with joy and gladness in the particular calling into which he has been placed—as long as he lives—somehow is overlooked. Although more than ninety per cent of Lutheran college graduates enter fields of service outside of the church, support for our colleges is frequently solicited entirely in terms of the ten per cent which they send to the seminaries or into some so-called "full-time Christian service." The glorious Lutheran doctrine of Christian vocation, which is actually at the heart of our program of Christian higher education, needs a rediscovery.

The heritage of the Lutheran Reformation must not be sold out to usurpers who would brand God's created world as an evil thing

[2]Kenneth Scott Latourette, "The Christian Understanding of History," *American Historical Review*, LIV (January 1949), 259-276.

and assert that the Gospel is a limiting and restraining force upon the human mind and spirit. The essence of the great commandment which Jesus taught was to love the Lord with all the heart and soul and strength, and *mind*. And the second commandment certainly projected the Christian out into his social environment when it admonished him to love his neighbor as he loved himself.

The liberal arts tradition, with its emphasis upon the dignity and nobility of man, his freedom and independence of thought and inquiry, and his potential for growth, is certainly not foreign to the Christian gospel. All of these things, plus the close personal relation with a gracious Heavenly Father who has created him, belong by right to the Christian man. Man is the crown of God's creative activity, formed in God's own image with creative potential second only to that of the Deity. Nor is there anything to suggest that the physical world which God created as man's dwelling place was anything but wholly satisfactory. "God saw everything that he had made," says the book of Genesis, "and behold, it was very good."[3]

To be sure, this masterpiece was corrupted by sin, and a sorry blot was made upon both mankind and the lesser created order. But man still remained as God's creature, and the universe as His handiwork. And in order that this blot upon it might be completely and entirely removed, God set into motion His great redemptive purpose for the whole of the created order, a plan the final consummation of which has not been fully revealed to us, but which centers in the Incarnation of Jesus Christ.[4]

Through His perfect life and His death, resurrection, and ascension Jesus Christ has broken down the barriers which have separated man from fellowship with God, and has opened the way to a restored sonship with Him, the relationship which God originally intended man to enjoy. This sonship is appropriated by faith, which is produced in the heart of the individual by the Holy Spirit of God. From the time of this re-adoption, the Christian man is launched upon a new life which is as rich in potentialities as the grace of God itself. Through the years there have been many Christian saints who have fulfilled these potentialities to a remarkable degree, but it is safe to say that the broad limits of this growth have never been approached in the intellectual realm, or in the social or the spiritual.

[3]Genesis 1:31.
[4]Romans 8:20-22.

I do not believe that the Lutheran tradition has permitted the full development of the concept of sanctification as it relates to the mind of man. We have emphasized the moral and spiritual aspects of growth in Christ (though even here it is all too easy for Lutheran preachers to become so immersed in justification that they never reach the positive implications of Christ's resurrection), but have shied away from the intellectual implications of the "abundant life" which Christ came to give. Paul wrote to the Corinthians that "where the Spirit of the Lord is, there is liberty."[5] And Jesus Himself pronounced the watchword of liberal Christian education when He said to His disciples, "If ye continue in my word, then are ye my disciples indeed, and ye shall know the truth and the truth shall make you free."[6]

The redeemed man is free! He is no longer subject to the narrowing, frustrating, crippling power of sin, but as the Holy Spirit empowers him, he speaks new languages, he assails new problems, he is free to think, to inquire, to investigate just as far and wide as it is possible for the human mind and spirit to reach. If the Greek ideal was a man of dignity, here is a man of Christ's own dignity, redeemed and restored to sonship with the Creator Himself. If the Greek ideal was that of a free man, held in check only by ignorance, here is a man with power at hand to conquer all things through Christ. If the Greek ideal was curious and inquiring, the Christian man has spread before him all the wonders of the universe, which he simply *must* examine if he is to be an honest steward of every power which God has given and redeemed. Surely the redeemed man, for whose sake God set His great plan in motion, cannot be less honorable, less dignified, less potent than the pagan. It must rather be that somewhere along the line part of the richness of the freedom of the gospel has been covered over and hidden from view.

Is this freedom to be found in the heritage of the Lutheran church? Certainly there is some of it to be seen in the fearlessness with which Luther challenged the citadel of spiritual authority in his day. There is some of it in his straightforward pronouncements concerning the liberty of the Christian man. Even Luther was not able to exploit this treasure of the gospel to the full, nor indeed has any person before or since. But insofar as we are able to follow the advice of Luther and find in Christ our central point of author-

[5]II Corinthians 3:17.
[6]John 8:31-32.

ity, we are free men. Even the barren scholasticism of the seventeenth century, or the equally constricting pietistic influences which have sifted down even into the twentieth century must not rob us of this rich bequest.

THE CHRISTIAN VIEW OF HISTORY

The very key by which man is set free is an event in history. Actually, from the Christian standpoint, the whole of the story of the human race centers in the Incarnation, the focal point of God's plan to set men free—to redeem them—and to empower them for a full and complete life *on earth* as well as in heaven. This great redemptive plan, conceived in the mind of God in eternity, is being worked out in time. Human history is the record of how man is utilizing this freedom in the affairs of this world, and of how he is managing his affairs without it.

Does history have a place in the Christian liberal arts? It is only through the entry of God into the historical process that we have Christianity at all, and thus the power which can free man's mind and his spirit for worship, for inquiry and investigation, and for service.

It is obviously very difficult to trace clearly the hand of God in every part of the historical process. A civilization may rise and fall, and while God may have decreed it, it is surely not possible to document such a decree by ordinary standards of evidence. Nor, incidentally, is it possible to document some other explanation of such an historical cataclysm so conclusively that no one may raise any further question concerning its finality. The historian must certainly follow some acceptable standards of evidence when he is gathering data on visible events, but if he refuses to recognize that there are other forces at work in the historical process which he cannot measure, he can scarcely do justice to history. Most historians, even though their training stresses the sanctity of these standards of evidence, eventually make their leap of faith and identify themselves with some standard of values as well.

The Christian historian's leap of faith brings him to the belief that God has created the universe, that He is actively concerned in human affairs, and that ultimately His own purposes will be achieved. The historian may seek as well as he can to discover

how these purposes are being worked out, but he can never conclusively demonstrate the Christian thesis. It has seemed to most
modern historians that the leap of faith required of the Christian
is somewhat more prodigious than that required by adherence to
some other interpretations of history. This feeling probably reflects
to some extent the continuing influence of the so-called "scientific
school" of historians in the nineteenth century, which conceived
their task to be that of amassing a sufficient amount of data so
that no interpretation should be necessary at all. Even if this school
betrayed its own ideal of "objectivity" in its treatment of such subjects as the rise of nationalism, its contribution of a careful methodology has done the profession of the historian a very commendable service. The reticence of many modern historians to give recognition to a Christian interpretation of history may also find a partial explanation in the abuses to which pious and zealous, but
often unlearned and even anti-intellectual Christians, have subjected
this view. The Eight Books of Miracles, written by Gregory of
Tours in the sixth century, are no more naive in their interpretation
of the role of God in history than some radio and pulpit expositions
of the Book of Daniel. Irresponsible excursions of this kind, which
mix prophecy and speculation with a minimum of historical fact,
and then blithely ascribe to their conclusions the authority of God
Himself make it very difficult for a reputable historian such as
Kenneth S. Latourette even to broach the "Christian Understanding
of History" before a group of professional historians.

Just as serious a danger lurks in the likelihood that professionally
trained historians who are teaching in Christian colleges may have
picked up the same suspicion of this Christian view of history as
the historians who are not in schools which specifically profess to
be Christian in outlook. Caught between personal identification with
a church school on the one hand, and the pressures of earlier professional training on the other, it is quite possible for the Christian
teacher of history to say, "Of course I believe in the Christian
faith," and then proceed to write and interpret history as if he
were an economic determinist. How much of this is actually done
in our Christian colleges would be difficult to say, but the dearth
of published material emerging from our colleges interpreting
either the liberal arts or individual disciplines in relation to the
Christian world view suggests that the problem is being conveni-
ently dodged.

It remains therefore to call attention to a few respects in which this Christian perspective can be summoned down from its lofty pinnacle of irrelevance and actually used to give clearer insights into the stream of historical events. I am not suggesting that the Christian historian boldly step forward with simple explanations of God's activity in the historical process. There is something essentially conceited about the notion that God's activities and purposes are so plain that anyone can discern them if only his heart is right. One of the first principles which ought to govern the Christian who views the historical process is that of humility. In the face of the overwhelming complexities of the physical universe and the intricacies of human actions and reactions, both individually and in groups, he who claims to discern clearly and assuredly the reasons for the rise and fall of nations and civilizations treads on dangerous ground. The Christian believes that God is above all, and that His purposes are being worked out in history, but he recognizes his own limitations in finding them out. With Augustine, he believes that the course of nations is governed by God, but that God's motives and methods are frequently hidden from our eyes.

The knowledge that man is not always able to discover or to comprehend exactly how God is working in history need not either frustrate or discourage. Armed with the conviction that out of the diversity of world events will ultimately emerge the triumph of God's redemptive plan, the Christian historian may turn with real spirit to learn as much as he can about the world in which he lives. Just as the Christian *man* must learn to understand the framework and the forces operating in the society in which he lives, in order that he may be a critical and constructive citizen, so also, with even greater thoroughness, must the Christian historian seek to understand the many different causative elements in human history. Without selling his soul to any other god, he may find value in the insights provided by almost any other view of history. One need not become an economic determinist to recognize the importance of economics in national programs of expansion. One need not subscribe to the dictum that "history is past politics" in order to appreciate the political aspects of history. He need not become a social determinist in order to profit from the observation of population trends. Even the conclusions arrived at by purveyors of these other viewpoints may be accepted in some cases, but always as partial or limited. Above and beyond all lesser insights into the nature of society and of historical causation stands his faith in the ultimate subjection of all things to the will of God.

LESSONS AND IMPERATIVES FOR THE CHRISTIAN HISTORIAN

Among the richest benefits to be secured from a careful study of history within the Christian framework is a deeper understanding and appreciation of the doctrine of man. History provides rich resources for observation both on the nature of man and of his behavior in the redeemed and the unredeemed state. It would be a strange Christian indeed who could study history and regard man as anything less than the crowning creation of God, into whom God Himself breathed the breath of life, and with it a dignity far above that of the lower created order. Granted that sin has besmirched this creation, God has actually entered the course of human history to restore man to sonship with Himself. Thus, whether a human being is personally a Christian or not, he is regarded by God as valuable enough to warrant the incarnation and crucifixion of His own Son. No Christian historian could therefore speak approvingly of German gas-chambers or Russian blood-purges; nor could he shrug off the tragedy of millions of famine victims in India; nor could he speak approvingly of a policy based on the assumption that Asiatic lives are cheaper than others. Nor indeed could a Christian historian countenance any policy, domestic or foreign, which minimizes the dignity of any human person. Quite on the contrary, a history which proceeds on this basic Christian presupposition will have a motivation for inquiry into entire realms of human experience which otherwise might be regarded as invalid. There is much yet to be learned about the nature and character of man, which the Christian historian, with his deeper sensitivity, could well explore.

There is a distinct danger that in embracing a Christian understanding of history, one may err at either one of two extremes. The Christian view of history may become such an other-worldly article of faith that it has nothing whatever to do with the course of this world's events. In this case, it actually becomes irrelevant. Or the Christian view of history may become so explicit that God is seen in every presidential election, and a moral is drawn from every economic depression. In this case, it is naive. If, however, it were not possible to point up certain developments in human history which indicate the reality of God's interest in human affairs and of the operation of His redemptive plan in the world as we know it, it would hardly be possible to speak of Christianity as an historical religion. The redemptive plan of God is cosmic in its scope, but it has dipped into human history directly, and we should therefore be able to observe some evidences of its work. Professor Latourette believes that evidence is accumulating as the centuries pass, that "measured by his effect on history, Jesus is the most influential life ever lived on this planet."[7] This influence, he asserts, is mounting, and at the present time "Christianity is more widely spread geographically than it or any other religion has ever been." The debt which western culture owes to Christianity, he claims, must be recognized in art, literature, thought, education, morals, institutions, and even science. The influence of the redeeming power of Christianity appears further in its promotion of literacy, in drives for peace and for world unity, in the battle against human slavery, and in behalf of improved medical care and the liberation of women. Moreover, says Professor Latourette, the transforming love of God is to be seen not only in collective movements, but also in individuals. "We know," he states, "that under Christian influence changes in character take place," and when such persons as Paul, Luther, Augustine, Loyola, and Wesley are changed, the influence of God's redeeming love has been channeled out to millions of others through them.[8] In this manner, through the Christian church, the Christian historian believes that the redeeming power of God has been and is actively in touch with human society. While the evidences he points out can never prove this faith, it can suggest strong probabilities for its validity. More cannot be said of empirical evidence submitted in support of any hypothesis.

From all that has been said thus far, it should be very clear that nothing in the Christian historian's approach to his subject matter releases him from his professional obligation to thorough workmanship, based upon academically recognized standards and utilizing all available sources. If anything, the Christian should have even a higher motivation for integrity and excellence than a non-Christian. Professor E. Harris Harbison in his Hazen Foundation study of the *Religious Perspectives of College Teaching in History* concludes that the Christian, who is also an historian, will be known less for his well-rounded philosophy of history than for his attitude toward history, "the quality of his concern about it, the sense of reverence

---

[7]Latourette, 272.
[8]*Ibid.*, 274.

and responsibility with which he approaches his subject."[9] It must surely be recognized that many a non-Christian has also approached historical study with reverence, and that a great many non-Christian historians have exhibited a far greater degree of integrity in dealing with their materials than many so-called Christians. But surely the nature of the Christian gospel fosters certain general attitudes toward people, toward events, and toward historical material which could have a profound and positive effect upon the writing of history.

Mention has already been made of the quality of humility. Generally speaking, this trait has not been overworked among professional historians. If one examines the book reviews in the *American Historical Review* or the *Journal of Modern History*, he cannot fail to note more than occasional evidences of a kind of Olympus Complex on the part of some reviewers. Unseemly though it be, historians, too, can be dogmatists, and very impatient with the "bias" of some other school of interpretation. Being a Christian is unfortunately not a guarantee of humility, but certainly, the realization that the destiny of the universe is in the hand of God ought to promote a spirit of humility in the making or the judging of any human conclusions concerning nations or movements or men.

Closely connected with humility is the spirit of fairness in judgment. This quality, so desirable in the historian, is not solely the property of the Christian either. Every historian brings to his work of investigation and writing his own personality and point of view. He cannot help being human. But one suspects that some of the great interpretive changes which are expressed by "revisionist" historians are not entirely the result of sensational discoveries of wholly new bodies of evidence which have entirely changed the understanding of a given set of events. Historians, too, are often influenced by the contemporary climate of thought and opinion, and unless they are men of great integrity, they may easily become "advocates" for one cause or another. The admonition to fairness given in Luther's explanation of the Eighth Commandment might well become a watchword for the historian as he shapes and molds his judgments. Putting the "most charitable construction" on the personalities and events of the past does not require an unwillingness to face the truth, but it does lessen the chances of besmirch-

---

[9] E. Harris Harbison, "History," *Religious Perspectives in College Teaching*, ed. by Hoxie N. Fairchild (New York: The Ronald Press, 1952), p. 94.

ing a reputation on the basis of insufficient evidence. There is a certain kind of temporary notoriety which gathers about the person of the muckracker, the "debunking historian," or the plain, garden variety of gossip. Righteousness and justice must be served, but nothing is lost, even in historical writing, if charity and mercy are allowed to temper the historian's judgments.

Professor Harbison speaks of realism as an attitude characteristic of both the historian and the Christian. He properly observes that it has been the "humanists" among historians who have been shocked by the excesses of human bestiality in history, rather than the traditional Christians. The unreality of the concept of man's perfectibility through his own knowledge and initiative has become glaringly real in the past half century. Greater gains have been achieved in science and technology than in any other comparable period in world history, but this gain has been paralleled by a virtually uninterrupted orgy of international violence. Philosophies of progress have been buried in the rubble of European and Asiatic cities, and modern historians are more than likely to be pessimists. Arnold Toynbee, not quite ready to admit positively that the doom of the West is at hand, solemnly reminds us that "we have no warrant for assuming that it is not."[10] Certainly the Christian shares the distress with which any serious minded man views the state of the world today, and because of his concept of man as the special object of God's creative impulse and of God's loving concern, he probably feels it even more keenly. At the same time he is not overwhelmed by the monstrosities of man because he believes in the positive reality of sin and evil. It was to redeem man from just this kind of fate that God entered into human history and identified Himself with man. The Incarnation was not undertaken for inconsequential reasons. No manifestation of evil in the world is entirely unexpected.

At the same time as the Christian views history in the clear light of realism, he brings with him also a sense of buoyant optimism, born of the forward thrust of his faith. The cosmic plan of God originated before time began, and will be consummated beyond the end of time. Exactly how this consummation is to be reached is not clear, but that God shall at last subject all things under His feet the Christian does not doubt.[11] This eschatological hope not

[10]Arnold Toynbee, *War and Civilization* (New York: Oxford University Press, 1950), 10.
[11]I Corinthians 15:28.

only enables the Christian to look beyond the conflicts of this world, but it also kindles within him a burning sense of urgency and responsibility to the world about him. The Christian historian need never hide his face from the stark realities of human history, but he has a faith which will never permit him to become a pessimist or a prophet of despair.

I realize that in these pages I have barely scratched the surface of the tremendous problem of the full relationship of our Christian faith to history. It is of course the same practical problem which every Christian in the world faces, or ought to face, but nowhere is the urgency of such a quest more imperative than in the institutions of higher learning of our church. One of my students remarked recently, "If the college itself doesn't know what it is trying to do, how shall the students discover it?"

There is certainly room for more integration, and for the enrichment of course offerings in the field of history. For example, at one college full-year surveys of Western Civilization and American history are offered on the freshman and sophomore levels. These are followed by an elective sequence of four standard advanced courses in European history, concluding with Twentieth Century Europe. In advanced American history, courses in the Colonial Period, the Civil War, and Recent American are offered, as well as Diplomatic, Constitutional, and Cultural history and a course on the American Frontier. Additional courses in British history, Latin American, Russian history, and the Ancient World complete the history offerings. It would also be of real value if a special course for history majors might be included, which would attempt to tie together and integrate the entire area, preparatory to a system of comprehensive examinations for graduation.

Devices such as this may be of some value in defining more clearly the meaning and function of the liberal arts within our colleges and in helping to relate the various disciplines, history in particular, to our overall educational objectives. The burden of responsibility, however, for the achievement of any success at all in the venture of Christian liberal arts education rests fundamentally with each individual professor.

CHAPTER 12

Music

by Bartlett R. Butler

The admission of music to academic status is a relatively recent development in the history of American higher education. At the time it was viewed with suspicion as the invasion by an applied art of the circle of the genuine liberal arts. Subsequently music has played an increasingly prominent role in student activity on our college campuses and has certainly found a comfortable acceptance among administrators, alumni, and the general public. So pronounced has been the emphasis on music in certain quarters that some educators have seen in it a detriment to the academic life of their institutions. Disproportionate emphasis on musical activity, inadequate educational philosophies concerning music, and actual injury to academic standards have brought a rather strong reaction against it, one which is compounded of justifiable criticism and serious misconceptions as to the place of music in a college curriculum. Although it can be argued that the usual musical activities—singing, playing, practicing, rehearsing, concertizing, method-learning, touring—are defensible from a number of viewpoints, the only really cogent reply to this criticism lies in the demonstration that the study of music is a *liberal* discipline and hence is thoroughly compatible with the goals of the liberal arts.

The discussion which follows assumes that there are at least two commonly-held attitudes toward music which, while respectable and reasonable in the face of present circumstances, have contributed to some of the inadequate philosophies of music in college. One attitude is that of the professional musician and teacher who knows his art thoroughly, loves it profoundly, and gives it his very being, for music is indeed his life. To study it ceaselessly, to perform well, to create well—even while living as fully as possible—this is all that is required. Such an attitude, whether consciously or unconsciously, tends to assert that music is self-contained and autonomous, bearing no relation to the rest of life except in the most elemental aspects.

The other attitude is often found among non-musician educators who firmly believe in the mission of the liberal arts in our colleges and yet are not sufficiently acquainted with the special problems of music to be able to see its potentialities as a liberating study. This attitude is willing enough to accept the value of music as a source of rich pleasure and deep satisfaction but is frankly skeptical of its worth as an object of serious study intimately related to the manifold facets of human life and thought. Neither this view nor that of the *l'art pour l'art* musician is able to provide a positive or constructive basis for the *liberal* study of music.

THE LIBERAL NATURE OF MUSICAL STUDY

The attempt to illustrate the liberal nature of musical study may well begin with a few references to the past, without, however, making any appeal to the authority of tradition. It is well-known that music was included in the *quadrivium* of the Seven Liberal Arts of the ancients and the Middle Ages. This, of course, is really quite misleading, for as such it was primarily a speculative study based on Pythagorean number-symbolism and was held to be a kind of bridge between the sensory world and metaphysical reality, a view perpetuated throughout most of the Middle Ages by the authority of men like Boethius and Cassiodorus. Living, sounding music had little or no connection with it. Nevertheless, Plato and Aristotle advocated the study of music for the development of character in accordance with the doctrine of musical *ethos,* though their conception of music was far closer to poetry than to music as we know it. Then, too, there was a common belief among the ancients in the healing effect of music, as in the story of Saul and David. The significance of all this lies in the fact that men recognized the intensely *human* (or divine) quality of the musical phenomenon. Similarly the medieval church was keenly alive to the power of music and watched it with a jealous eye. St. Augustine, who reveals in his *Confessions* how deeply music was able to move him, was careful to note his fear of its sensuous effects.

In contrast to ancient and medieval theory Luther's attitudes toward music were those of an enthusiastic, practicing music lover, and his testimony is so eloquent that it ought not be ignored. As Luther was unwilling to despise the wholesome joys of life and the beauties of nature but loved them as part of God's redeemed creation, he especially loved music as "a beautiful, gracious gift

of God,"[1] and declared ". . . I do not hesitate to say that, after
theology, there is no art to be placed beside music. Music and
theology alone are capable of giving peace and happiness to trou-
bled souls."[2] The first and last parts of *Frau Musica*, his song in
praise of music, run as follows:

> Of all the joys upon this earth
> None has for me a greater worth
> Than this I have from my singing,
> To set my voice sweetly ringing.
> There cannot be an evil mood
> Where good fellows sing,
> There is no envy, hate nor ire,
> Gone is through her all sorrow dire;
> Greed, care, and lonely heaviness:
> No more do they the heart oppress.
>
> .   .   .   .   .
>
> But thanks be first to God, our Lord,
> Who created her (by His Word),
> For His own beloved songstress,
> And for men of music, a mistress.
> For our dear Lord she sings her song,
> In praise of Him the whole day long;
> To Him I give my melody
> And thanks in all eternity.[3]

Luther insisted that music be taught in the schools, for it was
a "disciplinarian and moral trainer." Furthermore, no teacher
or minister was adequately prepared unless he had studied music.[4]

It has been said that none of the above should constitute authority for placing music among the liberal arts, for this should depend
entirely on the nature of music itself as subject matter and on the
nature and methodology of its study. On the other hand, it seems
possible at this point to formulate a proposition to be considered in
the major portion of this chapter: *That music has a place among
the liberal arts by virtue of its profound relationship to human life,
its prominent place in redeemed creation—a gift of God,—its nature as an increasingly significant achievement of man throughout
recorded history (especially in Christian cultures), and the fact*

[1]Paul Nettl, *Luther and Music*, (Philadelphia: Muhlenburg Press, 1948), p. 12.
[2]From a letter of Luther to the Swiss composer, Ludwig Senfl, quoted in Nettl, p. 24.
[3]*Ibid.*
[4]*Ibid.*, p. 34.

that its study is compatible with the aims and objectives of the liberal arts.

The following synopsis, though incomplete and merely suggestive, illustrates some of the possible divisions of music as subject matter:

I. The physical phenomenon: Music as patterns of air molecule disturbance, the province of acoustics.

II. The musical experience: The actualization of music in the human mind and its many ramifications.

NB. Although this experience is essentially a unity, its complexity is such that it will be approached indirectly through some of its components and its functions in the psychic life.

A. Elemental components and functions of the musical experience.
   1. The superficial appeal to the consciousness of musical pitch, tone color, and rhythm.
   2. The appeal to the awareness of logic, coherence, and beauty.
   3. The evocation of "affective experience," or qualitative states of emotional awareness.[5]
   4. The evocation of affective experience *by association.*

B. Derived, or resultant, functions of the musical experience.
   1. An illuminator: a source of self-knowledge.
   2. A humanizer: a source of knowledge about man and the continuity of human experience.
   3. A monument or document of human activity.
   4. An aid in Christian love.
   5. An aid to awareness of the Communion of Saints.
   6. An aid in worship.

III. The study of music.[6]

---

[5]The psychology and physiology of the emotional experience are still highly problematical areas of investigation, and the results thus far are hardly conclusive. However, psychologists generally prefer the term "affective experience" to the more common and often abused term "emotion" to denote qualitative states of emotional awareness, i.e., felt-emotion rather than expressed emotion.

Leonard Meyer, in *Emotion and Meaning in Music* (Chicago: University of Chicago Press, 1956), has discussed the various aspects of this problem in an illuminating and provocative presentation, which, however, raises many more questions than it answers.

[6]The danger in separating the study of an object, here a work of art, from the experiencing of it is much more critical in the fine arts than in other disciplines where the data have some concrete relationships to the environment of the student. In the case of the natural and social sciences he is constantly "experiencing" some aspects of these disciplines in everyday life. Also, speaking and listening involve some contact with the structure of knowledge and its communication, the provinces of logic, grammar, and rhetoric. (Mathematics, it is true, is indifferent, for it may well demonstrate in symbolic form what we may never experience directly, e.g., the curvature of space.) Even in theology experience is not

    A. Theoretical study
        1. Systematic
           a. Analytical theory: the components of style and form.
           b. Aesthetics of music.
           c. Psychology of music.
        2. Historical study: as a humanistic discipline.
           a. The history of music: a branch of cultural history utilizing other fields.
           b. The study of historical forms, styles and individual works to provide documents illuminating other areas.
        3. Music and culture: systematic and historical treatment of a variety of related fields. A few examples are:
           a. Music and art.
           b. Music and religion.
               1) Totems.
               2) Hymnody.
               3) Liturgy and worship.
           c. Music and drama.
           d. Music and literature.
           e. Music and the dance.
           f. Music and politics.
           g. Music and social customs.
           h. Music and medicine.
           i. Music and ethics.

    B. Practical study of music
        1. Creative work: composing and arranging.
        2. Performance.
           a. Solo.
           b. Ensemble.
           c. Conducting.
         3. "Appreciation."

THE RELATION OF MUSIC TO LIFE

It will clarify what has been called the relation of music to life if we consider the musical experience of a work where it first occurs—in the mind of the composer during the process of creation. Whatever his motives—the urge to create beauty, the hope of recog-

---

basic to theology *as theology;* "experience," of course, may transform it into religious knowledge or faith. But in the arts the divorce of the study of a work from an inner experience of it is contrary to the very nature of art, for a work of art is first and last an *Experience,* one which occurs in the mind of the artist and then, in varying degrees and in varying ways, in the minds of beholders and upon which the essential existence of the work depends.

nition, the desire for economic reward, the compulsion of a purely musical idea (or so he may think of it), or the conscious expression of an image of life—he is constantly reacting to his ripening creation and judging it according to the inner purpose he wishes to fulfill.

In this respect music is closer to the other arts than we are accustomed to think, for although the abstract sound of music seems far removed from the natural objects and shapes of painting, for example, actually a composition and a painting come into being in strikingly similar ways. Perhaps this is "to hold a penny candle to the sun," but for the sake of illustration let us imagine a painting of an apple. We say the artist has painted an apple, but a moment's reflection reminds us that the matter is not quite so simple. He has not really painted an apple at all. Rather, aware of an image of the apple in his mind, using his own senses, judgments, insights, emotions, etc., he then puts patches of paint on canvas in such a way as to satisfy him pictorially, interpretively, emotionally. We in turn respond to those patches of color more or less as he did (probably less), and have evoked in us the image of the apple and perhaps some of the other reactions the artist consciously or unconsciously intended.

With music, of course, the subject matter—if music has any—is almost never concrete. Because of its nature music can hardly use *external* experience as tonal material. But in the creative process a *relevant* state of mind is involved; it may be a generalized purpose, an emotional tone or mood, an image of experience, what Beethoven referred to as "ein Bild," or some other. This state, whatever its nature, like the image of the apple for the painter, profoundly conditions the choice of notes and their organization to achieve the desired result. Obviously the composer does not put feeling and experience *into* music, just as the painter does not really put an apple on canvas. In both cases, each artist strives to give the beholder, *in the first place himself,* the desired impression, whatever it may be. If he succeeds in satisfying himself that his expressive purpose has been achieved, then, given a certain common fund of human experience shared by composer and listener, it is possible that they may both share a similar response to the art work. If this occurs, artistic "expression" or "communication" has taken place by evocation.

It is not difficult to see how literature and the visual arts affect human feelings, but music, if one excepts technical details of form and style, seems to bypass the intellect and appeal directly to the senses and feelings. Hence, an analysis of the musical experience itself is extremely difficult. The approach which follows is too simple and schematic to have more than a suggestive and analogical validity.[7]

This approach is based on the hypothesis that affective experience, whatever its source in the mind, is perceived as a complex of nervous tension, release, and what we may call "ideal motion," i.e., an inner sense of motion or motor impulse, which may be fast, slow, smooth, jerky, calm, agitated. Within the framework of Western music certain aspects of melody and harmony have acquired the ability to produce such sensations of relative tension and release. Musicians speak of active and rest tones, "tension" points in a phrase, the "pull" of dissonance for resolution, the drama of climax. These are not merely metaphorical; they are keenly felt. On the other hand, the relation between tempo, rhythm, and style and motion and emotion is easily suggested by the many conventional performance markings, e.g., lively, grave, sweetly, at ease, joyfully, agitated. It is claimed that the patterns of tension, release and motion are responsible for the perception of felt-emotion in the listener. (Emotion as a result of association is another problem.) Clearly then, with such a wealth of variables, music has a nearly infinite number of shades of feeling which it can evoke.

To go a step further, it is also claimed that by careful introspection—given the common fund of experience mentioned above—one may infer the quality of the image of experience which *might* have produced an affective experience similar to that evoked by the piece of music. What is suggested here is that the musical experience may actually offer a kind of knowledge. It remains to be added that the listener's reaction does not *necessarily* depend on a conscious intent by the composer. Stravinsky, for example, has claimed that his music has no (external) meaning. If we take "meaning" to refer to evoked affective response by the process just described, he is very wrong. Stravinsky's music *may* tell us a good deal about Stravinsky.

This raises another question. Is there any way of knowing whether the composer has been successful in his attempt to mirror his psychic states in his music? Very likely there is not. However, this ability and the possession of psychic states which are truly significant are probably the critical differences between a great

---

[7]The writer gratefully acknowledges here his debt to his teacher, Dr. Donald N. Ferguson, whose rich thought is barely suggested in this summary.

composer and a merely competent one. Beethoven's sketchbooks are fascinating examples of the struggle to bring an idea to realization. We can see how he molded a theme from a bare, primitive state, changing here, adding there until. he "discovered" the final form with that quality of inevitability we call perfection. With vocal music, of course, it is much easier to judge the composer's success since the text gives us clues. Opera is full of compelling examples as, for instance, the late operas of Mozart in which he embodies in tones the subtlest differences in emotion and musical character-delineation.

Returning to the practical implications of affective response to music, it is clear that our theory, even if correct, has limitations, for the results are often disappointing. This stems from additional factors which must be considered. First, for music to be highly evocative the listener must be sufficiently familiar with music so that the barriers of style and convention will be minimal. It is analogous to genuine familiarity with a language, which involves not only a sure knowledge of grammar and vocabulary but sensitivity to connotation as well. This is acquired only by vivid experience and in the case of music by constant exposure to significant works. Second, it is necessary to realize that at a given stage of an individual's development his personal experience may not be rich enough for him to respond sympathetically to the emotional quality of works such as the *Mass in B Minor* or Beethoven's late quartets. And thus it is most important for us to keep in mind that the road to musical sensitivity is long and that college courses can only be a modest beginning.

Now it must be admitted that there is music—good music—which does not seem to have any characteristic affective tone beyond a very general mood. We may indeed say it is beautiful, but there seems to be no more definite quality we may ascribe to it. This may be evidence for the school of thought which maintains that music has no reference beyond itself and that its beauty resides entirely within itself. There is no authoritative reply to this, but it may be said, first of all, that the music referred to was often composed by those eighteenth-century composers who studiously avoided emotional tensions and sought the most delicate balance of elements in their music. Actually, however, such an equilibrium may well have a decidedly emotional as well as aesthetic appeal, as it certainly must have had for the aristocratic patrons of that age.

Secondly, it must be obvious that the source of musical beauty is surely not a formal scheme *per se*. Rather, form owes its power to the fact that it corresponds to fundamental human needs. For instance, *A B A* is a formal design embodying the principle of contrast and recurrence based on the need for variety, unity and coherence. Indeed, it could probably be demonstrated to an extent that all musical structures owe their effectiveness to such correspondences. Further, it is evident that one may analyze every structural detail of a work and yet not *experience* it: e.g., the satisfying resolution of dramatic tension in the recapitulation of a sonata, or the sweeping, cumulative effect of rhythmic composition in a painting. In the last analysis, then, the nature of beauty, however we may attempt to explain it, is related to the nature of man.

The discussion thus far has attempted to clarify the relationship of music to life, and it has suggested that this relationship implies more than the satisfaction of the desire for beauty. It has been inferred that great music springs from the depths of man's personality, involving his affective and psychic states—which may relate to intuition and insight—and that it can invoke similar responses in others. If this is anywhere near the truth, music should provide us with a peculiarly illuminating document which has been largely neglected up to this time. Its external features are of interest: its forms, its styles, its functions. But more important is what it reveals about the inner world of man, his view of life and not only his own but that of his milieu. And this suggests still another kind of documentary insight which music may provide, for it usually mirrors the changing tastes of the times as to what is "beautiful." This is particularly illuminating when there is a conflict between the ideals of a composer and the prevailing one of his age, e.g., in the case of Palestrina, Bach, late Mozart, late Beethoven, and our contemporary experimentalists of a few years ago.

It is this kind of study of music, music as a phenomenon dependent on and revelatory of human activity, that justifies its inclusion in the liberal arts, and therefore I would like to illustrate this in some detail.

Of the two main categories of music study—the practical and the theoretical—the practical will be touched on later. It is in the theoretical sphere that music is most valuable as a liberal art. Here it is viewed as knowable material related to many other areas of knowledge as well as being a documentary source of knowledge. The intellectual skills involved are fully as demanding as those of many another discipline. Furthermore the broadly human basis of music suggests that its study may also provide excellent opportunities for integration.

The systematic branches, e.g., musical aesthetics and psychology, but especially analytical theory, involve observation, experiment, speculation and statistical operations. Their methodologies resemble to some extent the sciences. It should be understood, however, that by analysis we do not mean the deduction of "useful" knowledge or normative criteria, but rather the attempt to describe systematically what there *is* in a piece of music.

Within the theoretical studies the historical approach is probably the most rewarding for the student of the liberal arts, provided it is treated as a humanistic discipline. Thus, the history of music becomes not only the study of musical developments and personalities, but a legitimate branch of human cultural history. Musical phenomena are not regarded as independent entities obeying their own genetic laws, but as integral parts of living cultures past and present. Therefore, virtually all the forces active in a given culture must be considered in order to understand its music most perceptively. A problem in music history will thus require help from contemporary literature, art, and sources of social customs; from political, economic, and social history; from philosophy, religion, and science, in order to achieve an integrated working-image of the milieu.

At the risk of illustrating the obvious I would now like to present some examples of this approach. The first concerns music in 14th century France.

During the 13th century the music of chivalry had been reduced to a trickle. Art music concerned itself with politics, satire, earthy humor, etc., the traits we associate with the middle class. But in the 14th century there appeared a recrudescence of the chivalric spirit in the musical style. The source of inspiration proved to be the anachronistic ideals of a declining nobility, whose purpose in society became increasingly restricted and whose status grew more and more insecure. With the loss of Acre in 1291 the recovery of the Holy Land remained a recurrent, but romantic dream. Threatened by the rising middle class, which aided the monarchy in its struggle for centralization, the nobility also found its wealth threatened by inflation. And ironically the glorious symbol of chivalry, the mounted knight, was forced to retreat before the efficient, versatile infantryman and the longbow.

Unwilling to face reality or, perhaps, even half-conscious of their inevitable fate, the nobility made a frantic attempt to revive the chivalric idea of the high middle ages and to breathe new life into the spirit and forms of the past. Reacting against the practical culture of the townsmen they pursued the courtly life, the refinement of manners, and the ideal of love-service; they surrounded themselves with splendor, objects of art, and music, all in the hope, it would seem, of convincing the world—and themselves—of their own vitality and the right to their position in the social order.

However romantic, unrealistic and artificial this revival of chivalry may seem, it did provide a powerful stimulus to artistic creation. Professional musicians were more eagerly called into the service of nobles and princes. But even more important than this patronage was the characteristic psychological world into which the musician entered, for this conditioned the needs he had to satisfy and determined the emotional tone he would reflect. The ideal may have been anachronistic; the material stylized and rigid, but the atmosphere vibrated with intense feeling. It was filled with a longing after past perfection, with dreams of heroism, honor, and ennobled love, so urgently cherished in order to soften the violent inconsistencies of the times.

The embodiment of this ideal in music was the work of Guillaume de Machaut, a poet and composer who was probably known to Chaucer. He chose to express the courtly ideal by reviving the old forms of the trouvères and adding to them the new art of free polyphony. The strange melancholy of this music, at first so foreign to the modern ear, becomes meaningful when understood in the light of the human situation from which it came. Then it is possible to respond to it and experience what one scholar meant when he said: "Machaut's art . . . has become an art of enchantment, which leads the hearer out of reality and seeks to entice him into a world of dreams."

The second problem is that of the development of a vital religious style in the Lowlands in the 15th century after a long period of relative quiescence. There is probably no one answer, but we can suggest a number of clues. The end of the Great Schism was greeted by a wave of optimism and confidence in the Church. The popes took a special interest in new art music. Duke Philip the Good may have stimulated the composition of sacred music to testify to the lofty spiritual ideals of the House of Burgundy on which his hopes for kingship seemed to depend. But perhaps more decisive than any one of these reasons was the intensification of religious feeling in the North as the aftermath of war, plague, and injustice. There was a definite rise in the sensibility of people to the Passion of Christ, a feeling which attached itself more and more to the Mass as the drama of Calvary.

It is also important to remember how large a part the northern lands played in Burgundian culture. The prevailing atmosphere there seems to have been imbued with the piety of an industrious and conservative middle class. The Brethren of the Common Life and the *devotio moderna* came into being about this time. As early as the 1390's Claus Sluter had brought his powerful emotionalism to the court of Philip the Bold.

As the religious element grew stronger in art and literature, the role of music took on special importance. Huizinga has described how the medieval mind strained to express the ineffable in words and images and how inadequate the results were felt to be.[8] The only solution was to rise above imagery, which seemed impossible. Not tied to images, music was perhaps the answer. In any case a religious music developed with all the intensity of the ancient chant enriched by polyphony, and it seems to have arisen in response to the desperate need of men seeking to experience the Divine.

These two examples show in a superficial way how some of the problems may be handled. Virtually any question of music history lends itself to an expansion into cultural history. One has only to think how inexplicable much German music would be without Reformation theology; or the development of opera without the Italian academies, preceded by Neoplatonism and its roots in Renaissance needs; or the shifts in style of 17th-century opera if its centers had not moved from the Florentine and Roman courts to Venice with her shrewd oligarchy and pleasure-loving populace; or Lutheran music without the Thirty Years' War; or Bach without the conflict of Orthodoxy, Pietism, and Rationalism; or Beethoven without the Enlightenment, Sturm and Drang, and the Revolution; or Wagner without socialism, Schopenhauer, and Nietzsche.

Whereas this type of study used the many facets of culture to clarify musical problems, a second approach uses music and the facts about music as documents of value to other fields. A sensitive understanding of music would certainly be an aid to the study of history or literature, for example, in helping recreate by means of

---

[8] J. Huizinga, *The Waning of the Middle Ages* (London: Arnold, 1941), p. 201 ff.

emotional tone the atmosphere of past ages. Many examples come to mind.

The vigorous, rhythmic German chorale—not the staid versions in our hymnals—suggests the strength and vitality of 16th century Lutheranism, as well as indicating how it was so effective in spreading the Reformation. To sense the austere mysticism of the Roman counter-Reformation one need only listen to Palestrina; on the other hand the Venetian style reveals the more sensuous appeal of Jesuit psychology. The music of the mature Bach is an extraordinary legacy of a man who was the product of the conflicts of his time but who transcended them by faith and produced some of the most sublime utterances of the human spirit in an age too frivolous to listen or comprehend. (Bach's son, Karl Philipp Emanuel, considered his father's music turgid and old-fashioned.)

In the music of Mozart we hear the polished elegance, the rational balance and clarity desired by the aristocracy. But in the late works, his passion, rebelliousness, and also his ideals of brotherhood—he was a Freemason, though a Catholic—are suggested. *The Marriage of Figaro* (1786) on the surface is 18th-century comedy, but in its overt sympathy for the servile classes it is a harbinger of revolution.

As a revelation of a human personality perhaps no music is so compelling as that of Beethoven. Titanic and demonic at one moment, warm and tender the next, above all it is deeply human. Beethoven's longing for brotherhood had no connection with Christian theology; rather it was a manifestation of his own profound need and of the hopes born out of the Revolution. But can the Christian ignore its intense sincerity and refuse to listen?

Nineteenth-century Italian nationalism found its spokesman in Verdi and his music. "Viva Verdi" was heard and seen all over Italy expressing love for the composer, but also concealing an acrostic of the words meaning "Long live Victor Emanuel, King of Italy."

And an example from the first part of the twentieth century might be Alban Berg's *Wozzeck*, a stark and pathetic document of despair bred in post-war chaos.

This should suggest some of the ways in which the theoretical study of music has a liberal basis and can be made to confront the student with a broad range of intellectual materials and can challenge him to integrate them.

On the other hand, it is less easy to demonstrate the value of the practical study of music in the liberal arts college. The usual attitude of our students is that musical performance consists of merely sounding the right notes at the right time and in the right way with pleasant results. The process is essentially mechanical and physiological. Very little intellect participates. This notion is seriously mistaken, for the truly sensitive performer must be both a perceptive human being and an expert knower of his art and its manifold relations. Musical performance requires as complete an assimilation of a work as possible; it must be genuinely *experienced*. It is thus a gateway to a truly profound responsiveness to musical values.

In the case of creative composition intellectual activity is much greater. There is a constant weighing of values, comparing results with intent, seeking methods of realizing an inner purpose, finding the logical course of a phrase, or the right structural plan. And in addition to its value as creative experience composition imparts first hand knowledge of the inner workings of musical materials as the student struggles with them himself.

To study music for the sake of appreciating and enjoying it might appear to be peripheral to the objectives of the liberal arts except as music enriches human experience; however, it can be justified in at least two other ways. First, the methods applied, in addition to guided listening, resemble the more rigorous ones of history and analysis and thus are intellectual. Second, an understanding of music and a knowing response to it are essential if the documentary value of music is to be apprehended fully, i.e., the musical document must be experienced before it can come alive in the mind. Most of us are aware, however, that perceptive listening rarely occurs automatically; it must be cultivated. Thus every student of the liberal arts should at least make an effort to appreciate the musical part of the cultural heritage.

Are there additional ways in which music may help realize the ideal of a liberal education? I am thinking of the contributions it makes along with the other arts to the life of the mind, apart from the theoretical ones already discussed. These contributions would thus be results of the artistic, or specifically, the musical experience.

Is there a relevant connection between the musical experience and reason? If the term "rational" is extended to include all the cognitive means available to man, including intuition, and if it is true that the workings of the mind are contingent on many factors not directly controllable, then I believe there is. In the latter clause

I am of course referring to the effects of unconscious attitudes, prejudices, and predispositions which may interfere with the free operation of the intellect. One can make no verified claims for music here, but perhaps the artistic experience can deepen and stimulate insight and imagination, can heighten sensitivity and awareness, can promote an intuitive grasp of truths about man and life in spite of these predispositions. It is a process which occurs on a sub-verbal level. Although thought, in the usual sense, is confined to the articulation of words, symbols, and images, we have all experienced the inadequacy of words, for example, to express certain states of consciousness. Until somehow articulated, intuition remains in the realm of feeling, and this is the realm which music may invade most directly and to which it may impart non-verbal "knowledge."

The experience of beauty itself conveys a form of knowledge about man, for it is a significant discovery to be reminded that men *do* respond to the beautiful. An intense experience of beauty also offers what we might call a "generalized" illumination, which helps clarify value perception and removes the dross accumulated by the pressures of everyday life. It may thus aid the intellect in seeing and pursuing the higher values: the true, the honest, the just, the pure, the lovely and that which is of good report (Phil. 4:8).

Finally, by its nature music may produce greater awareness and insight in some human situations. It may enliven known truths. A perennial weakness in man is his willingness to assent sincerely to some noble principle while failing to grasp inwardly its implications. (The person who loves humanity but cannot stand people is an example.) Music, as well as literature and drama, may awaken a man to his own contradictions and provide motive power to eliminate them.

THE SPECIAL RELEVANCE OF MUSIC TO CHRISTIAN FAITH AND LIFE

If what has been presented has some basis in fact, music has a rightful place in the Christian Liberal Arts College. But we have yet to see if there are ways in which its role has special relevance to the Christian faith.

It goes without saying that music, as a divine gift, should be dedicated to God, studied and practiced to His greater glory, and in the Christian college community it can, of course, be used to enrich worship and the devotional life in great measure. But in addition to the more usual functions of music in worship the Christian college might well make greater use of it to inculcate a living awareness of the meaning of the Communion of Saints, the Holy Catholic Church of the past, present and future. Our students should experience the pure theology and noble grandeur of the historic liturgies. They should learn to know and love the lofty religious musical utterances of the ages and realize that they sprang from a vital experience of faith. Eventually it should help counteract the self-centered legalism prevalent in the Church today.

Although there is the everpresent danger of aestheticism, against which we must constantly be on guard, we should not overlook the real power of beauty as an *intimation* of the transcendent.[9] In a strictly psychological sense—and we may assume that the Holy Spirit does not reject psychological assistance—music has a peculiar ability to suggest spiritual realities. Ordinary affective responses are dependent on stimuli from actual or expected experience. Music, however, may blend emotion-evoking elements without reference to external experience. Hence the composer of genius and spiritual insight may achieve a feeling-tone in his music which goes beyond the specific emotions of life and points to the reality and presence of God and His love. If music is truly God's gift, we should not fear or disparage its extraordinary power, but use it to build one another up and to offer our praise and thanks to Him.

Ultimately, the relevance of music to the Christian faith—and not just music, but the fine arts and all knowledge as well—depends on its relation to Christian love, for without love they are all as nothing. Therefore in what follows our concern is less with music alone than with love and the arts in general.

The love of Christ which redeems a man, also drives him out into the world to be a witness to that love. Paul commended the Scriptures to Timothy to perfect and equip him for good works (2 Tim. 3:15-17); similarly the Christian under the guidance of the Word seeks to understand God's world and human culture in order better to love and serve in the name of Christ. He studies in order to become an effective Christian in the use of his powers; he searches out the implications of faith and develops his critical

---

[9] It should be noted, of course, that differences in temperament and sinsitivity will modify the extent to which music can be effective here and elsewhere.

judgment, for good intentions are not good enough. He learns of the heights and the depths of the human predicament, and his complacency is transformed into compassion.

Although freed by redemption from the bondage of sin the Christian also knows that he is limited by his human nature, environment, prejudices, narrow vision, and experience. If he were somehow completely perfected, then the *insights* of art would be virtually superfluous; he would already possess the full comprehension of life; gratitude and love would have free course to do the will of God. But he is aware that by possessing intellectually the clear and simple answer to the meaning of life, he may become insensitive to the truly complex nature of life as it must be lived. He may be cut off from a grasp of the suffering, the needs, and the values of other men. Conscious of his weaknesses he will seek constant renewal of love through intensified awareness of the precious meaning of grace as offered through Word and Sacrament.

The Means of Grace are indeed sufficient in themselves, but it is possible that we may grow unresponsive to the familiar experiences and resist the power of the Spirit. Here then is a task of the ever-changing arts: to awaken through the senses a sensitivity to the meaning and power of the gospel, to create through the impact of articulated idea and beauty the awareness of the significance of life under God, to reveal ways in which Christ's love can speak through us. They can help us experience the glorious truth that freedom from the bondage of sin also means the freedom to love and serve Him who redeemed us.

Finally, it is most important to remember that these arts may be either "sacred" or "secular"; they may affirm faith or even deny and attack it. But if they are genuine products of human genius, they have something to tell us about life and man even though it be repugnant to us. A music of anxiety and chaos will not serve to strengthen a weak faith, but it can help a man comprehend the kind of world he must confront with the gospel. So little art and music today is "Christian" in its reference. Are we to shun it out of fear of soiling our spirits? Rather, a sympathetic and searching approach to the arts at all times is essential. To be alive to all serious forms of expression, to discover the kernel of meaning and value that is there, and to interpret this in the light of faith is, I believe, one of the principal responsibilities of a community of Christian scholars, for our Lord hallows all of life to those who love Him and seek to do His will.

CHAPTER 13

Visual Arts

by Arnold W. Flaten

It is dangerous for the Christian community to assume an attitude of indifference toward the total cultural pattern of its age. The consequence of such withdrawal is to lessen the effectiveness of its message. The obvious strategy of the church must be to bring the entire social and cultural structure under the influence of the gospel. "The Kingdom of God is like leaven."

To participate in this task the Christian artist must be a step in advance of his age. To follow from afar is not only humiliating but indicates spiritual lethargy, a lack of courage and initiative. The Christian artist must constantly assert the perennial freshness of the gospel message and the unlimited resources for adapting and varying its presentation for the changing cultural pattern. Inevitably this means the tension of a paradox.

The church is both conservative and dynamic. It is the custodian of eternal truth but at the same time it contains the dynamic creative element which challenges any tendency of a cultural synthesis to become static. The Christian artist must be aware of this tension. There must be a recognition of the continuity of cultural expression along with an openness and alertness to cultural change.

An ever-present danger to the Christian community is its inclination to identify itself with some past cultural style and assert for it a universal, timeless position. Any religious group guilty of this is doomed to a hardening of the arteries and eventual death. It becomes a kind of culture museum, an attraction for tourists. It leans heavily on archaeology.

CULTURAL SUICIDE

Recently on a trip through the eastern part of the United States I came across a strange version of such borrowings from the past. The Lutheran churches were invariably Gothic in style while the other Protestant churches were just as consistently Colonial (except for the tinted glass in their windows). One university had two campus layouts, one Gothic, and the other Colonial. The validity of either of these forms or any forms from the past to express our age can be successfully challenged.

The eclectic way in which elements from past styles are handled, the false structural members, the mingling of post and lintel with plastered arches, the lack of a consistent modular control—all indicate a haphazard handling. There is an unsureness, an arbitrariness about such structures which mark them as anachronisms, buildings out of step with their age. The Christian community which expresses itself in this manner steps out of the present and abdicates its right to cultural leadership. It has committed cultural suicide.

Eclecticism is a cultural disease. Some of its symptoms are a deficiency of imagination, a feeling of inferiority, an insensitivity to cultural change, the lack of spiritual vitality to integrate the borrowings from other cultures, an unsureness due to confusion of direction. Probably its most obvious characteristic is a putting together of unrelated bits which have little coherence.

However, to some eclectic expressions there must be conceded a kind of superficial unity. They are something like the nursery rhyme:

> There was a crooked man
> And he went a crooked mile
> He found a crooked sixpence
> Upon a crooked stile . . .

Such is the artificial unity achieved by a distribution of Gothic arches and tracery or by pasting on Greek facades and endless peristyles. It constitutes warmed-over architectural hash.

Eclecticism is accumulation without inner organic order. It is a product of intellectual aridity and emotional sterility. It repeats ad nauseam, and its attempts at original statement are forced and exotic. As in paintings by amateurs, there are occasional pleasant passages of color and pattern; but the overall impression easily distinguishes it from the work of a master painter who controls the total area of the canvas. The repudiation of historical imitativeness is a rejection of the eclectic's approach to the visual arts.

Complete imitation of the forms of the past is impossible. The language of art easily recognizes this by the use of the prefix "neo": neo-Gothic, neo-classic, neo-Byzantine, neo-Romanesque, etc. From the seventeenth century on, neo-classic and neo-Gothic vie for position in western culture. To explain the reappearance of these radically different cultural syntheses in the same epoch one must understand the prevailing romanticism of the arts of the period. Archaeologists a la Winckelmann and company teamed up with the romanticists and behold, all things became "neo."

For this period culture is not something organic. It is a product which can be turned out factory-style by paying proper attention to the measurements of archaeological discoveries. This is not an over-simplification. Check the course offerings of the architectural schools in the western world up until the last twenty-five years and the evidence is convincing.

The lack of any strong spiritually creative power is revealed in the arts. The intellectualism of the so-called age of enlightenment plus an unstable romanticism without theological anchorage took cultural refuge in the "neo's."

Each world culture develops its own aesthetic. To attempt a pantheon of all cultures and worship at all the altars is a futile syncretistic exercise. Each culture has its own style, its own aesthetic. While one might wonder at the Russian philosopher Berdyaev's statement that the physiognomy, the body of a person, is the form of his soul, still one can affirm that the visual arts and other cultural expressions do reveal the soul of a society. This cultural synthesis, this collective soul never occurs but once in the historical sequence. It dies with the extinction of the spiritual force which held the group together. All that is left is a graveyard.

HETEROGENEOUS MESS

The spiritual impoverishment, the lack of an indigenous cultural style of our time, indicates itself by the extensive diggings into this graveyard. Artists go through their Egyptian period, then Greek, then Romanesque, then Renaissance, and end with an enthusiastic embracing of Negro primitivism. Now, obviously, they did not worship the gods of these various cultures. By a superficial skimming they thought they could get some of the cream from all of them. It is said of Picasso that he has picked the bones of art history clean. This is not a disparagement of the intelligence and technical skill of this artist. But regarding the direction of western culture today, the Christian artist should challenge his position of leadership.

Secular artists today seem inclined to dip down the stream and forget the fountainhead of all cultural enrichment. The result is a conglomeration of aesthetic patterns, a heterogeneous mess. It is a pile-up of evidence showing the decline of any spiritually unifying force and the temporary ascendency of fragmentation and disintegration.

Cultural importation from the past is an admission of cultural inferiority. Prostration before the forms and styles of the past is a form of idolatry and has little to commend it Christianly speaking. Attempts to bring back the old may conform to the cyclic pattern of nature with its recurring seasons, but they are completely foreign to the dynamic eschatological view of a Christian philosophy of history.

There is no universally valid cultural form. It cannot be found even in Plato's heaven. All are defective and have either accepted the principle of transition or have become static and dead. Culture as well as man is on the way to a perfection which can never be achieved with any finality here. A slavish obeisance to past cultural styles is contrary to the Christian view. As Christians we look forward to greater things spiritually and culturally. Otherwise what do we mean by Christian hope?

The prevailing aesthetic credo of western culture from the fifteenth century on, besides its emphasis upon archaeology, has been the attempt to achieve the total illusionistic effect of nature; in other words to produce something very similar to color photography. It coincides with a gradual shift in the arts from a position of service to the church to an autonomous "art for art's sake" position. This divorce of the arts from the church is similar to that of the natural sciences. Each circumscribes its area and more or less isolates itself from the total cultural order. The artist preoccupies himself with the development of an aesthetic formula which was ill-fitted for the expression of spiritual ideas. His approach followed closely that of the natural scientist's interest in nature for its own sake. The first to dissect cadavers for the study of bone and muscle structure were Florentine artists. The pastorale, the depiction of landscape for aesthetic enjoyment, was a Venetian achievement.

This renaissance aesthetic was cradled in the church. The Psalmist's words, "The heavens declare the glory of God and the firmament shows his handiwork," plus the Apostle Paul's statement in the Letter to the Romans that "since the creation of the world God's invisible nature, namely, his eternal power and deity, has been clearly perceived in the things that have been made"—these encourage a reverence for the natural world on the part of those who believe the scriptures.

NATURE AS HOLY SYMBOL

Gothic Christianity saw nature as a vast and holy symbol. Often strange and ludicrously forced symbolic meanings were attributed to it. In their eagerness to relate the God of Scriptures to the God of nature they saw no harm in such pious imaginings. The book of nature was to be read with the same reverence as the Bible.

The Renaissance artists moved away from the Gothic position of nature as a divine symbol to nature as an absorbing study for its own sake. Spiritually it reflects a shift from an otherworldly view of life to an emphasis on this world. The organized church adopted an unsympathetic attitude toward change and incurred the ill-will of both artist and scientist; trying to block scientific research—Galileo, Copernicus, and others—and setting up restrictions for artists working in the church—Council of Trent in the Roman church, iconoclasm and Puritanical repudiation of the visual arts in the north of Europe. The result was a split between culture and the church, probably more disastrous for the arts than the sciences. The arts are fertilized by religion and grow sickly apart from it.

No longer in the service of the church, the artist turned his attention to the study of nature's visual phenomena and to the development of skills in presentation—light and shade, anatomy, linear and aerial perspective, special control, color theory, compositional patterns, psychological and emotional quality, an exciting field of aesthetic research, a game of infinite variety and charm.

The church watched this game with mingled emotions, sometimes of disgust but more often of indifference. It seemed all but oblivious to the fact that one of its most powerful means of proclaiming the gospel was frittering away its talents on worldly sideshows. It gave little encouragement to the artist in terms of commissions, and those given restricted the artist's freedom of expression by demanding conventional outmoded formulas. In this atmosphere not only the message of the church suffered in its total cultural impact, but the artist lacking theological direction went around and round the aesthetic circle, issuing one manifesto after another and producing a bewildering mixture of forms.

The present cultural schizophrenia is at least partially the fault of the Christian community. It alone has the qualifications for spiritual leadership to bring unity out of the present chaos of dispute and contending forms. Its first problem is a revision of the Renaissance aesthetic. It must find its contemporary expression in the area somewhere between the nature-illusionism of the Renaissance and the extreme cult of non-objectivity.

The non-objectivist's position must be rejected for the following reasons. Firstly, it is deficient as a medium of communication. It is a purist form and demands only a limited aesthetic response. Secondly, it puts too high a value on man's creative efforts. The artist in post-Renaissance times has been much overrated. With Leonardo and Michelangelo as examples, the idea of the artist-superman has been fostered. The church with its knowledge of man cannot accept such an interpretation.

Man's creative powers are decidedly limited. He does not create *ex nihilo*. The artist like all other mortals must humbly take his place within the total cultural pattern. His main function is to communicate visual meanings within the framework of spiritual values. The non-objectivist's position is too esoteric for the Christian artist.

While rejecting this position the church must never commit itself to the antiquated Renaissance formula. The Christian artist will always stand in wonder and admiration before nature, but he will recognize limitations of her use as a copybook. For holding a mirror up to nature the *National Geographic* and similar periodicals are quite adequate.

Basically the visual artist's field is the same as that of the poet. The poet's highest expressions are prophetic and his main tool is the metaphor. A new metaphor is a culture's greatest invention. It denotes a fresh insight; it puts things together in new relationships; it discovers a more vigorous means of communication.

The raw material of the artist is the visual world. Nothing fashioned by man can go beyond the limits of what the eye can actually see. The artist can rearrange, select, and distort but he cannot speak of "that which eye hath not seen." He should accept this limitation and become thoroughly conversant with nature's forms. For out of these he must shape the symbols, the visual metaphors of his age.

The church's stake in the visual arts is in their power to symbolize and communicate. The church should have a clear conception of what constitutes a good symbol. Important as the aesthetic and design qualities of a symbol may be, they are of secondary value. A symbol must signify, communicate. The artist is tempted to glamorize the symbol aesthetically or move into pictorialism and illusionism. The most effective symbols tend toward the abstract. This means the elimination of all extraneous elements, a selective simplification, and a geometric undergirding. This is a language quite different from that of Renaissance pictorialism and delight in things for their own sake.

A symbol is not an illustration. The dictionary is full of illustrations serving the purpose of definition. A symbol is a transitional form. It serves as a bridge of contemplation. A good symbol moves us rapidly from one plane of thought to another. It constitutes the main language of spiritual communication—often an area where all efforts at direct communication become inadequate. Only by analogy, metaphor, symbol can one break through to the world of spiritual meanings. A symbol can be a point of departure for a projection into the spiritual world. Such symbolic art becomes a "calculated trap for meditation." The church should apply itself to making better traps. It sorely needs them.

The church's main symbol in a community is its cult building. A full discussion of church architecture and its symbolism lies beyond the scope of this writing. It is surely true, however, that "too many churches cloister faith and vision behind outworn facades in a dim religious light of mystification and fantasy." This type of symbolism the church today should reject. Light, warmth, color, openness, strength, integrity in the use of materials and structural members, a sense of welcome and cheer should pervade the building both in the exterior and interior. For it is the place where the Christian celebrates the Resurrection of his Lord on the first day of the week.

The Christian artist today understands that the real value carried over from the cultural past are insights into the spiritual framework which produced vital organic expression in the arts. The great creative cultural epochs accepted the principle of transition. The artist's work appeared new and strange to his generation. But he approached his problem with assurance—assurance based on a religious position which he took for granted. There was a certain inevitability about the new form which won for it general acceptance over the old. The Gothic architect was as convinced of the ultimate rightness of his innovations as the Greek Phidias was of his. These men were not casting about in the past to find a ready-made style. They were not eclectic-minded. They were men of mature faith.

A near synonym of faith is courage. The sureness of one's convictions makes courage a natural trait of character. The timidity of the church in architecture and the arts is a poor witness. The church today should learn a lesson from its great past. It should admire and emulate those qualities of faith and courage which produced fresh, creative forms. It should avoid a timid, imitative approach. The cultural history of the past is for inspiration, not imitation.

In rejecting the imitative attitude, the Christian artist is not an anarchist. Like Jesus his purpose is not to destroy but to fulfill. The cultural style or pattern of Christianity will never be complete on this earth. It is always in the state of becoming; and the Christian artist shares with fellow pilgrims the mission of moving it toward its heavenly consummation. Like Abraham of old he goes out on faith, not knowing the land ahead, but sure that God will lead him. This is not haphazard meandering, but faith. Faith compounded of courage, initiative, and imagination always bears quality fruit with a total cultural impact.

If the church in the second half of the twentieth century can shake off the grave-clothes of historical imitativeness, discriminate wisely regarding the Renaissance aesthetic, and encourage an imaginative art of symbolic communication, the year 2000 A.D. should see it in its rightful cultural position—the leader and shaper of the cultural forms "in which we live and move and have our being."

CHAPTER 14

Natural Sciences

by Carl L. Bailey

It is our purpose to discuss how the teaching of the natural sciences may be matched with what we conceive to be the character of the Christian Liberal Arts college. Two general questions are involved. We must consider the relationship of the sciences both to the educational philosophy and to the religious setting of the college. The problem of the relationship to religion is perhaps more urgent, and more vexing, in the case of the natural sciences than in the case of any of the other disciplines.

THE NATURAL SCIENCES AND THE AIMS OF LIBERAL EDUCATION

We have defined the aims of liberal education as follows: to form the judgment and to teach fundamental truths concerning God, man, and nature. One might amplify this brief definition in the following terms: the liberal studies are those which help the student to know something of the nature of God, the world, and himself; to develop his powers of rational discrimination and critical thought; to know the methods of research in the broadest sense of that word; to develop his aesthetic sense and to awaken his mind to intellectual delight and curiosity. There are great implications in these brief statements; the applications of the liberal studies to one's religious life, to his life as a member of society, and to his personal life, can all be developed from these premises.

No academic discipline lends itself better to the aims of liberal education than the natural sciences. In them one finds knowledge which can help to form a world-view; boundless opportunity for exercising the critical powers; the need and the methods for discovering that which is unknown; beauty and depth which ought to inspire the desire to learn.

While it is certain that virtually every science teacher would agree with these aims of liberal education, it is by no means certain that every science teacher strives to attain them; and herein lies a shortcoming of our colleges. But justice to the teacher demands that we recognize his problems. Generally he has two tasks: he should strive to reach his liberal objectives, but he cannot afford to neglect the need for teaching factual knowledge and techniques. Those of his students who will enter the professional world must not, he feels, be placed at a disadvantage. The unfortunate result of this dilemma is that the liberal objectives are often neglected or lost sight of altogether; the teacher often feels that the time is not adequate even for limited technical instruction. The problem is difficult.

The curriculum and teaching methods in the natural sciences need to be based on the two classes of objectives mentioned above— technical competence, and the liberal aims. Each science department has its own responsibility to fulfill the first requirement as far as possible, within the limitations imposed by the total course requirements of the college. However, overemphasis on technical competence, at the expense of the liberal objectives, is to be avoided. This is not an easy attitude to maintain. Our science departments are sorely tried to achieve a fair level of technical competence in their severely limited time. But the scientist must remember that life is more than technical training, and that he is false to the principles of liberal education if he insists on producing narrow specialists, no matter how well trained they may be.

The instruction must continually stress the element of critical thought. No student will be stimulated or helped to think who is fed only doses of facts. Sometimes liberal education is conceived as being merely exposure to a wide variety of facts. But this conception falls short. Facts are important and cannot be neglected, but no education is liberal which is not passionately concerned with the awakening of the mind. The student must be faced with critical alternatives and paradoxes to be resolved through his own efforts. In courses in mathematics or physics he may be presented with beautifully organized logical structures of proof, but these will not teach him to be any more logical himself, unless he is made to exercise his own powers of analysis.

The instructor should continually try to impart to his students some sense of the beauty and grandeur of the natural order, to arouse their curiosity, and their sense of wonder. He should try to awaken them to the delight of learning and the excitement of discovery. He should make conscious and consistent effort to make them see the power of the scientific method of investigation but also (lest any man should boast) the limitations of its power.

One of the most important aims of liberal education is to teach research ability. This does not mean that the student must necessarily learn the technical methods of laboratory investigation. Rather, he must learn how to find out from books and other sources what he does not know, acquire the habit of seeking and using source materials, and learn to apply what he knows in new situations. One of the sharpest criticisms of vocational education is that it teaches people how to perform specific tasks, but may leave them helpless before novel problems or leave them without ability to supplement their knowledge from new sources. To the extent that we neglect this aspect of liberal education, we are justly subject to the same criticism. I remember a college graduate—her field happened to be home economics, but I do not mean to single out that field for attack—who, while teaching school, was asked to give a short course on the Farm Security Administration to a group of adults. Her somewhat amazing reply was that she could not, because she had never been taught anything about that in college. Evidently she had never learned that books exist and that one may read.

To a certain extent one may approach the liberal aims in science through courses specifically designed for that purpose. One may offer seminars in which philosophical problems or points of view on which science might bear are discussed, and he may offer courses in the philosophy of science. But none of these devices will replace the teacher who is awake to the aims of liberal study and passionately devoted to them. There is no academic field whatsoever in which some of the elements of liberal education cannot be deliberately and forcefully taught.

THE NATURAL SCIENCES AND RELIGIOUS FAITH

Since the Renaissance the war between faith and unbelief has increasingly been fought on the scientific front. It almost seems superfluous to recall the well-known truth that factual scientific discoveries, and the scientific habit of thought, have led to attacks upon the citadel of religion from many sides.

The kind of warfare between science and religion which most people know is that kind associated with specific scientific discoveries or ideas which have conflicted with specific doctrines of the Christian Church. Battles have raged over the structure of the solar system, over the age of the earth, over the theory of organic evolution, and so on. These disagreements have been taken very seriously, although they are actually superficial in character. It is more important to consider a more crucial kind of conflict between science and religion.

What are the essential elements of the Christian view of the universe? That God—the Creator and Governor of the universe—exists; that man is God's creature, an animal but more than an animal, the possessor of a will partly free and partly bound, an heir of sin but also an heir of eternal life; that the universe is guided by purpose, the purpose of God, Who is actively concerned with the course of human and cosmic history.

The real conflict between science and religion is concerned with these fundamental bases of Christian belief. If science can show that these axioms are false, then any other points of argument, such as the age of the earth, are quite trivial. Conversely, if science cannot demonstrate that these axioms are false, then science cannot destroy religion, although it may lead in some ways to an adjustment—a refinement, perhaps—of our conceptions. Consequently we must ask whether the findings of science have any bearing on these fundamental axioms.

Nineteenth-century physics was dominated by an essentially materialistic point of view. The laws of classical mechanics, which appeared at that time to govern all matter, had been discovered, and it was widely believed that all phenomena would ultimately prove to be explicable in terms of these laws. Consequently it was believed that an understanding of ultimate reality was within the grasp of the scientist through his laws and methods.

These materialistic conclusions from natural science had a profound effect on nineteenth-century philosophical and religious thought. If it is true that the whole universe is governed by mechanical laws, then it is obvious that divine purpose need not be considered to play any part in the history of the universe. Furthermore it is obvious that the whole history of the universe is determined. The laws of classical physics enable one to predict the future course of any material body which is governed by these laws, provided only that he knows the present condition of the body. Thus, a sufficiently clever scientist could describe the totality of future events if he knew everything about present conditions.

Of course there is no such person. But the present conditions do in fact exist, whether we know them or not. Therefore, according to this view, the future history of the universe is in fact determined by the fixed laws of mechanics.

Now a man is a material body. Therefore he also, if this view is correct, is governed solely by mechanical laws. Thus man becomes a machine, without mind or will, and with a future as hopelessly determinate—and as meaningless—as that of the most humble particle of dust. Only the material is real. All values, such as love, truth, honor, and the like, are illusions.

During the nineteenth century the materialist-determinist point of view became the dominant philosophy of the Western world. For many people, this philosophy settled the question of religion once and for all, for it denies, clearly and explicitly, all of the fundamental axioms of the Christian view. If God exists, He has no significance; the most He could have ever done was to set the cosmic machine in motion, and He has nothing to do with present or future. The notion of divine purpose in the universe is completely overthrown. Man could not be said to possess the sort of dignity affirmed by the Christian tradition.

The strict deterministic point of view is not considered intellectually respectable nowadays. Therefore, one might think that to attack it is, so to speak, to knock down a straw man. But this philosophy remains the guiding view of many. It appeals to the uneducated or unreflective because of its apparent common sense and its implications are often not fully realized. In our colleges, even, it is not impossible to find science courses taught in such a way that this point of view is favored, not so much deliberately as unconsciously. Furthermore, as has often been remarked, common sense today generally follows the science of a generation ago, and modern man has become conditioned to the philosophy of an earlier time.

The materialistic philosophy of the nineteenth century was to a considerable extent based upon the findings of classical physics. So when we see, as we do today, that this philosophy is no longer so respected, we are not surprised to learn that physics is again partly responsible. Events in the history of physics, which began just before the turn of the century and are still continuing, have caused a spectacular change in the world-view of that science, with a corresponding effect on the philosophy of materialism.

We have learned that the materialistic point of view of classical physics was childishly naive. Suppose we say, for the sake of argument, that there exists such a thing as ultimate reality; then scientists now clearly see that we can never understand ultimate reality through the powers of science. The best we can ever do, in any scientific investigation, is to construct for ourselves a "model" or "analogue" of reality. We may say that our model resembles the "real thing" more or less closely, but we shall *never* be able to say that we "know" all the features of the "real thing." Today we know that we may pursue the truth, but we also know that the pursuit is endless.

An excellent historical example of how this change in point of view has occurred is furnished by the work on atomic structure. A century ago, the physicist was content most of the time to think of an atom as a hard sphere, because for the most part the then-known behavior of atoms could be explained by that hypothesis. Later observations led to the conclusion that an atom "really" consisted of a miniature solar system with a central nucleus and some circulating electrons. Still later observations have forced us to adopt a still more complicated model, in which the old "electron orbits" have been discarded in favor of a scheme of "energy levels" and "probability densities" which cannot be briefly described. Today no physicist would dare to claim that he knows the real structure of an atom. Even less can he claim that he knows the real nature of the nucleus and electrons themselves; these bodies appear to have enormously complicated structures. Truly one must say that the more closely we study the atom and its parts, the more we realize that we do not understand them.

We must thus recognize that we have no hope of reaching the end of our investigations. Behind the appearance of any material body—behind the appearance of any natural force—behind the appearance of any natural law—there must lie some unobserved substratum.

Other recent developments in physics have also forced us to the same conclusion from a different direction. We now realize that scientific investigation cannot be separated from the problem of epistemology—the problem of *how we know*. It is not possible to separate the observer and his instruments from the thing observed, so that our picture of the world is in part the product of our means of perception. This again amounts to the admission that we cannot actually apprehend reality, but only appearances. The hard pieces of matter have disappeared from modern physics. Sometimes what we used to think was matter seems instead to be a projection of the mind of the observer. So the foundation of the philosophy of materialism has been undercut.

Now our scientific investigations are limited to the order of space and time, and our knowledge of that order must always be regarded as incomplete. But we must admit even more. We have no guarantee that there are not orders of reality which cannot be exhaustively analyzed in terms of space and time. It is affirmed by many that the existence of beings inhabiting a higher order of reality, and capable of acting upon us despite our inability to act upon them, has the most profound consequences for thought and life. Of any non-temporal, non-spatial categories of existence, our scientific investigations can tell us nothing. Some would say that as long as we cannot investigate scientifically any such order of reality, the question of its existence is meaningless. But such an attitude is childishly arrogant.

Modern physics, then, teaches us that science can say nothing about ultimates. The physical arguments which formerly appeared to prove that religion was false have themselves been shown to be wanting, and modern physics can take no less favorable an attitude towards religion than the attitude of neutrality.

The old-fashioned scientific determinism is also open to attack from many other directions. In the first place one recognizes that the mechanical argument, namely, that the course of the world is fully determined by the known laws of physics, is really only a *presupposition*, the product of a swollen pride. Only by assuming that our spatial-temporal categories comprehend all existence can we make this argument have meaning. But it is just this very assumption that we have no right to make. If we say, for instance, that it is "impossible" for a dead man to come to life or for a virgin to give birth, we are then arguing that our sphere of existence cannot be invaded, or at least that the laws we know are all the laws there can be. The intellectual arrogance of such a point of view need hardly be mentioned.

Living organisms also pose an exceedingly difficult question for the believer in materialism. Living beings surely resemble machines in many ways, and the laws of physics and chemistry can account for many aspects of their behavior. But if a living being is *nothing but* a mechanism, it is a very subtle one indeed; for every such being has the ability to reproduce itself and furthermore the ability to repair damage to itself. It is an interesting question whether it would be theoretically possible to design a mechanical device which would have these properties. It is likely that such a machine, if it could have no help except for supplies of raw materials and energy, would have to contain infinitely many parts. One therefore suspects very strongly that living organisms, while mechanistic with respect to many of their functions, cannot be regarded as *nothing but* mechanisms.

The so-called mind-brain problem has been argued for centuries, and today we still have little or no progress to report, in spite of modern research techniques. What is the nature of thought? What are ideas, and where do they come from? Do men really make decisions, and if so, how? Surely thoughts and ideas reside in the brain; but are thoughts and ideas *nothing but* the result of the physical-chemical functioning of brain tissue, or is there some more subtle, non-material factor?

Surely materialism cannot answer these questions. For, if our brains are nothing but mechanisms, we must (1) deny all freedom of will, and (2) suspect the validity of all reasoning.

The reason for the first conclusion is obvious. The "decisions" of a purely mechanistic brain would be determined by its conditioning, so that a man could no more perform an act of will than an adding machine could willfully change its answer to a sum.

The second implication is somewhat more subtle. If the functioning of the brain is determined by its conditioning, then the conclusions of a philosopher are not reached by what one would usually call "reasoning" at all, but rather through inevitable mechanical processes. Another philosopher might reach quite different conclusions by equally inevitable processes. There would be no possible way of adjudicating the disagreement. In a word—if the mind of man is fictitious, then the philosophy which proclaims it so must also be fictitious, for it was produced by minds.

No one can claim that man's will is entirely free. But every man feels within himself the elements of will, and few of us are willing to concede that this feeling is an illusion. True enough, this intuitive opinion is not subject to scientific measurement, but I suspect that it is valid all the same.

There is at least one possible approach to this question which might prove fruitful. To explain this approach, I need to discuss some physics. One of the most fascinating and baffling chapters in the history of physics is the one concerned with the nature of light. At the time of Newton, two opposed points of view had about equal support—the "corpuscular" theory which held that a beam of light consists of a stream of small invisible particles something like pellets, and the "wave" theory according to which light consists of a wave motion in an all-pervasive medium called luminiferous ether. Gradually experimental evidence piled up; by the middle of the nineteenth century it was obvious that light could not possibly be corpuscular but was certainly wave-like. Then suddenly some quite new evidences appeared; these new experiments could not be understood at all in terms of the wave theory, but only in terms of corpuscles. A baffling contradiction existed—indisputable evidence which says that light cannot be corpuscles but must be waves, and equally indisputable evidence which says precisely the opposite. Physicists were forced, as an oft-quoted remark has it, to "use the wave theory on Monday, Wednesday, and Friday, and the corpuscular theory on Tuesday, Thursday, and Saturday."

The modern point of view does not really resolve this puzzle, but essentially consists of the admission that the "real" nature of light is a mystery that we shall most likely never solve; it is another example of the modern point of view that we cannot fully apprehend reality. We say that the "real" nature of light is somehow a synthesis of its wave properties and its corpuscular properties; under certain circumstances, light *appears to us* in the form of a wave, and under other circumstances it *appears to us* in the form of a corpuscle. It is not correct to ask which of these appearances represents the "real" nature of light, for each of them is only a partial revealing.

We might approach the mind-brain problem in the same way. We see the mechanical aspects of the brain by means of external observations; under quite different circumstances, namely the introspective processes, we see the non-mechanical aspects. The "real thing" may be somehow a synthesis of these apparently contradictory aspects, and *appears to us* in one way or the other, but not in both ways at once.

MUTUAL MISUNDERSTANDINGS IN THE RELATIONS BETWEEN RELIGION AND THE NATURAL SCIENCES

One might get the impression, from what has been said, that the findings of science are never to be considered as having any bearing on religious questions. That impression would be wrong. Scientific findings cannot, in the most general terms, be used to criticize the validity of the religious point of view, but they often are relevant to opinions or doctrines held by religious people. We all know that there is a long history of disputes of this kind. While these disputes are essentially trivial, there is a sense in which they are important, for many a person has been lost to faith because he could not accept what the Church told him about the age of the earth, or the virgin birth, or the structure of the solar system, or the miracles of Jesus.

Clearly it would be impossible in a paper of this kind to discuss all these disputes in detail. Some general remarks, however, can be made as to the attitudes of both the disputing parties, for both have made errors.

The defenders of the faith have often been at fault. A glaring example, and one which ought to teach us something, was the persecution of Galileo for saying that the earth was a planet revolving about the sun, rather than the opposite, as the church contended. That controversy only made the church look ridiculous in the eyes of informed people, and helped to undermine its authority. The ecclesiastical authorities could not see (1) that their attitude was not really Biblical, or (2) that the scientific truth had no essential bearing on the Christian faith. The tragedy of the affair lay in the fact that the dispute was entirely unnecessary.

In more recent times we have seen similar affairs, like the controversy over the age of the earth. About all one can say is that we must be wary of reading the Bible as though it were a textbook in science, or of clinging to interpretations which are not really relevant to the validity of the faith when such interpretations are shown to be incorrect.

One most dangerous and indefensible result of this kind of intellectual intolerance on the part of the church is that it may lead to a suppression of certain areas of study in church-controlled colleges. We have heard the charge that students and teachers in church colleges are not free to seek the truth; sometimes this charge has unfortunately been justified, although we have happily largely outgrown it.

Occasionally an even more serious charge has been justified: that the defenders of the faith have deliberately distorted or withheld facts. It would be a very grave matter, were any such behavior to come from our church or college leaders; in a college it would be particularly intolerable. If "Lutheran physics" means that the facts are to be twisted to fit Lutheran doctrine, then we want no part of "Lutheran physics." Christians surely need to have the faith to be willing to expose their beliefs to honest and objective criticism; after all, the refusal to admit criticism betrays, in a subtle way, a lack of faith.

Other intellectual crimes committed in the name of the defense of the faith are obvious to any person reasonably versed in science who reads some of the "scientific" books which appear on the shelves of our religious bookstores. Many of them only excite the laughter of informed people; and if the reader is uninformed, they fill his mind with errors which may later be uprooted at the expense of painful disillusion. One may perhaps classify the mistakes made by some of these writers as follows: errors of fact, errors in interpretation of fact, adoption of untenable hypotheses based on bias, refusal to accept validated experimental results, and refusal to admit that scientists' results are usually reached in good faith. No good scientist should resent criticism of his work, or skepticism about his results. But the criticisms of scientific findings made in some of these books are often ignorant or biased, and sometimes amount to nothing more than the statement, "I don't wish to believe that." One could wish that the religious book publishers would have these works reviewed by qualified scientists before publication. Earlier it was pointed out that scientific knowledge is always incomplete. Some religious people have stretched this fact into the doctrine that all science is what they call "pseudo-science" unless it happens to agree with their point of view on some religio-scientific question. This kind of bias hardly needs refutation.

But not all the sins are on one side. The proponents of the scientific view are often to blame in various ways. I have mentioned that the materialistic attitude involves a presupposition which often leads to inconsistency or circular argument. For example, a typical criticism of the Christian position might argue that miracles are impossible, because we have never observed them; therefore, the accounts of miracles in the Bible are unbelievable because miracles are impossible.

Some persons believe (1) that God exists with power, and (2) that miracles are impossible, simultaneously. We notice this particularly in the case of "liberal" theologians who boggle at such things as the virgin birth or the resurrection, apparently because they think that science has demonstrated that such events are impossible. How anyone can entertain such a simple inconsistency is a mystery. If we admit that God exists with power, how can we exclude on scientific grounds the possibility that He might intervene in our affairs? It is true (as men have always known, of course) that virgin births and risings from the dead do not normally occur; but to say that they cannot occur is to put upon God the limitations of man.

I once heard a high school teacher say that the Flood was impossible because it could not rain for forty days. The pupils nodded agreement; they were conditioned, as most now are, to the naturalistic philosophy: nothing can occur unless it is scientifically permitted. But they did not realize that *before* they can say that the Flood was impossible they must *first* establish that God has no power.

In their disputes with religion the scientists have not always been innocent of intolerance. There is a tendency towards an impatient rejection of criticism when it comes from those who, as far as science is concerned, are laymen. Of course one plain mark of an intelligent person is his willingness to hear criticism, and this quality is perhaps even more important to the scientist than to most others. The principle is obvious: criticisms must be honestly judged on their merits. A teacher—in any field—must exemplify this virtue at all times. Of course what I have just said must not be considered to absolve the religionist from his responsibility to make his criticisms informed.

One product of nineteenth-century science and philosophy was the notion that all the problems of mankind—war, poverty, crime—would soon be solved. If we only waited for the scientists and engineers to write down the next decimal place, we should be in paradise; the glittering chrome-plated world which would be created by technology would be a world of peace, joy, and light. The twentieth century has taught most thoughtful people to abandon this fatuous optimism; an exclusively scientific society is more likely to be a chrome-plated jungle inhabited by urbanized savages. But many people still talk as they did fifty years ago, forgetting that technology cannot create morals.

I should not like to leave the impression that the only contribution of science is the neutralist conclusion that it cannot be used against us. Although we can never use scientific findings to provide positive *proof* of religion, they can for the believer reveal the glories of God. Sometimes, they seem to confirm what we have already thought; as for example, archaeological discoveries have confirmed certain parts of the Old Testament, and psychology has revealed the depravity of man's nature with ghastly clarity. Viewing from the point of view of physics the fantastically intricate and yet beautifully organized structure of matter, and from the point of view of biology the almost unbelievable elegance of the design of living beings, one is breathless with awe before the wonders of the world and is almost forced to argue that such ineffable creations must have had a Creator.

At the same time this warning must be sounded: one must never base his religious beliefs on any *specific* scientific doctrine. For the doctrine may be overthrown, and the religious beliefs go with it. The man who wishes to use science to prove his religion must proceed with the most exquisite caution. The one thing we can say with certainty about science and religion is that the modern conviction that science cannot decide ultimates or give us a knowledge of ultimate reality will not change.

I think it is now possible to see that to a considerable extent our liberal and religious aims, in our college teaching, overlap. Critical thinking, openmindedness, intellectual honesty, and the ability to make discriminating judgments, are important constituents of the point of view from which the problems of science versus religion must be approached. If in our teaching we emphasize humility and wonder before the creations of God, the limitations of human powers, and the incompleteness of human knowledge, we shall have not only taught liberally but shall also have contributed to religious understanding. If our teachers are well-informed, and are left free to teach their subjects without interference or limitations, and if they permit free and uninhibited discussion of all opinions, they can be both liberal arts teachers and religious teachers.

REFERENCES FOR COLLATERAL READING:

C. S. Lewis: *Miracles.*

E. A. Burtt: *The Metaphysical Foundations of Modern Physical Science.*

G. G. Simpson: *The Meaning of Evolution.*

W. Stace: *Religion and the Modern Mind.*

P. E. Sabine: *Atoms, Men, and God.*

M. Schlick: *Philosophy of Nature.*

M. Otto: *Science and the Moral Life.*

B. Russell: *The Impact of Science on Society.*

C. E. M. Joad: *Guide to Modern Thought.*

A. N. Whitehead: *Science and the Modern World.*

D. F. Swenson: *Faith of a Scholar.*

K. Heim: *The Transformation of the Scientific Worldview.*

H. Margenau: *The Nature of Physical Reality.*

J. W. Krutch: *The Measure of Man.*

CHAPTER 15

Sociology

by Albert F. Wessen

The purpose of this paper is to consider some of the interrelationships between three entities with which higher education must in some way deal. One, sociology, is a relatively new and heterodox academic discipline which has come to have both implications and connotations for the conduct of life. A second, Christianity, while above all a way of life, is both the source of content for an academic discipline—"religion"—and a pervasive source of intellectual problems with which all of the academic disciplines must in some way deal. Liberal education, however, is not in itself capable of being translated into a discipline in the academic sense of the word; it is rather a somewhat inchoate ideal of what all the disciplines together should be, a set of values which seeks to relate the educational process to the good life.

It is perfectly possible to deal with each of these three concerns of education in such a way that they have no discernible relationship to one another. Liberal education has frequently been conceived in such a way that sociology is excluded from its substance and Christianity removed from its purpose. Sociology has usually not been directed toward serving the ends of Christianity or liberal education, and in terms of both has frequently been regarded as a naughty step-child in the curricular family. And Christianity has been content at many times and in many places to withdraw from the implications both of sociology and liberal education. Moreover, if it has often been the case that there has been little interaction between any two of the three concerns of this paper, it has been positively rare to think of all three as so symmetrically interrelated that each has fruitful implications for the others. It is this position, however, which is the thesis of this paper. We suggest that sociology can provide productive insights which have a place in the practice both of liberal education and of Christianity; we contend that the values denoted by liberal education can enable individuals most fully to explore the implications of both Christianity and sociology; and we believe that upon the ground of Christian conviction both the aims of liberal education and the progress of sociology can best be implemented.

THE NATURE, AIM, AND METHOD OF THE SOCIAL SCIENCES

Historically, sociology was a part of the intellectual harvest of Enlightenment philosophy. As such, its intellectual affinities were primarily with the metaphysics of positivism. The very word "sociology" is credited to Auguste Comte—and from the beginning, sociologists were his disciples, at least insofar as a fervent belief in the efficacy of scientific method and in the delusions of theological and metaphysical thinking was concerned. The second principle historic source of inspiration for sociology—Nineteenth century Evolutionism—maintained and intensified the peculiar philosophical bias which was the environment for the developing social sciences.

It can cogently be argued that this positivistic bias, with its ecclesiastically displeasing partisanship in the "warfare between science and theology," was historically necessary for the development of the social sciences. Nothing less than a methodological revolution, with its inevitable consequences of doubt and disavowal of traditional ways of thinking, could persuade intelligent men of the need to supplement their heritage of ethico-rationalistic thought about human behavior. The prestigeful and seemingly infallible model of Newtonian physics (usually as transmitted by popularizers and not by personal involvement) was necessary to inspire pioneers to essay the goal of creating a social science. And the Nineteenth century's satiety of traditional Christian formulations led many to the conviction that they should cast their lot with a new and hopeful science rather than with suspect dogma. The intensity of motivation engendered by these currents of thought was considerable; and if it sometimes made the works of pioneer social scientists read like secular sermons, it at least encouraged them to attempt a social science.[1]

The very idea of science, with its appeal to empirical reality

---

[1]We are adumbrating here the "motivational bridge" concept so useful in the analysis of culture change. For three examples of the use of this concept, see: for the Enlightenment, Carl Becker, *The Heavenly City of the Eighteenth Century Philosophers;* for science, A. N. Whitehead, *Science and the Modern World,* ch. I; for modern capitalism, Max Weber, *The Protestant Ethic and the Spirit of Capitalism.*

and consequent frequent repudiation of traditional and rationalist construets, was corrosive of the theologically imperialist world-view of the Middle Ages. Since belief in this world-view—especially in that part of it pertaining to social behavior—seemed a necessary testimony to the verity of religion, the rise of science almost inevitably gave rise to heterodoxy and heresy within the Christian community. Although theologians joined battle against new formulations in the natural sciences, so long as science could be restricted to physics adjustment could be made to it. Thus Cartesian dualism, the Kantian distinction between the phenomenal and the noumenal, and the academic distinction between *Naturwissenschaft* and *Geisteswissenschaft* each in its own way made it possible to believe both in traditional theology and in scientific dogma. When, however, science invaded the domain of *Geist*, the intellectual fortresses of theology seemed imperiled.

Yet it was the historical function of the social science movement to declare the distinction between *Naturwissenschaft* and *Geisteswissenschaft* invalid, at least insofar as this dichotomy involved a radical difference in methodology. The social sciences assert the possibility of arriving at probabilistic generalizations concerning human behavior by means of controlled empirical research. They assert that events which fall within the scope of their body of verified theory can be explained without recourse to other philosophic categories. However, the assumption that the data of human behavior can be reduced (at least analogically) to fit the theoretical model of the physical sciences is probably no longer the majority view among sociologists. As sociology and the other behavior sciences have grown toward maturity, they have increasingly developed new theoretical models of their own, designed to take cognizance of the unique matrix of human behavior.[2] Thus they have attempted to preserve that which is sound in positivistic distrust of unbridled speculation while coming to grips with the truth that lies behind the idealistic insistence on the irreducible uniqueness of human nature.[3]

"Sociology," then, denotes a system of analytical theory with reference to social behavior that is subject to empirical verification. The same can be said for the other behavioral sciences (psychology

---

[2] E.g., theory utilizing such sociological concepts as *culture, role, status, value, orientation, definition of the situation,* and the like.

[3] For the historical development of the social sciences in the direction of this paragraph, see Talcott Parsons, *The Structure of Social Action,* 1937.

and anthropology) and for economics. What is significant about this definition is that it restricts the scope of the discipline. Sociology as a science is thus neither a program for action nor a normative philosophy. It is an integrated system of generalizations. And, increasingly, it is agreed that these generalizations pertain to *functional relationships*. This is to say that they describe empirical clusters of fact—that when one kind of behavior is observed, other behaviors and conditions of behavior will probably be associated with it. In the field of sociology, these functional statements typically deal with the interrelationships of various components and their relationship to behavior—components of *culture*, e.g., beliefs, expectations, norms, values; components of *society*, e.g., groups and group structures; and components of *personality organization*, e.g., motivational patterns, emotional set, intelligence. (These of course are considered in relation to relevant facets of the physical and biological environment as well.) What the sociologist does, then, is to utilize *structural categories* which represent analytical aspects of society, culture, and personality, and attempt to relate these functionally to each other and to observed behavior.[4] The technical problems of the discipline center around the construction of theoretical categories, their operational definition in empirical situations, and verification of their interrelationships. The significance of sociology for contemporary culture lies in the insight it can throw on the "mechanics" of human behavior—on the way societies function as integrated wholes, the effect of malfunction of parts on the whole, the probable effect of specific kinds of change on the society, and the like.

It is crucial, therefore, that in a discussion of this kind a rigid distinction be drawn between sociology as a self-contained theoretical system and the philosophical implications and connotations which have grown up around this system. As we have pointed out, sociology grew up in the rigorous philosophical climate of positivism, and sociologists have more often than not united positivistic

---

[4]Space does not permit giving concrete examples of the way in which sociologists work. A few classical and modern examples, however, are: Emile Durkheim, *Suicide;* Max Weber, *Gesammelte Aufsätze für Religionssoziologie;* W. G. Sumner, *Folkways;* B. Malinowski, *Argonauts of the Western Pacific;* E. E. Evans-Pritchard, *The Nuer;* A. B. Hollingshead, *Elmtown's Youth;* P. K. Whelpton and C. Kiser, *Social and Psychological Factors Affecting Fertility;* for a general text utilizing this approach, see Robin Williams, *American Society.*

bias with their theory and research in a most dogmatic fashion. Insofar as the discipline has come to approach the status of a mature science, however, it has overcome this confusion and realized that a science is valid regardless of the *Weltanschauung* of the scientist. In the field of religion, for example, it has outgrown its early positivistic aim of explaining religion away. Rather, it has come to accept religion as a given factor in human behavior which —regardless of its ontological status—plays a functional role in society that should be analyzed.[5] Thus, ideally at least, there is no difference between "Democratic sociology" and "Republican sociology;" and a "Christian sociology" is as much an academic monstrosity as a "Christian chemistry" would be.[6]

This is not to say that the Christian will draw the same implications from sociology as will the humanist. It is not to assert that in the teaching process the line between science and the philosophical implications of science can or should be drawn. It is not to deny that there remains in the accepted corpus of sociological theory much unverified and biased "metaphysical" matter.[7] Our purpose is rather to suggest that insofar as the social sciences have achieved their ideal, their relation to values is objective in the sense that they do not presuppose specific value positions in a detached and neutral fashion. Therefore the relation of sociology to liberal education and Christianity is similar to that of the natural sciences.

This point of view involves two corollaries. First, it makes necessary a critical approach to the statements of sociologists. Are they remaining faithful to their scientific ideal, or have their philosophical and policy biases been disguised by a scientific mask? By the scientific criteria of empirical verification and theoretical consistency is it possible to accept this or that statement as truly sociological? Sociological chaff must be winnowed from the good grain both

---

[5]For this development, see T. Parsons, "The Development of the Sociological Theory of Religion," in *Essays in Sociological Theory.*

[6]As Weber observed long ago, however, even when philosophical bias is overcome within the technical research situation, it still exerts itself in terms of the *selection* of problems for research. In this sense, the Christian sociologist will not always behave exactly as the positivist because he will consider a different range of phenomena of importance for theory and research.

[7]This is not to deny that the argument of the present paper has its own peculiar metaphysical and epistemological postulates. Briefly, it involves the position that verified sociological theory represents a *facet* of reality, but because it is only an analytical aspect of reality, sociological theory as such is compatible with any of several broad metaphysical positions.

for the progress of the science and for the sake of its optimal contribution to the world. In this reckoning, the historically sanctioned froth of positivistic bias will no doubt be blown away. Second, because of the traditional conflict between science and theology, the relationship between sociology and Christianity is likely at times to be difficult. Just as the development of modern astronomy necessitated the removal of theological sanction from the Ptolemaic cosmology, developments in the social sciences may compel the Church to rethink some of the implications of its theology.[8] From a contemporary vantage point, however, it appears that the social sciences in no way call into question the validity of the gospel as the center of theology.[9] And the sociologist who is Christian must have as one of the articles of his faith the belief that ultimately the knowledge of science and the knowledge of revelation are compatible. He will look for the reconciliation of apparent conflict either in the imperfections of science or in the misapplication of theology.

THE SOCIAL SCIENCES AND THE LIBERAL ARTS

The ideal of a liberal education seems easier to define in terms of what it is not than in terms of what it is. Despite its historical roots in the classical *trivium* and *quadrivium,* liberal education as a concept which mobilizes the convictions and passions of educators seems to be relatively new. With the overthrow, during the Nineteenth century, of the classical curriculum and the simultaneous broadening of the educated population, traditionalistic values in education tended to be supplanted by utilitarian ones. And the conviction that education "is worth money" came to be a dominant American belief.[10] With the rise of this belief, the doors were opened to all sorts of vocational courses, and, to some, the American high school and college seemed in danger of becoming trade

---

[8]Thus, for example, the development of modern psychological and criminological thought has rendered the theological distortion which equated criminality or insanity with evidence of election to damnation impossible. Sound theology would probably reach the same conclusion—but it is a fact that it was the development of the social sciences which put the *coup de grace* on this idea.

[9]Just as they do not testify to it.

[10]See G. S. Counts, *The American Road to Culture.* For contemporary evidence for and about this doctrine, see Havemann and West, *They Went to College.*

schools. "Liberal education" came to the fore as the rallying-concept for those who oppose both the dominance of utilitarian motives in education and the implementation of this value through "vocationalism."

It is more difficult to define the positive values and disciplines which the proponents of liberal education desire to place in the curriculum. It is apparent, however, that this group almost unanimously sees instruction in the humanities as central to a liberal education, and wish through it to implement such basic values as democracy, freedom, creativeness, morality, the good, the true, and the beautiful. Liberal education is normally defined as that kind of education which provides the basic skills for living and not merely the facility for earning. There is a tendency, if one can take the Andover, Harvard, and Yale reports of curriculum studies as representative, to equate liberal education on the college level with general education, and thus to denounce the evils of "specialism."[11] Usually, therefore, advocates of liberal education find themselves in the position of advocating some kind of controlled curriculum rather than a free system of course election.

Perhaps because ours is a pluralistic culture—and probably because of the educators' abhorrence of being called sectarian—liberal education is usually defined only in a minimal sense: it must be solid and intellectual, and it must "free" its students to enjoy the good life in the fullest and highest sense of the phrase. (Its opponents would add, "it must be useless.") Thus it usually means in practice a curriculum in which the humanities and the natural and social sciences are accepted, while the applied arts and sciences are for the most part rejected.

The social sciences are usually granted a place in the framework of a liberal education, although theories differ as to how great it ought to be. Because some feel that the social sciences are inevitably iconoclastic, they would minimize their place in liberal education or eliminate it altogether. Others, feeling that the aims of liberal education can best be achieved through consideration of the classics, tend to dismiss the social sciences as secondary or actively to oppose them because their abstractions typically do not emphasize human creativeness. Still others see the results of man's study of

---

[11]Thus President A. Whitney Griswold of Yale: "The very term 'liberal arts' has given way in professional academic usage to the term 'general education,' with its obviously broader implications as to content and method." *Report to the Alumni of Yale College,* 1952-3.

man as vital to the ideals of liberal education, and hence see the social sciences as a necessary supplement to literary, philosophic, and historical studies.

For good historical reasons the allegation that social sciences are often iconoclastic is, as we have seen, true. Moreover, one of the difficulties of teaching sociology stems from the fact that since its method involves the *imaginative* effort to suspend one's own value commitments for analytical purposes, it is easy for students to assume that sociology preaches value neutrality or debunks traditional values.[12] It is true, too, that the method of sociology involves emphasis on statistical statements with regard to probable behavior of groups rather than on the unique individuality of each actor. It tends, too, to attempt to define as clearly as possible the limits of human freedom which the conditions of the human situation impose. There is thus justification for the charges that sociology does not directly foster ultimate values and that it tends to play down the sphere of human freedom and creativeness. It may be, therefore, that the burden of proof is upon sociology to justify its claim to a place in the curriculum of liberal education.

It has a claim, we believe, both in terms of the skills it fosters and the content it teaches. Like all the sciences, sociology tends to emphasize specific techniques—and it is easy to become lost in the morass of sociological jargon and methodology. There are, however, certain basic skills and qualities of intellect which lie behind the technical aspects of sociology. These are directly relevant to what a liberal education ought to involve.

Perhaps the most basic skill the sociologist ought to possess is that of acute *observation*. Of all people, he ought to be perceptive in his appraisal of the meaning and dynamics of social situations. Despite the fact that sociologists are often sadly lacking in this quality, the discipline serves to foster it in several ways. Emphasis is placed on the painstaking description of situations as they actually are. Through the technique of direct observation, "participant-observation," interview, and questionnaire, the sociologist attempts to accumulate data which will reliably describe reality situations. It is a truism that the secret of successful observation lies in knowing what to look for; and the theory of the social sciences should help professional and layman alike to have some idea

---

[12]This suspension of value commitment is analagous to the suspension of reality judgment which fiction demands of its reader.

as to what will be significant in appraising a social situation.[13] The sociologist, in observing social situations will usually be particularly interested in describing typical behaviors and expectations of behavior, in describing who interacts with whom under what conditions, and in searching for background factors that will explain the regularities in his observations. He will also attempt to gain insight (*Verstehen* in Weber's terms) into the subjective meaning of the situation for those involved in it.[14] Insofar as sociology fosters skills such as these, it should help students better to appraise and function in the social situations in which they find themselves. And successful social living is a *sine qua non* of the enjoyment of the good life.

If the sociologist observes social behavior, he does so in order to have an empirical basis for his reasoning. And the particular kind of reasoning which the social sciences utilize is, we believe, in itself a contribution to a liberal education. Like all sciences, sociology attempts to create a synthesis between the empirical and the theoretical. It is, therefore, constantly in a state of tension. The sociologist is bound to determine the meaning of all the facts which face him in terms of his theories, and each new theoretical insight must insofar as possible be subjected to the ruthless check of confrontation with observed facts. He therefore must learn to distinguish between his theories and the data which support them—and our experience has been that this is a hard lesson for students to learn. Thus, one goal of the social sciences ought to be to teach students, in thinking about human behavior, to try to avoid both the reactionary cocksureness of pure empiricism, and the radical certainty of speculation.

The logic of the social sciences is, as we have said, a logic of functional relationships. Students must therefore be taught to approach social phenomena with an eye to seeing things as interconnected and as *Gestalts*. They must be encouraged to examine things in terms of the functional consequences of their presence or ab-

[13]Sociological and psychological research have shown, for example, that *informal* organization of workers is related to work efficiency in industrial plants just as surely as is the formal work organization and external working conditions, thus correcting one-sided opinions previously held by management engineers. Cf. Roethlisberger and Dickson, *Management and the Worker.*

[14]Here, too, the sociologist must use some of the same skills as the good novelist. It is for this reason that novels can be of great value in the teaching of sociology.

sence to the whole of which they are a part. They must learn to distinguish this kind of evaluation from making normative value judgments—and to appreciate the use and value of both. Always with the tentativeness of science they must learn to do these things with data which is, for the most part, familiar to them, that is, data to which they normally react with little reflection and often with much emotion. To learn the logic of science in dealing with the commonplaces of social behavior is both to see new worlds open up on *terra cognita* and to learn something about oneself.[15] The social sciences can help students mature by leading them to understand that *how* is sometimes as important a question as *why*.

The materials of sociology are not always familiar; there are, for example, the findings of social anthropology. To the sociologist, anthropological data is particularly valuable for answering theoretical questions precisely because of its comparative perspective. Such data provides "living laboratories" in which sociological variables are arranged in different patterns. To the student, they offer the opportunity to examine cultures other than his own, which are motivated by value systems different from and frequently contradictory to his—and yet functionally more or less efficient. It is a liberating experience to learn that one's ways are not the only possible ways. And for the student, as it was for Sumner, it is also a liberating experience to learn that "the mores can make anything right."[16] The relativity of culture is an observed fact that must be faced; but the functional perspective of sociology ought to help the student see in it something other than an invitation to "throw the mores over." For the lesson of *anomie*[17] is also a lesson which the data of sociology drive home again and again.

Sociology is a synthetic science as well as one with its own

<hr>

[15]To participate in a small group communications experiment is usually a learning experience in both the theoretical and the personal senses. And to send a student interviewing in slums which he has passed every day of his life is usually a profoundly educative experience. Not only does a student learn sociological facts and techniques, but he acquires both a kind of social insight he never had before and the art of establishing rapport with strangers.

[16]Cf. W. G. Sumner, *Folkways.* It is good to know, perhaps, that the justification of our sex mores, for example, is not that they are the only workable ones but the only possibility our value system allows us without undue guilt and pain. At least, knowing this, we ought to be able to deduce that sex mores are corollaries rather than main theses in human life!

[17]For the original elaboration of this concept, see E. Durkheim, *Suicide,* and *Division of Labor in Society.*

method and factual domain. It provides a theoretical context into which the problems and findings of other social studies—economics, political science, history—may be placed. It provides a check to overgeneralization of the utilitarian results of economic and power analysis by showing that economic and political man is also family and religious man—and by demonstrating that the intimacies of the primary group may be more influential for human behavior and satisfactions than the contractual relationships of marketplace and forum. At the same time, it is insistent that thinking man is also eating man, and that the intellectual aspect of life and the higher emotions alike are grounded upon a substrate of basic and animal drives. In a word, the very logic of sociology drives one to protest against an education which is exclusively intellectual and classical or which is exclusively utilitarian. Just as the functional approach makes any simple determinism impossible at the level of theoretical explanation, it protests against a curricular imperialism which exalts any one way of knowing or one kind of skill-for-living at the expense of adequate communication of the rest.[18]

The facts of sociology, therefore, should be valuable for their utilitarian as well as for their theoretical significance. The student—whether his destined vocation be teaching, medicine, social work, the ministry, or a career in business—inevitably lives in a social world, and the net result of his sociological training should be to make him better equipped for life in the world. His study of American society should make him a citizen more perceptive of his country's problems and more discriminating of its culture. His training should make him both critical of social panaceas and intelligently aware of what is involved in social action. His understanding of the havoc that asymmetry of role expectancies can create[19] in social

---

[18]The sociologist, of course, must not be blind to the danger of a sociological or scientific imperialism. His training too often tends to make him anti-individualistic, uninterested in fields other than his own, and, ironically enough, anti-cultural.

[19]Here sociological jargon is more concise than literary English. The basic idea is that human behavior is played out in series of complementary roles—husband-wife, doctor-patient, speaker-audience, etc.—and that men come to situations with cultural expectations concerning what will be expected of them and of their *alter*. When these expectations differ, they are said to be asymmetrical—and normally social difficulties arise if the asymmetry is not overcome. In the field of medicine, see L. Saunders, *Medicine for Spanish Americans*, T. Parsons, *The Social System*, Ch. X, A. Wessen, *The Social Structure of a Modern Hospital*, Ch. IV.

relationships should make him concerned in his own roles to understand the expectations of others, and therefore to avoid mutual misunderstanding. And his appreciation of the function of norms and values in human living should make him intelligently committed to those which are his heritage.

SOCIOLOGY AND THE LIFE OF THE CHURCH

We must now look briefly at some of the implications of sociology for theology.[20] As indicated above, sociology itself can neither affirm nor deny any theological or ontological position; it is a tool subject, the results of which can be used for various ends, depending on the values of the user. For the Christian, however, sociology ought to serve a purpose which accords with his belief. As a tool, it ought to be used in his hands for the furtherance of the Gospel and the glory of God; it ought, in a word, to be useful to the Church.

The most obvious use of sociology in the church's service would seem to be in the study of the institutional life of churches. Not only can sociological knowledge be applied in church extension planning[21] or to bolster the factual knowledge of church commissions on social issues, but it can shed light on the dynamics of church life itself.[22] Why is one church flourishing while its neighbor is slowly dying? What differentiates the active churchman who is faithful and consecrated in his service from his backsliding brother? Admitting the truth of the theological distinction between those who are enlivened by the Holy Spirit and those who have not received Him, these questions are still valid sociological research questions. There is little doubt that the varied backgrounds and experiences found in even so homogeneous a group as a congregation, together with the institutional malfunctioning of well-meaning souls, can account for the building and razing of barriers to Christianity among men.

For the idea of the gospel as the Word of God means that God

---

[20]For another discussion, see Talcott Parsons' Hazen Foundation pamphlet, *Religious Perspectives in the Teaching of Sociology.*

[21]Knowledge about population trends, migration, community potentials and the like would be useful here as well as expertness in sociological field techniques.

[22]E.g., H. P. Douglass, *1000 City Churches,* Joseph Fichter, *Southern Parish.*

comes to man through human language, under the forms of culture[23]; in this sense the Word is joined to Sacrament in ever-contemporary assertion of the doctrine of the Incarnation. And just as Jesus as man was the victim of the misunderstandings of men who could not recognize who he was, so it is possible for the gospel to become unintelligible as the church fails to understand the common life which swirls around it. As stewards of the mysteries of God it is not the function of churchmen to hide their trust behind the formulae of institutional rigidity or the gibberish of cultural lag, but rather to proclaim them so clearly that all men will know their height and depth.

If this is so, sociology must have implications for the church insofar as it has anything to say about the workings of human society and culture. Its word will of course not be the last—but it should have the sharp edge of a critical tool, enabling the church to prune from itself the excrescences which allow some men to label it a "survival."

Thus the sociologist may wish to investigate the nature of the Christianity that is actually believed and practiced in a community. For example, he might inquire whether the people's understandings of the great theological words—"sin," "forgiveness," "atonement," "grace," and the like—are congruent with those of the preachers. And if he finds that sometimes they are not—if, perchance, the preachers define sin as alienation from God through self-centeredness while the people think of sin as a multitude of little transgressions (usually sexual)—he will ask why this is so. He will attempt to discover why by looking at the institutionally sanctioned practices of the church itself as well as the culture as a whole. If, to carry our example to its conclusion, he finds that the church has dissipated its energies in little crusades against smoking or movies or dancing, he will suggest that there is truth in the proverb that "actions speak louder than words."

He will be interested, too, in describing the day-to-day life of church workers. What role conflicts does the pastor face in his day-to-day work? For what is he prepared adequately, and at what points does his training fail to guide him? Could it be that wiser counsel would have enabled him to serve more acceptably than he is? At what points is he reaching his people—and in what different languages must he speak to reach them all? How, indeed,

---

[23]He comes to man directly through His Spirit, too.

can he weld into a true community, and what are the dangers of
doing so? To all of these questions detailed sociological study of
the parish at work could provide suggestive answers.

Because the sociologist is interested in the analysis of culture,
he will be interested in assessing the impact of Christianity upon
contemporary culture[24] and of culture upon the expression of
Christianity.[25] As one who attempts to deal analytically with various aspects of culture and society, he will be especially interested
to keep Christianity and the culture within which it is expressed
analytically separate. Thus, he will compare the various manifestations of Christianity in time and space with other aspects of the
cultures in which it has found itself. He will wish to see, for example, whether congregational polity is merely an influence of
the political values of certain nations upon their churches. Conversely, he may wish to discover how denominational preferences
affect voting behavior. From his studies of the interrelations of
Christianity and culture, he will likely conclude that Christianity
is in certain respects incompatible with other aspects of contemporary culture—and that this will have certain predictable consequences, given the structure of the church as an institution.

The matter of cultural relativity is relevant at this point. In
Western culture, Christianity has been for centuries identified as
the accepted religion, and likewise has identified itself with the
culture to a greater or lesser degree. It has sanctioned various systems of European political organization, sanctified the Western
family system, and become the arbiter of our civilization's morality.
As H. Richard Niebuhr has noted, it has become both the expression
of various Western cultural types through denominationalism,
and has sought to wrestle with and transcend culture in its theological expression.[26] The consequence of this is that the church
has not only had to accommodate itself to the cultures within which

---

[24]This he will do in several ways. He will attempt to measure the distribution
of Christianity among the population; he will estimate its influence upon culture as measured in cultural production; and he will assess its importance in
cultural development. (e.g., Gordon Allport, "The Religion of the Postwar
College Student," *J. Psychol.*, 25, 1949; M. Weber, *The Protestant Ethic and
the Spirit of Capitalism*, and R. K. Merton, "Puritanism and Science in Seventeenth Century England," *Osiris* v. 4, 1936.

[25]Cf. E. Troeltsch, *The Social Teachings of the Christian Churches*, A. Faucet,
Black Gods of the Metropolis, V. E. Daniel, "Ritual and Stratification in Chicago Churches," *American Sociological Review*, 7, 1942.

[26]Niebuhr, *Social Sources of Denominationalism*, and *Christ and Culture*.

it has been placed, but that it has inevitably acquired a severe case of cultural myopia; it has become culture-bound. Western Christianity has, it is said, become fixated on the Roman flair for rhetoric, while the Eastern church has retained some of the classical Greek feeling for drama; each thinks its ways are ordained from above. Western missionaries seek to preach Western marriage forms, Western technology, and Western medicine with their Gospel not only as a means of influencing people to Christ but because Western ways are "right."[27] The general assumption is that the sanctioned ways of the culture are right in the same way that gospel is right—and volumes of theological rationalization have buttressed this assumption.[28]

It is precisely the comparative vantagepoint of the sociologist which makes him insist upon the radical distinction between revealed religion and the body of human culture. Lying behind, yet distinct from, our cultural expression is the Word—a God become flesh for men, suffering, dying, and rising again for their justification —and beyond Scripture's eternal verity, the inspiration of fallible men must translate that Word into relative cultural form. That in doing so men identify what the mores make right with what God makes right (if conflict is not too obvious) is perhaps understandable. Yet these specific cultural embodiments become confused with the Word and men cling to them with the fierceness of martyrs; wars have too often been fought over theological argument. "We see through a glass darkly" now—our vision is clouded by the immanence of our culture—and we need a cross-cultural perspective with which to behold the darkness of our glass.[29] This the social sciences are able in some degree to provide, if they will.

The fact that the applications of Christianity to contemporary culture are not automatic or ready-made—and hence are fallible—

---

[27]The cost of some of their preaching to the pagan society as a whole has filled monographs on "cultural disorganization among primitive tribes."

[28]It is interesting to see how time and culture-change relativize these arguments. Theological justifications of the divine right theory in government carry little weight for moderns—but the theological reasoning which seemed so correct three centuries ago is not less so now. It was probably irrelevant both then and now.

[29]One such darkness is the assumption that Christian sanctioned culture patterns must *function* better than other ones. This is not necessarily so. The justification of Christian ethics must lie in the field of principle rather than of efficiency. When the church forgets this, it becomes confounded with its culture in a peculiarly insidious way.

should give us pause. It does not, however, excuse the Church from making them. And as it makes them, sociology should be able to contribute much from its body of facts concerning social behavior. Effectiveness and efficiency is a virtue even in holy places—and the church should stand to profit from infusing its thought with the data of the social sciences.[30]

The peculiar character of Christianity as a religion of Incarnation means that it of all religions should have the least conflict with science. Because God created the world, the facts of natural science should attest to His glory. Because He manifested Himself in human form, the discoveries of the social sciences should testify to His nature as well as to the nature of man. And because He manifests Himself through His Word and through His church, they should—as studies of society and culture—be His hand-maidens in a special way. For insofar as they fulfil their ideal of describing that which is real, they will both be testifying to the glory of God and teaching others something of how to do so.

CHRISTIANITY AND SOCIOLOGY WITHIN THE CONTEXT OF LIBERAL EDUCATION

We have described something of the character of contemporary sociology, both as it is and as it tries to be. We have sought to assess some of its implications for liberal education and for Christianity. It remains to sketch briefly the convictions underlying our remaining theses.

We contend that the values denoted by liberal education can enable individuals most fully to explore the implications of both Christianity and sociology. Despite the fuzziness of the concept, the motive of liberal education is clear enough. It wishes to provide an atmosphere in which man's skills and aptitudes can be developed to the fullest in order that his aspirations may be of the highest. Its ideal is that of the Renaissance—*l'uomo universale*. To achieve this goal it must free man from his ignorance and from his inertia, and it must free educational institutions from their bias and their mediocrity.

The prescription of what should go into a liberal education cannot be discussed here; suffice it to say that it places severe demands

---

[30]The application of sociological theory to the field of religion and the work of the church has hardly begun.

on both student and teacher while offering unparalleled rewards. If what we have said here has validity, however, we can say that both sociology and Christianity—insofar as they are what they claim to be—belong in this prescription.

Christianity is a faith which does not require erudition: it is a faith which can sustain both the laborer and the philosopher (and it may be that it can reach the former more easily than the latter). Nonetheless, Christianity is a faith which demands all that the Christian has to give—even to the extent of a cross. It therefore must demand the best that education can produce—and it is this that liberal education aspires to do. For this reason alone Christianity must be interested in it. Yet, as the faithful know, Christianity is a faith the intellectual depths of which are not easily sounded. Its richness takes on new dimensions with increasing study; this should be true both with regard to the study of the faith itself and to Christian study of the world and culture. For the implication of the religion of Incarnation must be that the study of life must throw out constant insights on Christianity to the believer.

The environment of a liberal education ought then to be the most adequate one for the growth of a Christian, not because it excels in the indoctrination of dogma and cultural values, but because its freedom and comprehensiveness is best calculated to express the manifold relevance of Christianity to life. And the aspiration of a Christian college should be not merely to turn out more zealous Christians—professional and otherwise—but to broaden the horizons of all its constituency through the many-gauged quest for truth which a liberal education involves.

Sociology, too, can best thrive in the environment of a liberal education. As the Nazi and Soviet experiences alike show, science cannot live in other than an atmosphere of intellectual freedom. But it is possible for this freedom to be compromised in the educational structures of a free land. They are compromised when the dogma of one philosophy—be it sectarian or secular, positivistic or idealistic—becomes the required institutional or professional creed which the scientist must hold. They are compromised when the problems of technique and professional recognition occupy the scientist's attention to the exclusion of broader issues. They are compromised when the scientist is interested in the data of his science to the exclusion of the findings of other disciplines. Science—natural and social—therefore ought best to thrive in the atmosphere of freedom that a liberal education strives to provide.

But sociology is particular—because it is a synthetic science and because the study of man is old while it is young—needs the comprehensiveness of liberal education in order to develop. Its students need a broad philosophical background in order to understand the nature of the sociological enterprise and to avoid some of the pitfalls to which it is prone. They need the insights of great art and literature in order to develop the *Verstehen* they seek to apply with the rigor of science. They need, as innocents abroad on a jargon-infested sea, clarity of thought and expression which the "skill disciplines" can teach. And above all, they need a broad knowledge of history, that basic source of sociological data and explanation. Sociologists, self-conscious after the fashion of an adolescent intent upon using his new-found faculties of manhood, need to live in an atmosphere in which there is opportunity to appreciate the maturity of other and older disciplines than their own.

If sociologists need a liberal education in which to thrive, non-sociologists need it in order to appreciate the promise of sociology. They need it as background. They need it as supplement; the social sciences, for all the professional enthusiasm which they may exude, are only a small part of the making of an educated man. Above all, the layman needs the intellectual adventure that a liberal education ought to provide in order that he may assimilate the excitement of the new horizons to which the social sciences now point.

And we believe that upon the ground of Christian conviction both the aims of liberal education and the progress of sociology can best be implemented. This belief is the basis for the vocation of Christian sociologist.[31]

It should be apparent from what has been said thus far that sociology has much progress to make: it is at the beginning of its career as a science in fact as well as in desire. It should be apparent, too, that its history has provided it with biases which complicate its intrinsically difficult task. We have argued that it might well have been necessary for a positivist revolution to come about in order for sociology to come into being. We shall now argue that in order for it to come to maturity the metaphysics of positivism must be transcended. The development of sociology has shown this to be the case. The unsolved problems of sociological theory today are especially those which the canons of positivism dismissed as

---

[31]We aver that this *vocation* must exist, even though we deny the existence of Christian sociology as a special discipline.

unreal.[32] It is because a narrow positivistic viewpoint seems today to be a reactionary force in sociology—leading to the avoidance of crucial theoretical concerns and to preoccupation with methodological refinement at the expense of substantive enrichment—that we feel a Christian is particularly well equipped to make a contribution to sociology. He is a realist—and sociology needs realists. And he knows (or should know) what all scientists need to remind themselves: that their science is as partial as it is tentative. The Christian, therefore, ought in principle to be less easily buffeted by the winds of "scientistic" dogma than the non-Christian; he, of all people, ought to work most zealously for the creation of a sounder sociology.

From what we have said, the reasons why a liberal education ought to be grounded on Christian conviction should be obvious. The ideals for which liberal education strives require much of man —and of all people the Christian ought to have the necessary motivation. It is he who is to live a life of vocation in all that he does. It is he who is, in faith, free to enjoy life to the fullest. And because he is free in faith, he can be free to learn, to discriminate, and to utilize all of the truths that man has thus-far discovered.

---

[32]The problems of the sociology of religion are an excellent case in point. The fact is that we yet know very little about the interrelations of religion and other aspects of culture. Part of the reason for this lies in the unwillingness of many social scientists to recognize the possibility that religion might be more than the expression of tradition. Another crucial area about which we know little is that of the subjective components of culture.

CHAPTER 16

Psychology

by Olaf W. Millert

The purpose of this paper is to consider problems of psychology in a liberal arts college with a definite Christian commitment. We shall endeavor to argue that contemporary psychology is capable of contributing to essential goals of the liberal arts tradition, consistent with the basic tenets of Christianity.

First we shall define our main concepts and limit the areas of discussion. Second, contemporary trends in psychology will be subjected to a critical analysis. Third, we shall examine the phenomenological approach to modern psychology in relation to the suggested objectives of the liberal arts and the basic beliefs of Christian religion.

For reasons of time and space, we shall confine our efforts to the principal questions of agreement and disagreement between psychology and Christian liberal arts education.

ON LIBERAL ARTS, CHRISTIANITY, AND PSYCHOLOGY

By liberal arts education we mean two things: an *attitude* of critical open-mindedness toward historical and present-day ideas and issues, and a substantive *content* of significant facts and modes of explanation. Ideally, an individual with a liberal arts background will manifest this attitude by his insatiable desire for evaluating new ideas, relating the new to the old, and possibly modifying the learning of the past in the light of the new. A liberal arts education would include, in the purest sense, the disciplines of communication (languages, arts, logic), the disciplines of natural and social phenomena (natural and social sciences), and the disciplines of normative significance (ethics, aesthetics, metaphysics, theology). Admittedly, this categorization is devoid of clearly delineated contours. The fields of study which prepare for specific occupations and which frequently are incorporated in the liberal arts curriculum, reflect a compromise with the prevalent philosophy of pragmatism and utilitarianism. Furthermore, training of the body, regardless of its undeniable intrinsic value is not a part of but a complement to the liberal arts conception.[1] The ideal outcome of liberal arts education is the individual's keener understanding of himself, his cultural heritage, and the physical and social world of which he is a part. It includes a groping, but unavoidable answer to fundamental normative and cosmological questions. Liberal arts education has no license for indoctrination. It provides building blocks to link the past with the present and tools to draw blueprints for the future. The ultimate integration, from the educational viewpoint, lies in the learner and thinker. Psychology, as a separate discipline tries to determine how a person perceives the world and himself. We believe that in this particular area psychologists can make a unique contribution to the liberal arts education.

Christianity is a generic term which lends itself to a variety of definitions. We shall define it as a theistic belief in a Supreme Being revealed through Jesus Christ. The essence of Christ's teachings is expressed through the Sermon on the Mount. A Christian commitment entails acceptance of Christ and His message as recorded in the Scriptures. We do not dare to contend, as the neo-Thomists do, that scientific evidence proves the existence of God.[2] Our definition of science is narrower and more limited than that of St. Thomas and his contemporary followers. Both religion and science are seeking truth. We believe that the revelatory truth of religion and scientifically arrived truth will ultimately be in perfect accordance. However, science is incapable of making assertions about the first principles of religion. They simply do not fall under the purview of science. The neo-Thomists, in their broader formulation, describe science in two ways: as a body of subject matter and a set of techniques. The non-Catholic scientific psychology restricts the meaning of science to the use of certain established and accepted methods. There are no methods of science capable of ascertaining any ultimate premises. The fundamental assumptions of religion rest upon faith which flows from the grace of God. A logician would consider this as a good example of a circular

[1] A provocative essay, entitled *Morals, Religion, and Higher Education* by Robert M. Hutchins, published in the University of Chicago Round Table pamphlet number 617 (January 15, 1950), offers good food for thought, although it is difficult to agree with the author's rather one-sided emphasis on Great Conversation.

[2] The Roman Catholic viewpoint on science and religion was succinctly voiced by Pope Pius XII in his address delivered on 22nd November, 1951, to the members of the Pontifical Academy of Science cf. P. J. McLaughlin, *Modern Science and God* (New York: Philosophical Library, 1954).

definition, which is quite correct. However, we submit that *a priori* postulates are causally indefinable unless we either assume a transcendental power or a vacuum which accidentally emitted a hydrogen cloud as a basis of the cosmus. The terms accident or chance simply denote our ignorance. A confirmed positivist would maintain that the notion of a transcendental power is just another term for ignorance. Yes, but this ignorance is indicative of the limitation of man's cognitive capacities. We cannot know God completely through our reason. Nor can we experience Him completely through our emotions. We can commune with God only through the ground of our being.[3] Consequently the answer to the ultimate question is necessarily ontological. Yet the intense pursuit for an answer may well be a psychological datum.[4] Investigation of religious behavior —a neglected area in current scientific psychology—could be a significant potential contribution of psychology to Christianity.

DEVELOPMENT OF CONTEMPORARY AMERICAN PSYCHOLOGY

Contemporary American psychology strives to attain a scientific understanding of behavior and experience, with the explicit hope of eventual prediction and control. Since the times of Wilhelm Wundt and William James, who in many textbooks share the distinction of being called the fathers of psychology in Germany and America, respectively, psychology has divorced itself from philosophy. It refused to exist as merely a minor branch of another discipline whose speculative techniques were considered unfruitful and unpromising. Psychology became a poor and self-conscious relation in the family of science and vigorously embraced its basic methods. Consonant with the *Zeitgeist* of the era of a booming technology and the home-grown philosophy of pragmatism and competition, American psychology secured a modest room in the mansion of the natural sciences between its budding neighbors biology and sociology. Physics, with its increasing prominence and prestige, became an idol and a model for many leading theoretical psychologists. Physiological research, exemplified by the rigorous

---

[3]In this connection Paul Tillich's work is perhaps the best example of relating psychology, the liberal arts, and Christian thought.

[4]A penetrating and lucid analysis of the form and origin of the religious sentiment has been achieved by Gordon W. Allport, *The Individual and His Religion* (New York: The Macmillan Co., 1952).

methods of Pavlov, Bekhterev and their followers, paved the way for John B. Watson's rebellion against introspectionism and subjectivism. Behaviorism was born.

In the heart of continental Europe, Sigmund Freud exploded the Victorian taboo about sex and turned the floodlights of clinical observation on the powerful unconscious drives which, he thought, determine behavior. A third movement which left its traces in American psychology was likewise an imported product from Europe. It has been called Gestalt psychology. The theories of behaviorism, psychoanalysis, and Gestalt constitute three major frameworks which, broadly speaking, provide a crude but still illuminating picture of current American psychology. Although these movements have influenced each other, their fundamental assumptions, their techniques of analysis and theory construction, their central concerns and affiliations are sufficiently different to warrant a separate examination.

Psychoanalysis opened Pandora's box and released countless mysterious drives and man's repressed memories. It can be defined in two ways: a theory of behavior and a set of rules for therapy. The proponents have refrained from making extravagant claims and invoking science in their support. Only recently attempts have been made to erect a bridge between scientific psychology and analytic theory. Psychologists usually consider psychoanalysis as an intriguing art with mystical elements rather than as a science. As a theory it is heavily biased toward abnormal behavior. Despite the fact that it is purely speculative in nature, many keen insights of its founder have made their way into the body of widely accepted psychological facts and principles. Psychoanalytic theory has passed through various stages of modifications. The most vocal and theoretically-minded American analysts deviate considerably from orthodox Freudianism, which was strongly materialistic and positivistic. Theories of the late Karen Horney and Erich Fromm have minimized the emphasis on biological drives and stressed the cultural and social factors of behavior. It is interesting to note that a number of leading American religious thinkers have absorbed notions of depth psychology in their works.[5] With regard to theoreti-

---

[5] A marriage of ontology and depth psychology has taken place in Paul Tillich's *Courage to Be,* Yale University Press. Paul Tillich was a close personal friend of the late Karen Horney. He reviewed favorably the latest book of the analyst and ethical humanist Erich Fromm in the November, 1955, issue of *Pastoral Psychology.*

TABLE I

EMERGENCE OF CONTEMPORARY AMERICAN PSYCHOLOGY

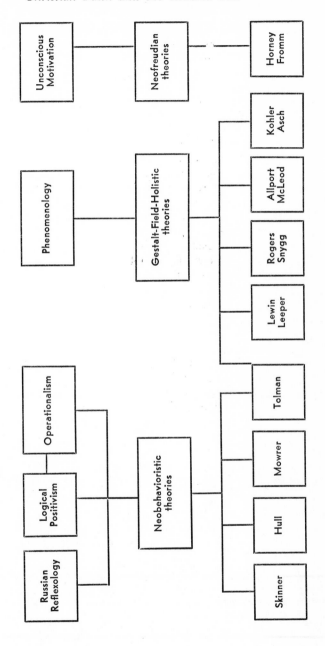

cal and academic psychology, psychoanalysis is primarily concerned with motivation, personality development, and pathological behavior. On the undergraduate level in educational institutions it plays only a minor role. Freud's personal antagonism toward organized religion is well known. Carl Jung, a Swiss psychiatrist and prominent early dissenter, has given much weight to religion in his theory of personality. Nonetheless, his writings are heavily charged with symbolic and enigmatic abstractions bordering on mysticism, and his personal religious commitment is equally obscure. From the treatment point of view, the analyst's values and attitudes play a significant part. Since the analyst is directly involved in the personality restructuring process of the patient, questions of faith assume prime importance. We feel that a student in a liberal arts institution should have a broad understanding of psychoanalysis in view of its past and present impact upon the American cultural scene. It is also imperative that a liberally educated person would not confuse psychoanalysis with psychology or psychiatry. In psychology it has always remained in the background and has never been fully accepted; in psychiatry it constitutes a specialized branch. Many practicing psychiatrists have no use for a couch in their offices. Students should be cautioned not to use the three terms interchangeably.

Neobehaviorism is the orientation which undoubtedly encompasses the largest segment of *bona fide* American psychologists. In all likelihood, only a minority of them have consciously and cheerfully accepted that label. Others have simply been exposed to neobehavioristic teachers and training centers long enough for successful penetration of a behavioristic frame of reference. By association they have also assimilated neobehaviorism's philosophical twin brothers, logical positivism and scientific humanism[6] with their fundamental assertions concerning the criterion of meaning and the principle of operationalism. The former contends that knowledge consists exclusively of tested and verified scientific propositions; the latter requires that all concepts have to be defined through a set of concrete operations. Metaphysics, aesthetics, ethics, and

---

[6]This movement is related to unified science, logical empiricism, empirical rationalism, and scientific empiricism. An easily readable exposition is Herbert Feigl's "The Scientific Outlook: Naturalism and Humanism," which appeared in *American Quarterly*, 1, 1949. An equally illuminating but more technical article by the same author, "Scientific Method without Metaphysical Presuppositions," was published in *Philosophical Studies*, February, 1954.

religion are thrown to the winds as emotive and meaningless utterances. It is a philosophy to end all philosophies in the name of positivistic metascience. Exaltation of scientific reasoning and the glorification of the omniscient scientist, who is created in the image of the high priests of the school, make it very dogmatic indeed. The movement disclaims any metaphysical presuppositions. Despite the cleverness of arguments and built-in self-corrective devices, we must reject neopositivism on the ground of presumptuous epistemology and rigidity of outlook. More specifically, it is a highly questionable metaphysical premise to assert that nothing exists beyond physical events or operations. The contention that propositions are meaningless according to a rigid principle of verification is clearly an unpalatable *tour de force*. For instance, let us suppose that Mr. X wants to make a verbal statement that he is in love with Miss Y. Now this assertion is meaningless until it has been tested and verified. It can not be subject to an empirical test until all concepts are operationally defined. Very likely we would have no difficulty in defining Mr. X and Miss Y by physical descriptions or measurements. But how can we operationally define the complex concept of love? Is love an intense emotion and *ipso facto* a meaningless "emotive" utterance, or can we translate it unequivocally into a set of concrete operations? We are baffled and have to admit our inability to verify the statement, but Mr. X keeps proclaiming that the statement is profoundly meaningful for him. We have to agree with Morris Cohen that although "verification depends on meaning—in the sense of logical consequences—meaning does not necessarily depend on verification."[7] The neopositivist meaning-criterion creates a wholly artificial duality of verifiable and unverifiable propositions and ignores an infinite array of intermediate propositions amenable only to partial verification.

Neopositivism has emptied traditional ethics of meaning and replaced it with an ethic of scientism.[8] Although science does not dictate value standards, it provides the individual with scientific tools to compare different values in terms of their consequences.

---

[7]Morris R. Cohen in his little volume, *A Preface to Logic* (London: Routledge, 1946) takes exception of the logic of neopositivism.

[8]The principal writers of the neopositivistic school are, next to Carnap, Herbert Feigl and Gustav Bergmann. The latter has compiled a number of his more important articles into a book *The Metaphysics of Logical Positivism* (New York: Longmans, Green and Co., 1954).

From a number of possible alternatives the person selects the course of action which best meets the contingencies of the particular situation. But what determines the choice of the best action? The one which science has tested and confirmed to be the best. It seems that the line between means and ends becomes almost imperceptible and the argument inevitably leads to an endless circle. It is impossible to overcome that impasse without a tacit assumption of some preexisting values. The neopositivist would go along but reject the labels of absolute or immutable. To the scientific humanist these values may well be justice, peace, and relief from suffering. We realize that these terms are charged with many variant connotations and as such are highly ambiguous. Without the specific referents to a given situation or an absolute valuational statement, neither peace nor justice is intelligible. We can distinguish between three points of anchorage: (a) a value is extracted from a metaphysical position independent of man and society, (b) a value stems from a valuational statement sanctioned by society, a group of society, or an authority, (c) a value emerges from the rational and/or emotional judgment of the actor himself without specific reference to society or a metaphysical position. Although the three categories are capable of considerable refinement, we might say that the focal point is either an ontological agency, a person's immediate environment, or the person himself. If we start in the reverse order, the third possibility is called into question by a leading, systematic neobehaviorist who writes ". . . science does not confirm the assumptions of freedom, initiative, and responsibility in the behavior of the individual . . ."[9] If man has no freedom, how can he make independent value judgments? The second possibility becomes problematical in the light of historical evidence. Neighboring societies may hold radically contrasting values and even one society may hold simultaneously or successively mutually incompatible values. Cultural anthropology has accumulated a vast amount of empirical data to subdue our hopes to find uniform values even in geographically limited areas.[10] There remains the third possibility to derive our values from a transcendental system which is not subject to the idiosyncrasies of men or eccentricities of changing cultural periods. It seems to be the most promising and

[9]B. F. Skinner, *Science and Human Behavior* (New York: Macmillan, 1953), p. 449. The quotation is lifted from its context, but the idea it expresses is the unavoidable conclusion of the author's thinking.
[10]Attention is drawn to the well known South Sea studies of Margaret Mead.

consistent approach we could reasonably adopt. In the Western civilization Christianity has provided a system of values which transcends individuals and cultures.

Logical positivism has brought to the open forum many ambiguous issues. It has clarified methodological difficulties and at the same time reified principles of objectivity, operationalism, and parsimony. It has challenged many and horrified some of the traditional philosophers. The neopositivists have spoken, written and published profusely and, paradoxically enough, with a strong conviction amounting to unsuspected dogmatism. For the challenge, the stimulation, and the scholarly controversy we can be thankful. It can be said that good many things have been clarified and improved in the philosophy and methodology of science due to the direct or indirect influence of this movement. On the other hand, their metaphysics or lack of metaphysics and their unlimited faith in man and science offers nothing which seems even remotely better than the time-tested ethics of Christianity. Therefore we can not subscribe to the philosophical presuppositions of current neobehaviorism. But we are still confronted with the fact that explicitly or implicitly neopositivism is presently the dominating school in psychology and sociology.[11]

Behavioristic psychology is also characterized by accepting the simplest molecular level as a starting point in the study of behavior. The irreducible stimulous-response unit is selected as the empirical ultimate. For reasons of economy and simplicity, behavioristic psychologists have carried out their theoretically crucial experiments in animal laboratories. The bulk of empirical data which is built around and in support of stimulus-response models is taken from experiments with animals of various levels of complexity starting with the paramecium and ending with the anthropoids. This immediately raises the question: to what extent can we generalize from the simplest to the most complex form of behavior? We are sitting on the horns of a dilemma—anthropomorphism in reverse. How far can we go in drawing analogies from animal behavior? How about the highly intricate nature of symbolic processes which unquestionably goes on in man? Behaviorists have failed to come up with adequate answers to these vexing questions.

---

[11]The neopositivistic trend is discussed by George A. Lundberg, "The Natural Science Trend in Sociology," *The American Journal of Sociology*, Nov., 1955.

A third movement parallel to neobehaviorism on the American psychological scene can be loosely connected under the heading of phenomenology. The Kantian distinction between phenomena and noumena was purified by Husserl and developed into a psychological approach by Brentano. Modern formulations of the central datum of immediate experience have been proposed by Gestalt psychologists and their offspring and brothers-in-arms known as field theorists, holists, organismic, and personalistic psychologists. Their main quarrel with behaviorists focuses upon what they call the reductive fallacy. They reject the so-called psychological atomism and its methodological ramifications. Edward Tolman, a psychologist who developed an elaborate system of neobehaviorism, introduced the terms molar and molecular. The first deals with larger functional units or patterns of behavior, the latter refers to simple, irreducible units. The kernel of phenomenological thinking is expressed in the notion that reductive analysis distorts behavior forms or phenomena. Molar units have laws of their own which do not function at a molecular level. Guided by this assumption, phenomenologists have been relatively unconcerned about lower animals. They prefer to take the human person as their subject and start out with peculiarly human activities like reasoning, creative thinking, and perceptual organization. Knowing and organizing are the key words of the phenomenologically oriented psychologists. The methodological range varies from strictly empirical researchers at one end of the continuum and the more or less philosophical psychologists at the other extreme.[12] They have been less concerned with strictly quantitative relations and more apt to be sympathetic toward descriptive and explanatory language which resists numbers and mathematical equations. The phenomenologist has not only examined individual behavior; he has also illuminated group behavior which is evident in the ingenious approach developed by the late Kurt Lewin.

SOME IMPLICATIONS

It would be superfluous to say that there are irreconcilable aspects which separate neobehaviorism from the tenets of Chris-

---

[12]It is impossible to do justice in a short paper to the vast number of fruitful notions which have evolved from the phenomenological framework. An excellent summary can be found in Chapt. III of Gardner Lindzey, *Handbook of Social Psychology*, Volume I (Cambridge: Addison-Wesley, 1954).

tianity. A number of psychologists apparently live in logic-tight compartments: they are behaviorists methodologically, decline to take a stand on neopositivism, and support their church regularly on Sundays. The inconsistency is obvious. The phenomenological approach, particularly in the applied region, has worked hand in hand with religion without disturbing frictions.[13] Likewise, phenomenologists do not attach tags of "meaninglessness" to subjects and areas which constitute the core of liberal arts tradition. In fact they tend to draw from those disciplines new hypotheses and subject them to test in their social and experimental laboratories. We need not belabor the inescapable fact that the methods of the arts and sciences and the methods of religion are fundamentally different. But they also overlap in practical life-situations. They need not be rivals or mutually exclusive. In the liberal arts college setting they are supplementary. In a Christian college we have a special obligation to see that the sciences, and this includes psychology, would not encroach upon theological statements which science can neither prove nor disprove. The sciences can at best provide us with a partial picture of the world. Religion provides the roof for the house and unity inside.

In summary, it appears that with greater tolerance and magnanimity we can find an important place for contemporary scientific psychology in a Christian liberal arts college. The phenomenological approach is offered as one which seems to be in best accord with the traditions of liberal arts and the tenets of Christianity.

POSTSCRIPT

During the four years which have passed since the original essay was written, several ideas incorporated in the discussion have come to a sharper focus in the writer's mind. An improved formulation of them would probably contribute to the clarity and cogency of the argument. However, we wish to uphold our original thesis that a strictly behavioristic or a traditional psychoanalytic approach could not do justice to the conception of man which underlies the notion of liberal arts and constitutes an integral part of the Christian

---

[13]Attention is directed to Robert MacLeod's essay in *Religious Perspectives in College Teaching* (New York: Ronald Press, 1952) which brings in points not discussed in this paper.

faith. Both of these movements have been unnecessarily zealous in rejecting all ties with traditional philosophies. A new and broader perspective is needed. Modern behaviorism and psychoanalytic theory have joined hands in attacking rigorously and sometimes quite effectively small and limited problems. But we tend to forget that the most vital and significant events in human life and experience such as love and grief inevitably elude the conventional methods of the natural sciences which behaviorists prescribe. Their methodological exclusiveness does not seem justifiable. Our knowledge and understanding of human behavior cannot grow if we surrender unquestioningly to restricted philosophies of science which themselves are open to serious doubt. On the other hand, the phenomenological, holistic, and personalistic lines of thought in contemporary American psychology, although yet voices crying in the wilderness, do offer an alternative approach which could harmoniously coexist with the humanities and the ethics of Christianity in a liberal arts college and enrich the insights we gain from the great literature of our civilization.

CHAPTER 17

Political Science

by Kenneth W. Thompson

It is said that first-class problems attract first-class minds, and in these terms it is reassuring that the content of the liberal arts curriculum has occupied the attention of small but able groups of scholars around the country. Less attention has been paid to the problem of liberal arts in colleges which from their founding have given religion a central place. Yet the proportion of the nation's political, economic, and military leaders, to say nothing of its religious spokesmen, who owe allegiance to these institutions is substantial and impressive, indeed. Their educational contribution cannot be measured, of course, merely by the attainments of graduates, for a "university" is primarily a place of intellectual growth and cultural enrichment for *all* its students. Nevertheless the Christian liberal arts college, simply from the standpoint of the nation's leadership, has established itself as one of the pillars of a strong and durable social structure. This makes the question of including or excluding political science from the curriculum a vital issue, because the increasing scope of the political sector is a stubborn reality of modern life.

THE PROS AND CONS OF INCLUDING POLITICAL SCIENCE IN THE LIBERAL ARTS CURRICULUM

The answer to the question should not be sought, however, only by assessing the importance of things political. It must also take account of such practical questions as the nature of the liberal arts, the competing claims of other disciplines and the possibility of teaching government or political science to young people in their college program. Here the pros and the cons are set forth vigorously by both the champions and opponents of political studies. It is possible to summon impressive evidence both ways, and it may be useful to review the central arguments in the debate.

Those who doubt the wisdom of exposing young men and women

to political science point out that it has been, in some aspects at least, a graduate school subject. Public administration and public finance as advanced studies can be heavily weighted on the side of specialization. Both the principles of the subjects and their application are more designed for someone looking to career service than to the needs of the private citizen. For example, the minutiae of administration may have less value for the ordinary student than the recurring issues in a discussion of the meaning of justice in philosophy or political theory. If there is a reply to this criticism, it is that political science is more than public administration and some awareness of the modern structure of government is vital to everyone in a free society.

The question is also raised whether the study of politics is as basic in the formation of young minds as more general studies like philosophy and history. Philosophy deals with the perennial problems of man and society, of nature and truth, of free will and virtue. History seeks to understand the major eras in the unfolding of man's social record and the discrete events in this experience. Is it not more logical to ground any liberal arts curriculum in these fundamental disciplines? Since the student is restricted in what he can do, he must choose, and philosophy or history are more basic than political science. They provide the essential preparation necessary to a wide range of pursuits in which students subsequently may engage, including political science.

Another proposition that is superficially convincing is the claim that the study of politics is a heady wine, that it tempts students to assume they are masters when all they have is command of fragments of knowledge, and that it produces dilettantism. There is a tendency, at one extreme, for students to become pundits and authorities on each emergent crisis merely because they possess a smattering of knowledge about the political system. Or they may retreat to a semi-mystical contemplation of the methodology of political science, shunning concrete political problems as being unworthy of the true scientist. Whichever course is taken, the result is scarcely of the kind best calculated to produce students keenly alive to the great issues.

It is also argued that political science is a field in flux with many of the basic problems still unresolved. More research is needed to ascertain the chief characteristics of *homo politicus*. Behavioral science is at the threshold of a breakthrough, much as the physical sciences had to await their Galileos and Einsteins before true progress was possible. The most rudimentary knowledge about political behavior has long been impossible because of the prevalence of armchair philosophers but now with more exacting research designs and precise survey techniques, the science in political science has come of age. However, we need more data about electoral behavior, legislatures and legislations, and decision-making before an adequate corpus of tested political information will be available.

Then there is the view that the ambiguities and subtleties of politics are too overpowering for young minds. Confronted with the more sordid stuff of politics, the give-and-take, compromise and bargaining, and political infighting, young men may lose faith in the society in which they live. To avoid the training of cynics, it is better to concentrate on mathematics and leave politics for a riper and more mature age. Plato was himself disposed to feel that the fine arts, logic, and mathematics were more appropriate than metaphysics for the young, and his thinking is mirrored in this more modern attitude concerning the study of politics.

Beyond this, the limits of curriculum restrict the choices that are open to undergraduates. They must be trained in languages, history, the natural sciences, and perhaps in more general survey courses before they can turn to a specific social science. It is difficult for many of the better liberal arts colleges to maintain a separate political science department, and more often than not it becomes part of a history or philosophy or economics department. A premium has to be placed on versatility in a smaller faculty, and the possibility of a historian doubling in political science is greater than the other way around. In consequence, political science has tended to hold the orphan status of a subject too important to be excluded altogether but, for a variety of reasons, not important enough for major emphasis.

Finally, in all institutions, but particularly in denominational colleges, political science runs the risk of being caught up in political crusades. It hovers perilously near the brink of indoctrination. Professors become special pleaders, and political platforms come before political philosophy. Students seek answers to the painful choices of contemporary politics, and the instructor may find the moral burden too great of restricting himself to teaching how to think rather than what to think. The distance between a Platonic dialogue and a political diatribe is sometimes the distance between the pedagogical model in political science and the reality.

However, the critics of political science and those who argue against its inclusion in any liberal arts curriculum have not had the field to themselves. There is also "a case for political science" which must have a hearing. In the twentieth century politics has become an increasingly vital sector of our national life. For Republicans and Democrats, Conservatives and Laborites, and Christian Democrats and Social Democrats, the public sector of the economy has increased not primarily because of the machinations of a handful of greedy bureaucrats but in response to modern social realities. Moreover, whatever the uncertainties and ambiguities of politics, the whole electorate, including young men and women, are required to act. They must choose periodically among alternatives on which they can have but limited information. If they are denied the opportunity of "going to school" with responsible political scientists, they will take their training from others less objective and fair-minded in their approach. The McCarthys will always be with us ready and willing to offer instruction in the "truth." When political education is lacking, special interest groups will fill the gap much as youngsters deprived of responsible counsel on social relations and sexual behavior seek it covertly where they can. It will not do to say that politics is not for the young, for the kaleidoscopic movements of modern life place political decisions in the hands of us all. If the colleges do not provide political training, young people will go to school elsewhere and oftentimes their fare will be meager if not malnutritious and harmful. There are countless examples of the account being skewed by demagogues. Nurtured on such a diet the young grow old and cynical and apathetic before their time. The purveyors of political insights on radio, television, and some of the newspapers are seldom as well-trained as university people for whom political studies are more than a side-line. The half-educated interpretations of politics by some of our public oracles shorn of any cultural roots commonly destroy the natural curiosity and interest men have in the political and lead to a sense of fatalism and futility on what is possible in public affairs. In this situation one can imagine a modern Jefferson calling upon the universities and colleges to redress the balance against this unhappy development by providing the school for the statesman and citizen.

This line of reasoning has a corollary in the belief that most Americans tend badly to underestimate youth. The notion that they must be spared the harsh realities of social life lest the natural idealism of the young be blotted out is probably a misreading of the times. Cynics are made not so much from exposure to reality as from the sudden discovery that the fairyland world in which they had thought they were living is vastly different from the actual world. Moreover, it must be remembered that the liberal arts colleges under discussion produce the great bulk of the nation's leaders and for many of them their one exposure to economics or political science occurs during college days. If one type or another of social studies is missing, these prominent Americans bring less to the world than would otherwise be true.

Furthermore, political science at its core is not a specialist subject. It deals with fundamental issues that touch the universal. It considers the most basic problems in man's relations with man. It strives to give content to concepts like justice and order, freedom and equality, and authority and power. It must come to terms with these issues wherever there are political observers—in the United States or Europe and in Asia or Africa. In every case there are aspects of political behavior that are unique, but since politics is essentially a laboratory for the study of human nature there are universal foundations.

In this connection, the religiously oriented liberal arts college doubtless has a unique contribution to make. Political science is most profound when it touches the garments of theology and moral philosophy or general philosophy. Someone has said that these realms of learning are best able to help political science to save it from itself. For theology or philosophy can teach the social scientist to live with the problems and dilemmas he is otherwise tempted to believe are easily soluble. Cut loose from its historical and philosophical moorings, political science floats aimlessly on the waves of current illusions. It becomes an instrument of progress in the age of progress and a method for the realization of a predictable order in a scientific day. A liberal arts college has a better than even chance of marrying politics to philosophy and preserving its necessary links with history and theology.

It is also true that political participation is feasible for undergraduates in liberal arts. From mock political conventions and United Nations Assemblies to precinct work in the local community, the opportunities are considerable. I would feel personally that this approach should not be pushed too far, but as a supplement to the study of politics it can serve to bring the classroom and the student closer to the political arena. Thus it can provide a safeguard against the not inconsiderable risk of the divorce of theory from actuality. In the same way that medical research must not be separated too much from the patient in the sick bed, the political scientist can never afford to lose sight of the voter. But these contacts must be informed by a clear conception of the questions the scholars wish to ask if the most useful utilization is to be made.

Every college or university will have to draw up its own balance sheet of the pros and cons of including political science in its curriculum, but in some form or other, I believe, the aforementioned issues will come into play. Furthermore the balance will tip this way or that as more or less weight or credence is given to certain elements in this check list. There is a case for political science, but the real issues must be faced at each particular institution in the light of the problems and opportunities that this field of study presents.

THE DISCIPLINE OF POLITICAL SCIENCE: ITS HISTORY

Political science as a separate field of study goes back to the turn of the century. In 1903 the American Political Science Association was founded, and an organized approach to the subject stems from that date. Four major phases in the history of political science can be identified, and each period has had its inception in a response to some major historical event.

The origins of the study of political science have roots in a major reformist movement which roughly covers the period from 1890 to 1914. This was the era of muckrackers, the exposé, the discovery of crime in politics, and the political boss and party machine. The aim of the reformers was a civil service and career opportunities for qualified public servants. In their utopia, administration would replace politics and the expert the spoilsman. The stress was on more perfect institutions, and spurred on by the philosophy of the nineteenth century Enlightenment the reformers were confident that the city manager plan, the initiative and referendum, or the public commission would usher in an era of unlimited progress.

Throughout this early period, political science was continually drawn beyond the classroom. Every problem of the body politic was the business of the scholar. He approached them all in the spirit of the philanthropist Andrew Carnegie, who urged the Trustees of the Carnegie Endowment to look to the problem of war and when this had been solved to consider the next most troublesome issue that had appeared on the horizon. Boundless optimism and faith in human perfectability pervaded the new discipline.

This spirit continued through a second stage which roughly spanned the two decades beginning in 1914. Scholars viewed reality through the spectacles of legalism and rationalism, two trademarks of the twentieth century American "Weltanschauung." If the problem was war, the solution was an international covenant—the Kellogg-Briand Pact of 1928—outlawing and making war illegal. If the peril was international "aggression," a legal formula proscribing and defining it was the goal. If states trembled in insecurity, reassure them with security pacts heaped one upon the other. It has been said of the League of Nations and perhaps the United Nations, that they represent an attempt to apply rationalized procedures in the form of new machinery for the international order. One rather acute critic has noted the tendency to believe that there exists or can exist a card index of situations or events to be consulted for the appropriate and already prescribed action whenever the event or situation turns up. It is charged that in this approach standardized procedures are valued more than prudence and the perfection of machinery more than political wisdom.

A third phase that more or less parallels the second but continues down to the close of World War II is the current-events viewpoint. Political scientists constituted the fire-brigades that answered the call of the state. If the emergency was the decline in the quality of the public service, they rallied to the side of the President's Committee on Administrative Management. If the crisis was in the international realm, they constituted themselves the Commission to Study the Organization of the Peace. Social security, public administration, and the elimination of war were three focal points. Political science in this period was clearly not irrelevant to the major issues of government, but whether or not it was also systematic, comprehensive, and consistent with its principal objectives is at least a debatable question. For whatever the scholar may be, he is probably not ideally a pundit. The peril for the political scientist in modern society is that he is often required to act as if proposing and disposing of each consecutive current problem were his essential role.

Following World War II, the fourth phase in the history of political science has displayed at least half-a-dozen characteristics. It has endeavored more self-consciously to model its science after the envied stature of the natural sciences. The goal before it has been to discover methods and techniques through which problems could be made susceptible of validation and verification instead of remaining unique and idiosyncratic. Second, it has concentrated on the behavioral aspects of politics—phenomena like voting, electoral behavior, and public opinion—in which the use of scientific methods seemed most within reach and in which the progress of science could be expected to be most rapid. Political behavior has emerged as the research interest of a growing and ambitious group of political scientists who are particularly zealous of attaining scientific standing.

Third, a strong trend typical of contemporary society has been the growth of specialization. In scholarly societies, professional journals, and research institutes, the movement has been in the direction of a narrower and narrower point of focus. In the study of international relations there are journals for international law, comparative law, world politics, and international organization. With respect to political behavior, separate journals treat the problems of public opinion, conflict resolution, and the power-elite. Some political behaviorists concentrate on political parties, others on decision-making and still others on communications theory. In order to reach scientific exactitude, the subjects of study become increasingly limited, circumscribed, and, some would say, trivial. Indeed, there are obvious risks in selecting a research topic merely because it is quantifiable. The story is told of an inebriate whom a police officer found one evening searching for a lost watch under a lamppost. Asked whether he had dropped the watch there, the drunk replied, "Of course not, but I have light here to see what I am doing." In history, the analogous case is the historian who does research on a problem merely because there is an abundance of documentation. Fourth, the years after World War II have witnessed a revival of interest in political philosophy. One of the ironies of political behaviorism as a prevailing trend has been the growing disenchantment with some of its tenets. Natural law philosophers speak out against it because of its vulgar empiricism, which they say has the result of reducing political values to numbers or disregarding them altogether.

Fifth and sixth, two rather fundamental controversies arise from the struggle between the two prevailing tendencies of political behaviorism and political philosophy. One is the facts-value controversy. Behaviorists maintain that facts can be identified as conditions of reality about which testable propositions can be advanced. Values can neither be proved nor disproved and exist for the theologian or metaphysician but not for the scientist. The aim of political science must be to attain to a value-free discipline. Political philosophers, by contrast, are dubious about a value-free social science, for they note that every scholar carries with him a heavy baggage of assumptions and value-commitments. His selection of a research problem, the importance he gives it, the relative weight he ascribes to its parts, the purpose of his enterprise as he sees it, and the ultimate use to which it is put are all value questions to a greater or lesser degree. All questions of fact are in some measure value-questions and in most social problems facts and values are inseparably intermingled. According to the political philosophers, the fact-value dichotomy is based on a too-simple view of social reality.

The other controversy which results at least partly from the present state of political science is the debate between liberalism and conservatism. Liberalism has been the ground on which most American intellectuals, including political scientists, have chosen to join issue whether with antagonists of the left or right. Historically, liberalism was associated with the claims of a rising middle class, but its tenets of majority rule and individual rights were extended at least ideologically to other social groups. Both by virtue of the identity of the liberal creed with the claims of the middle class and by virtue of the prevalence of concepts like progress and perfectibility that inhere in the Enlightenment, liberalism came to stand for the best of all possible worlds. Needless to say, in an industrial age with society on the march such a creed symbolized the wave of the future. More recently, however, the failure of modern man to eliminate the ravages of international conflict and cope with the setbacks appearing in the guise of totalitarian democracy have led to a reexamination of political ideas. Conservatism going back to Edmund Burke has aroused much interest and for some its more somber view of man and the universe has seemed more appropriate to the times.

THE COMPONENT STUDIES OF POLITICAL SCIENCE

If intellectual main currents like reformism and liberalism have shaped the broad outlines of political science, its major component studies have evolved with some measure of consistency and coherence. At least it is true that over a fairly long period of its history, political science has included political theory, international relations, comparative government, public administration, political parties, state and local government, and public law or jurisprudence. Sometimes the reason for adding a field had more to do with convenience or ambition than with reason, and occasionally there has been a tendency to add a subject merely because no one else was filling the need, e.g., administrative law, public finance, etc. Moreover, some of the component studies bear little if any relation to one another and the offering of some departments have a patchwork appearance about them. Students sometimes ask what connection there is between public personnel and the political theory of Aristotle or local government and public finance.

However each college or university must choose for itself, and theoretically, at least, one can map out the salient studies in a program for liberal arts undergraduates. Political theory or political philosophy should of course be the core of the science. In any discipline that is worthy of the name someone must synthesize the various separate studies and generalize from them. It is theory which asks the questions which give meaning to an intellectual discipline. The theorist from his broader perspective strives to place partial insights and limited research findings in a more meaningful context. In practice, political theory has not always scaled these heights. Instead American political science has sometimes done no better than a venerable political theory that was merely a recitation of selected ideas from philosophers beginning with Plato and ending with Winston Churchill.

More recently, political theory has been reinvigorated by a threefold development. On the one hand, political philosophers prompted in part by scholars of foreign origin like Leo Strauss and Hans J. Morgenthau of the University of Chicago have undertaken to bring political theory closer to systematic philosophy. On the other hand, political theorists have attempted to deal with concrete problems in such subject matter fields as international relations, political parties, and public administration on a broader conceptual basis. In spite of variation in approaches, political theorists seek to cope responsibly with the great issues that are not readily measured by behaviorists, like state and society, freedom and order, and majority rule and individual rights. Their task is to treat an important realm of thought through reason and judgment when the methods of pure science are not available. It may be a sign of the times that outstandingly able younger scholars are turning increasingly to political theory. If a college or university were limited to but one course in political science, I would suppose political theory should be that course. The increasing attention to political theory is reflected both by the increase in writing within the familiar categories of political theory and the increase in the quantity and penetration of theoretical studies in subject matter areas.

The second broad area from which any liberal arts curriculum may profitably draw is international relations. The position of the United States suddenly catapulted into an inescapable role of world leadership has called for qualities of high political intelligence and moral judgment. Unlike England, this country has not had a long apprenticeship in world affairs and its policies are endlessly subject to passion and impulse. Despite this, two administrations since the War have evolved policies that were moderately consistent and realistic. Nevertheless, one of the nation's most essential tasks in the present and immediate future is to train up a people capable of grappling with the stubborn and persistent problems of world politics. Earlier, international relations suffered from an intellectual climate which hoped to shift these burdens to international institutions or eliminate them through legal pacts and treaties. The postwar writing in the field has been characterized less by legalism and utopianism, more by political realism. Studies of national security, economic development, and the forces that mold foreign policy have taken their place alongside monographs in international law and organization. Most colleges seek to include courses in international politics, American foreign policy—sometimes in conjunction with American diplomatic history—and international law and organization. Seen in this perspective, American foreign relations become merely another chapter in the long history of efforts of nations to accommodate their interests to one another. From this approach, the historic tools and "laws" of diplomacy become relevant to American practice and the young student sees more clearly the need for patience and persistence in America's world leadership.

Comparative government shares with international relations a primary emphasis on foreign politics. Educationally, it helps to fix attention on non-American political institutions and practices with a long and respectable history. The study has been marked by lively debate and soul-searching especially within the past half-decade as the focus has shifted from the comparative study of institutions to a comparison of equivalent functions. For example, the Prime Minister in Parliament is not comparable in every respect to the American executive, and in underdeveloped countries the prospect of readily identifying executive, legislative, and judiciary is still more tenuous. The study of the governments of non-western areas has stimulated the reaction against culture-bound comparisons. American scholars have asked themselves if the approach was sufficient in which the governments of other countries were held up to their mirror of the three branches of governments in the American federal system. The little book by Roy Macridis, *The Study of Comparative Government,* is perhaps the single most illuminating discussion of the trends in the comparative field. At least an introduction of students to the comparative approach to political reality has much to recommend it. Historically, four or five westernized countries—Britain, France, Germany, the Soviet Union and one other—have comprised the unit for comparison. With the growing trend toward international interdependence, the case for including one or more non-western countries has become strong even though the basis for comparison becomes more difficult. The link between international relations and comparative government is obvious and a forthcoming volume edited by Gabriel Almond and published by Prentice Hall is designed to treat the making of foreign policy in eight countries on a comparative basis. It is useful to study foreign governments but even more profitable to compare functions which are genuinely comparable.

The other component studies in political science include American Government, public administration, public law and jurisprudence, public opinion and electoral behavior, political parties and pressure groups, and state and local government. Obviously an awareness of the rudiments of the American system is at least as basic as a knowledge of foreign systems. In one sense, American government is taught in the interstices of every course; it may also be appropriate to launch the undergraduate with a survey course in which the fundamentals are treated. The other courses in administration and politics are largely American, and most institutions pick and choose from among them as educational needs and intellectual and other resources dictate. For undergraduates, I should think public law and jurisprudence might be more basic than state and local government, but this question will be governed by countless circumstances. In any event this is the scope of political science as I see it and the component studies which go to make up the discipline. For most undergraduates, the subject matter courses are probably more meaningful than a heavy dose of so-called methodology. For a limited curriculum, political philosophy, international relations and comparative government, American government and politics, and public law might be considered the salient component studies.

THE DILEMMAS OF POLITICAL AND THE LIBERAL ARTS COLLEGE

Because of the special problems that crowd in on any society in the conduct of its political life, the denominational college has a unique opportunity. This inheres in the fact that modern society is embarrassed by the prevalence of the ethical problem that intrudes upon the most vital political questions. The technological ethos which has conquered so much of American thinking has small place for values or higher ends. Indeed its every effort is turned to reducing the need for judgment or wisdom through procedures that restrict the human factor to a minimum. It seeks for methods and formulas that are testable, repeatable, and precise and that will cancel out the need for unusual imagination and insight. The college with its roots in a religious heritage is less vulnerable to the infectious attractions of this simple view, and its devotion to the humanities and theology tends to immunize it against a type of scientific outlook which the better scientists would themselves reject.

One example of the kind of problem for which the modern technological outlook is singularly unqualified is the central issue of political morality. Most discussion of this theme runs to one or the other of two extremes. Either too much or too little is claimed for ethical principles. Both secular and religious thinkers alternately deny that morality influences politics—"politics is a dirty business" —or affirm that virtue is the sole criterion. A well-known evangelist affirms that a certain nationalist Chinese leader could never have tolerated corruption because "he prays three times a day." Another present day religious movement imagines that all our personal and political problems could be wafted away through "positive thinking." One is reminded of William James' comment that the trouble with religious people was that they were forever lobbying for special favor in the courts of the Almighty. However, secular thinkers who espouse doctrines of commercialism and cynicism, progress and success, or militarism and nationalism are no less blinded to the essentials of the moral problem.

A responsible analysis of political morality must begin with the recognition that it is political morality, not abstract morality, that calls for study. It must recognize that while religious ethics places self-interest in question—man must lose his life in order to find it—political ethics takes self-interest for granted. Thus the goal of political ethics must be to canalize and direct the national interest, say, in ways that are most conducive to international peace and order. It can never assume that responsible national leaders will transcend the national interest by loyalty to a cause that would throw national survival in jeopardy (although the United States fought for the principle of democracy in two world wars, this is hardly an exception, for with the prospect of Europe being overrun by a single power, national security was at stake). The highest end in political morality is to find the point of concurrence between self-interest and some higher end or purpose. Perhaps a religious scholar is more likely to have the fortitude to undertake this task than one filled with all kinds of rationalistic or technological illusions.

Significantly enough, democracy is another subject for which study goes on appropriately in a religious setting. Some modern writers insist that democracy flourishes best in a secular state and point to non-democratic societies in Latin America and Europe to prove that religion is basically antagonistic to the democratic state. There are other religious writers who claim that democracy is a direct outgrowth of Christian faith. However, it is historically more accurate to say that both secular and Christian forces played a part in the rise of democratic political institutions. On the one hand there are traditional non-democratic Christian cultures which are to the right of free societies. They prove that the Christian faith does not inevitably yield democratic fruits. On the other hand, free societies like our own seem to be a fortunate product of the confluence of Christian and secular forces. In the United States, Christianity and Judaism contribute a view of man that is incompatible with his subordination to any political system. In addition, there are secular forces which act to assure critical judgments of human ends and ambitions and those false idolatries that characterize modern tyrannies. It is as wrong to decry either the religious or the secular component of democracy. The Christian concept of human dignity makes any effort to fit man into a political program, even in the name of social engineering, morally ambiguous and offensive. The idea of a source of authority from which the individual can defy the authorities of this world—"We must obey God rather than Man"—is one of the cornerstones of individual freedom. At the same time, the Biblical insistence that the same radical freedom which makes man creative also makes him potentially dangerous leads to those requirements of restraint or equilibrium of social forces upon which effective democracy rests.

But this is but one side of the story. The other involves the hazards inherent in the relation between Christianity and democracy and the positive contributions of secular thought. There are grave historical and psychological perils in associating ultimate religious truths with immediate and proximate causes. The religious theory of the divine right of kings is only a particularly serious example of some of the abuses that are possible. Moreover, the ascribing of secular (or non-religious) content to non-sacred objects and ends of society has endowed a multitude of lesser activities with a practical moral respectability and at the same time discouraged the premature sanctities in which both traditional societies and modern collectivism abound. Yet a too explicit secularism disavowing reverence for the ultimate may itself generate false idolatries such as the worship of efficiency or the wholly self-sufficient individual. Compared with the noxious idolatries of modern totalitarianism, these dogmas are fairly harmless, but they show that any too explicit denial of the ultimate may itself become the basis for a secular religion with excessive pretensions and sanctities of its own.

Democracy and political morality are but two of the cardinal issues of political life on which there is reason for expecting a special contribution from a denominational liberal arts college. For this reason, I believe political science should probably be included in any liberal arts curriculum which seeks to realize its purposes and goals.

Index

INDEX OF NAMES

INDEX OF SUBJECTS

INDEX OF SCRIPTURE REFERENCES